Lit crit

Afterwords

Afterwords

Novelists on Their Novels

Edited by Thomas McCormack

St. Martin's Press
New York

Library of Congress Cataloging-in-Publication Data:

Afterwords : novelists on their novels / edited by Thomas McCormack.
    p.   cm.
    Originally published: Harper & Row, 1968, c1969.
    ISBN 0-312-01382-5 (pbk.) : $9.95
      1. American fiction—20th century—History and criticism.
2. English fiction—20th century—History and criticism.
3. Fiction—Authorship. I. McCormack, Thomas.
PS379.A34 1988   87-27341
813'.54'09—dc19   CIP

Contents

Introduction to the Paperback Edition

I WROTE THE introduction to the first edition of this book in 1968. In the twenty years since then, I've been increasingly involved in a study of the editing—and the writing—of fiction. One effect of this is that if I were sending the author-invitation now (the one described on the first page of the introduction), I'd probably be much more specific and concrete about the questions I'd like the writers to address.

I concede that might not be a good thing; it would stress 'technical' concerns, and I suspect this could have had two results: The pieces might have been drier, more abstruse, and somewhat dehumanized. Compelled to focus on crafty problems of structure, selection of characters and circumstance, narrative control, and the like, the writers might have left out the reports of personal turmoil and triumph that currently make some of the accounts as embracingly intimate as autobiography.

The second result would probably have been: fewer essays. There are, in here, lots of ruminations about technical matters, but it's striking how often the writers actively recoil from any notions of technical planning or control of their novels. They all want to think the books are indeed controlled, but there's a centipede's wariness about trying to codify what the controls are. It reminds me of the story told by the football player Brian Piccolo, who seldom got to play because he was second-string to the great Gale Sayers. "Gale," Piccolo inquired, "when you run with the ball do you think about it, or do you just *do* it?" "I just do it," said Sayers. "Well," Piccolo asked, "would you mind thinking about it?"

Still, my feeling now is that in my greater innocence of twenty years ago, I surrendered too much to the magic of art. (I'm also certain that twenty years from now I'd look back on the me of 1988 and wince at this year's ignorance.) Novelists frequently reconsider past novels of theirs and lament that they went wrong, and their analyses are almost always in terms of mistakes that a clear-eyed craftsman (with sensibility) might have spotted at the time.

Twenty years ago I was interested in the drama, the sensation of the writer, as the novel was written. I still am. But today my second interest has increased immensely—the interest in craft, the teachable things that can guide a writer to spot and remedy early faults that would forever hamper the development of his offspring. I stand by the line of twenty years ago: No one can tell an artist how to do it, but there *are,* potentially, tips on how to allow it to get done. I won't accept that nothing can be taught about writing except grammar, or that the whole idea of craft is a pedant's invention. So now I wish I'd probed further into these writers' craft, chased down certain technical hints they dropped, asked more questions.

A second change in me over the twenty years has come with the tweezing hours I've spent badgering editors to read more actively, to respond as though every line is important, to realize that *not* to question a writer is a kind of disrespect because it implies that if he or she hasn't got it right it doesn't make any difference. In 1968, disarmed by my groupie greenness and dazzlement, I couldn't see that an editor has to be more than a white-collar messenger between the writer and the typesetter. So I didn't dispute, as I would now, almost every line by William Gass in the first part of his piece, the part that canonizes meta-fiction and condemns orthodox narrative—not because I disagree with him (which I admit I do) but because his argument is so fuzzy, faulty, and mean. With Price, on the other hand, though I'd push hard on some phrases and judgments, twenty years of increasing understanding of his subject would allow me to raise a more appreciative croon of praise for his insights. This means, say I, that I'm now able to take all these writers more seriously.

But my sentiments about the value of craft are, I realize, idiosyncratic, and maybe if I take two aspirins they'll go away. I hope not, because if I'm right there's work we can do that will help editors be more useful and writers less accident-prone. That curriculum can't be spelled out here. This new introduction is meant to do only two things. The first is to reassure those close readers who are vexed to find in these pages critical, pregnant words and notions that are never pursued or clarified but which are essential to answering that key question: How did the writer decide what to put in and what to keep out? I still enjoy the *Paris Review* interviews, but these days I jerk feverishly to my feet when the author says, "At a certain point, of course, you figure out what your premises are and what you're doing." Which means, evidently, discovering the controlling factor in deciding what to put in and what to keep out. "Wait!" I squeak. "That's important!" And then I dance in frustration as the interviewer lets the author slip away without ever explaining 'premises' or 'what you're doing'. To all of those who feel agitation at such a moment, the message is: You're not alone.

The second intention of this new introduction is, happily, more positive, more celebratory. It's to say I still enjoy the pieces, admire their authors, am fascinated by their tales of tales. Sure, you can go too far in abandoning reason in the presence of mysterious art, but in the end there *is* something that no mere craft can summon up, something deliciously awesome to contemplate—especially when conjoined with these testimonies that it arises in beings as human as you and I, worried about their families and their gardens, wondering what's for dinner tonight.

I hope that, after reading this volume, you can agree with Robie Macauley, who said in *The New York Times Book Review* those twenty years ago, "*Afterwords,* finally, ought to be a good book for a writer's shelf—especially young writers and isolated writers. America . . . has not very much of that shared kind of experience about the making of a novel that young writers are often so desperately anxious for. The silent struggle to tell it and be heard—this is what *Afterwords* is about."

—Thomas McCormack
1988

Introduction

"I CAN'T DO IT," said one writer. "For me the writing of a novel is a prolonged lunatic binge, and much as I'd like to describe the event, I find it's impossible." "I'd do it," said another, "if I knew where to begin. I don't know where to begin, therefore I can't do it." "Hey!" said a third. "I happen to have five thousand words already on paper about my experience in writing my novel. . . . I'd like to polish and expand it a bit. . . ." Alas, when he had finished expanding his piece it ran to 60,000 words, and he had written another book.

The three men were responding to invitations to contribute to this volume of after-the-fact prefaces. Take one of your novels, the invitation said, and write about it; give a sort of craftsman's journal, a report describing the campaign of the book—how it began, what it looked like to you at various stages, what problems came up and what solutions you devised, how explicit were the considerations of craft we think we see—in other words, what was *going on* when you worked.

The book could be valuable in several different ways, the invitation said. For one thing, it seemed an apt and allowable way to satisfy readers' appetites for details about the writers and the writing they admire. For another, its description of how a writer has seen and solved technical problems could be helpful to students of the craft. For a third, it could be an aid to appreciating what a writer has done: It's the rare reader who has what the writer would feel to be a perfectly placed focus on a book, and this was the writer's chance to adjust the lens. A final virtue, said the letter, is that the making of a novel can be a dramatic thing, a structured tale altogether worth preserving for itself. These seemed to be four of the reasons why the likes of Henry James's prefaces and the *Paris Review* interviews are such a delight to read.

Well, the fourteen people represented in this book wrote their pieces for their *own* reasons, and they are far more personal, more driving than any suggested in the supporting brief of an invitation. The reasons vary because writers vary. Reading these complex, disparate pieces calls to mind the old truth that there is nothing, absolutely nothing, that is discernibly common and peculiar to all writers. On the first (and possibly, as Ross Macdonald points out, the most deceiving) level, the fourteen aren't even doing the same thing, aren't working in the same genre: One or two are historical novelists, one a detective-story writer, one the most intimate of autobiographers and another the remotest of fabulists, one is talking about a short story rather than a novel, another—John Fowles—is talking about something that isn't quite anything yet, he deals with a work-in-progress.

A novel-in-progress always means work indeed, but no one makes it seem less so than Louis Auchincloss. For some, the chief effect of his piece on *The Rector of Justin* will be to confirm their long-term suspicion that to be a writer is a gloriously simple thing. By his own testimony, and that of people who know him, he does write with ease and speed. A friend of his once told me how Auchincloss, while hosting a party at his home, managed between chats to sneak to his desk, dash off a scene in a current novel, and return to the social doings with his jacket still on.

At first glance his strong suit seems to be glistening intelligence, a magnificent reasonableness, a lawyer's problem-solving mind. Notice how he appears to *figure out* how his book must go. Yet buried in his account are the telltale phrases: "I was caught up for a while by a fancy theory. . . . The first version had to be scrapped entirely when his personality got out of hand. . . . I had a sudden inspiration. . . ." There are 300,000 lawyers who can figure things out, but only one who can write as Auchincloss does. The fact is you can't *figure out* what the characters should say next, but Auchincloss always knows. And even if you can figure out what a sentence must say, you can't figure out what it must *do,* or what its shape must be, and yet Auchincloss always knows that too. "I am neither a satirist nor a cheerleader," he says. "I am strictly an observer." No; not if this means a mere recorder. He *observed* Endicott Peabody and Learned Hand, but Francis Prescott is something else.

In his long and good preface to his novel *One Day,* Wright Morris talks of many things, but perhaps principally of the way observed details, daily facts—details minute, and facts enormous—intrude themselves into an artist's work, just as they do into all of our lives. Facts enormous: the day in *One Day* is November 22, 1963, and much of the book is about the way that public calamity intruded, and still intrudes, on us all.

He also talks about understanding one's own gift. "My talent, such as it is, finds its realization in the creation of *characters,*" says Morris. This is an important thing to know about oneself. Perhaps the primary task of any artist—any person?—is to discover what he or she can—and cannot—do. Morris wishes he could write a simple novel—clean, cool, clear as mountain water: "I like them—but they are not the books I am bidden to write."

From one angle, the most optimistic item in the original invitation to these writers was the suggestion that there are hints on *how to write* that they might impart. It sounds like asking for hints on how to grow tall, but it isn't quite that. There are *mechanical* moves that can make things easier for those with innate talent to develop. But it is true that these tips can never be keys to how-to-do-it; at best they can only tell how-to-allow-it-to-get-done. A novelist once told me that the best advice he'd ever received about writing was: Fold the paper down the middle, and write only in the right-hand column; that way you will have the whole left-hand column for making changes and additions.

Morris gives at least one practical tip, an old one, but worth repeating: If you're stuck for what comes next, don't assume that the best, the professional thing to do is to chain yourself grittily to your desk until something breaks. "The writer who stops to smoke, pare his nails, abuse his wife, or just pace up and down the creaking floor of the kitchen, is wooing the bird of flight to sing and the chances are that song, not a singing commercial, will be his reward."

Anthony Burgess is a natural gusher, and his first task is to cope with the flow, channel it. He says in his preface: "I planned *Nothing Like the Sun* as a binary movement with a brief epilogue . . . this sort of arithmetic proportioning is not so cold-blooded as it appears. Nobody regards the sonnet-form as too artificial to express passion. . . . A lot of contemporary fiction would be better for the constrictions of a mould, however artificial."

Among other things, it's Burgess's welling, jumping gusto and vitality that make his preface—and his book—such a pleasure. "*Nothing Like the Sun* was . . . a literary task almost hemorrhoidally agonising, and it must have consumed yards of paper and thousands of cigarettes." We believe it, but we don't believe it. The fact is, Burgess's piece succeeds marvelously in conveying just how much *fun* writing can be.

Robert Crichton, once he got going, obviously enjoyed himself too. His preface to *The Secret of Santa Vittoria* gives an idea of how hard *beginning* can be—and it also provides a unique solution. The tale is told of Rilke's making woe to Tolstoy about the difficulty of writing, the monstrous burden of one's art, the terrible confrontation with the blank page, the insurmountable beginnings. To which Tolstoy responded, "*Voulez-vous écrire? Alors, écrivez! Ecrivez!*" Crichton took the advice in his own way. He had stalled on the very first line of the book, was unable to get into the thing at all, no matter how often he charged the gate. Then, one day, "I began to write the story of Santa Vittoria in the form and style of a Dick and Jane first reader." And it got him going; at least it gave him something he could revise: "through Dick and Jane I had outflanked art."

The Secret of Santa Vittoria required on-location research, and Crichton has a tip about that: When you're there, write lots of letters home. "Months later . . . it was the letters that turned out to be filled with the kind of information I needed. My notes were mostly useless."

A third tip from Crichton is a variety of Ernest Hemingway's advice for maintaining day-to-day momentum: "When I am going good but have worked enough for the day," says Crichton, "I stop before finishing a paragraph I'm anxious to finish and then I stop in the middle of a sentence."

Fourth tip, but with no foolproof directions for carrying it out: Get *immersed* in the book. "Immersion" is Crichton's word for an absolute, almost hallucinatory involvement that allowed him to rewrite 447 printed pages in 23 days—a performance to boggle the mind of any publisher.

Mark Harris, who teaches college English, scandalizes a thousand straitlaced colleagues in his preface to his first novel, *Trumpet to the World*. With irony, and yet without irony, he titles his piece "How to Write." And the "how" sounds very like Tolstoy's *"Ecrivez!"* With the first novel Harris learned "the value of speed, of writing fast and planless." That way some things will occur "by faith and by process as [they] never could occur by plan. Until the writer has experienced that process and acquired that faith he will have a hard time going on, and I am thankful I learned it very young . . . [I] have tried to tell other people about it ever since, for it is the only way to live." Though I'm not sure this "flailing, planless, using my writing to discharge my furies" assault will work for everyone of talent, I'm certain it's precisely the right advice for some. And certainly it has an almost physically salubrious effect that more sedate writers will never know. It's hard, though, on those writing teachers whose aim is to impart discipline to their students.

Mary Renault, a seemingly Spartan woman, writing of Minoan times, is the only true historical novelist represented in this book. She chastens those who falsify, even if it is fiction: "it is inconceivable to me how anyone can decide deliberately to betray [the truth]; to alter some fact which was central to the life of a real human being . . . in order to make a smoother story, or to exploit him as propaganda for some cause."

Like Auchincloss, she is less totally cerebral a writer than a quick reading of her piece might suggest, I think. "Two discrepant images had thus been wrestling in my subconscious imagination." The winner was the one with logic on his side, but it was imagination that put him there in the first place. It does not necessarily diminish the imaginativeness of characters if they are reasonable possibilities—especially in historical fiction.

William Gass's long letter to his editor David Segal about *Omensetter's Luck* reminds one of Stuart Gilbert's study of *Ulysses:* You read it and you are seized with a need to get back to the book itself.

Gass recalls Joyce for other reasons. Both men are theoreticians of art. Joyce, chased to the margin with Jesuit scholasticism, wrote incredibly determined books, with structural dictates reaching into every cranny. Gass, who teaches philosophy at Purdue, shows a similar commitment to metaphorical interlock. After explaining an episode in *Omensetter's Luck* he writes: "This explanation is very tedious and wooden, and certainly unconvincing. But Henry's suicide remains convincing to me because it is esthetically necessary. Given the character of the image system of which he is a part, his death and the exact manner of it, are inevitable." The fiction produced by this approach is something different—as Joyce's was.

Reynolds Price refuses "to contract with readers on horseback, racing by," and in his preface to *A Generous Man* he says many things worth slow pondering. He notes that the book was badly received by those who came to it with preconceptions about what a novel is supposed to do. They'd read *A Long and Happy Life* contentedly enough, but now his new novel found them baffled and inflexible: Snakes that think? Ghosts that change tires?

Price's piece is unusual for its intensity of concern about a *title* for the novel, and a category. At first he gave his book the subtitle *An Escapade,* and then he thought of *A Romance.* These mullings show, I think, that Price sensed ahead of time he was going to have trouble with readers expecting an orthodox tale. He wanted to raise a warning flag: "*A Generous Man* is not a novel. . . ." Price and Gass are remote from one another, but together in their estrangement from a kind of orthodoxy shared by the other writers in this volume. None of the others would have occasion to say: My book "proceeds under no law except its own— the demands of its meaning. . . . The form of [the] story is . . . miraculous."

In "Discovering the Dangs" George P. Elliott tells how the first, clamorous image for his story came to him while he was prostrate with a fever. He had a virus and with it he bugged his own unconscious: "Abruptly I imagined. . . ."

That first, feverish vision of Elliott's was a donation from the mind's netherworld. What followed had to be worked for. In Elliott's case the craftsman's job was less one of expression than of exploration: "I was bent on discovering what complexities of meaning were latent in that image. . . ."

Like Elliott's (and Gass's and Mailer's), Truman Capote's piece was not written expressly for this book, and in some sense, being much more sheerly personal reminiscence than an examination of the craftsman at work, it is outside this book's intent.

But it does add another persuasive voice to this book's testimony that the first rule for the would-be writer is to be possessed, catch a fever, get struck by creative lightning. Having arranged that, the rest comes hard. "Lightning" is Capote's own word: "Excitement—a variety of creative coma—overcame me. . . . Usually when a story comes to me, it arrives, or seems to, *in toto:* a long sustained streak of lightning that darkens the tangible, so-called real world, and leaves illuminated only this suddenly seen pseudo-imaginary landscape, a terrain alive with figures, voices, rooms, atmospheres, weather."

"Detective story writers are often asked why we devote our talents to working in a mere popular convention," says that master of the genre, Ross Macdonald. "Our answer is that there may be more to our use of the convention than meets the eye." After reading Macdonald's preface to *The Galton Case* I think most observers will agree that indeed there is. Macdonald cites Brigid Brophy's remark to the effect that the detective story "cannot be taken seriously because it fails to risk the author's ego and is therefore mere fantasy." It seems the judgment could hardly be more off the mark in Macdonald's case. Miss Brophy would never have guessed that a detective-story writer might junk a first version because "Neither structure nor style was complex enough to let me discover my own largely undiscovered purposes." Nor could she expect him ever to report, "I remember the rush of invention that occurred when the emotional and imaginative urges, the things *The Galton Case* was to be about, were released. . . ." This isn't a cool technician merely playing with a literary Tinkertoy; there is a great deal of ego on the line here.

Macdonald is a technician as well, an expert at his craft, and he is especially interesting about the mechanics of his genre. The techniques of detective stories hold for other stories too; consider Macdonald's two paragraphs on the occasional value of letting "a character and his story divide." It's a lesson that anyone interested in the craft of fiction—and drama—might profit from.

Partly because of its short-entry form, John Fowles's preface to his work-in-progress *The French Lieutenant's Woman* is a feast of provocative remarks. Just a few: "All the best cutting is done when one is sick of the writing." "Follow the accident, fear the fixed plan—that is the rule." "The nightmare of the writer is that all his worst private fears and self-criticism will be made public." He is especially strong in his defense of the novel against exaggerated reports of its death. "One has in fact only to do a filmscript to realize how inalienably in possession of a still vast domain the novel is; how countless the forms of human experience only to be described in and by it."

Fowles believes that an obsessive search for new forms in fiction can blind the searcher to what accepted forms can do. He's right about this, I think; it *can*. But there is an argument that new forms must constantly be sought after because each age is a different subject, with different insights, tensions, rhythms. (Fowles notes how the very shape of our dreams is conditioned by our having been brought up on movies.) Forms in art are like dialects of time. They become identified with eras, and when we're not of the era, though we can listen appreciatively, we find the sound doesn't really fit the contours of our own moment. The gavotte is grand, but it isn't the dance we're doing.

Very much of his era is Vance Bourjaily, and his *Confessions of a Spent Youth* is a book of remarkable timeliness for his generation. His piece about its writing has much of the same intense honesty, body-heat personalness, and here-in-the-room-with-you aural quality of the book itself. The description of the innovations that went into the book has great technical fascination.

In one sense it may be misleading. When he tells how much of the book was meant to be a fictional critique of myths of fiction, or how its structure was like a series of topical shingles, each advancing in time beyond its predecessor, we might expect the novel to be a chilly quadrille of writing. It's anything but that.

If anyone matches the tone of his time the way Bourjaily does, it's Norman Mailer. They are—or have been—closer in voice, stance, and preoccupation than any other two writers in this book, perhaps than any other two major writers of these decades. Hemingway and Fitzgerald loom large in both their backgrounds. It was John O'Hara who once said the greatest single influence on postwar American fictional style was the author of *The Last Tycoon*.

In his marvelously rich and winging *Crack-Up*-like account of *The Deer Park*, Mailer says as much himself. For my money, Mailer's explanation of why he went through the last draft of *The Deer Park* taking the polish *off* the style is one of the most illuminating of all possible lessons on what it is to be a worthy writer. Mailer describes his glossy original version as "a style which at its best sounded like Nick Carraway in *The Great Gatsby*." Which meant, because Mailer's man was not Carraway, that it was wrong, that it must "blur his character and leave the book unreal." This immensely important insight is a reply to at least part of John Fowles's defense of old forms. The very great danger of received forms is that the writer is apt to listen to the form rather than to life.

This concern about voice is strong in both Mailer and Bourjaily, and it's important to see that what's on their minds is something much deeper than verbal finery. There are three kinds of writers: The kind who write and always will write in no-style, a functional timber as characterless as the flap copy on the jacket; the kind who seem to have been *born* with a style, the natural athletes of art who are wildly, triumphantly individual without ever having thought about it—Dickens, for a prime example; and, that great majority of good writers, the kind that has to find a style. How does one *find* a style? The most important thing is probably to focus one's eyes beyond the scrim of the masters to the real goings-on. Of course, it isn't just eyes, and it isn't just ears (though to a writer's sensibility there is nothing more seductive than rhythms); it's also the kind of "sensitivity" that gets chosen, that is, those observations about people and the world that are taken to be most important. The most blatant imitators of Hemingway and Salinger did not embarrass us nearly so much by their sound as by their attempt to impersonate a soul.

Each of the four reasons given the writers for why they should do these after-the-fact prefaces turns out to be at least mildly supported. There are things in here to satisfy that lover's hunger for news from the inside. There are some technical tips worth considering. There are genuine aids to understanding better what the writers were after and what they actually did. And there are some good stories about stories in here. In the end, though, we have to be glad that the writers had those other reasons of their own.

—THOMAS MCCORMACK

Afterwords

LOUIS AUCHINCLOSS

The Rector of Justin

Writing *The Rector of Justin*

FROM MY TWELFTH to my eighteenth year I was a student at Groton School, an institution then approaching the end of the fifty-five-year administration of its veteran headmaster and founder, Endicott Peabody. Dr. Peabody had, more than any person I have ever known, the quality which military men like to describe as "command presence." He was not only physically large and imposing; his character and personality were sustained by a vibrant religious faith that, so far as I know, was never clouded by a doubt. He had been educated in England where his father had been the London representative of the Morgan Bank, and he seemed to belong more to the nineteenth century than to the twentieth. As a headmaster, he was in the tradition of Arnold of Rugby whose revolutionary idea of a church school had been that the church should be first and foremost.

In those years my imagination was at its most impressionable, and it was utterly engrossed by a school where I was at first abysmally wretched and later moderately content, and where at first I did everything badly and ultimately a few things well. Sooner or later I knew that it was bound to provide me with material for the fiction that I had started writing as early as fourteen. I had only to consider the vast number of boarding schools that populate American and English fiction. And indeed in later years I did begin to write of schoolboys, but I always reserved the subject of a headmaster for the time when I should feel ready to handle it. I already had an inkling that it was going to be my major theme.

What troubled me most was the personality of Dr. Peabody, which for a long time massively blocked my embryonic story. Of course, many of the Groton family are convinced to this day that my Rector of Justin, Francis Prescott, was modeled directly on Dr. Peabody. This kind of identification among a writer's acquaintances is inevitable, and, as one member of the Peabody family told me, it showed how little people remembered him. My difficulty with the shade of Dr. Peabody was not that I was unwilling to use him as a protagonist, but that I *could* not. His character had been too simple and too direct for my purposes. I had become convinced that the central problem in all New England Protestant church schools of his day was the conflict between the piety and idealism of their inspirers and the crass materialism of the families from which they drew not only their students but their endowments. I found some evidence that Dr. Peabody, in his retirement, had come to a troubled awareness of this dichotomy; but during the bulk of his active life I am sure that, beyond a mild disappointment that so few of his graduates went into the church and so many to the stock market, he was happily unconscious of how far his reach had exceeded his grasp.

Furthermore, he had never been an intellectual man; he had never quite trusted the arts. He had seemed to think that they were like tobacco or alcohol, all right if not taken in excess. He once protested that his boys wasted their time in Christmas vacations at the theatre because they were more interested in the "pulchritude" of the actresses than in the message of the play, but as one acute graduate pointed out, Dr. Peabody himself would have been the first to look askance at the boy who was more interested in the message than the actress. In my youth I had been a passionate admirer of Dr. Peabody, but I could not acclimatize myself as a mature novelist to the prospect of a fictional headmaster who would be unmoved by Jane Austen or Balzac and who might have even raised his eyebrows at the sublime sonnets of Shakespeare.

No, to dramatize the troubled story of the Protestant church school my headmaster would have to be a much more complicated character than Endicott Peabody. He would have to have moments of doubt to balance his faith; he would have to see his school as a mountain of vanity as well as a monastery; he would have to be intellectual, cultivated, occasionally cynical, sometimes cruel, always clever. If Dr. Peabody had his moments of despair, they didn't show. I wanted my man to be tortured in his brilliant success by constantly having to question its validity, and at times to despise even his own teachers and pupils for their failure to make his ideals seem as shining as he had aspired to make them. I wanted him to be humble and vain, to be St. Francis of Assisi and King Lear on the heath. I wanted him to express the agony of failing ridiculously when he wanted at the very least to fail magnificently, and I wanted him to raise the question—no more than that—if he had failed at all.

The greatest man whom I ever had the good luck to know was the late Judge Learned Hand. He offered here and there a clue to what I wanted, and in the final characterization of my Francis Prescott I put in more than one of his traits. I even inserted a couple of stories that he had told me, but when the novel appeared, this was only noticed by one of my correspondents. I might parenthetically make the suggestion to incipient novelists that, if they wish to disguise a character drawn in any part from life, all they need do is change his profession. To most readers the word "fiction" is an utter fraud. They are entirely convinced that each character has an exact counterpart in real life and that any small discrepancy with that counterpart is a simple error on the author's part. Consequently, they are totally at a loss if anything essential is altered. Make Abraham Lincoln a dentist, put the Gettysburg Address on his tongue, and nobody will recognize it.

As I began gradually to make out my headmaster, I began also dimly to discern my school. It would have to be more characteristic than special; it would have to be large, more like St. Paul's than like Groton, and have a dash of English public school toughness, for the eastern seaboard, at the end of the last century, was inclined to be Anglophile. It would have to embrace the best, and some of the worst, aspects of the New England Protestant church schools, and, most importantly of all, it would have to arouse in the reader a genuine question as to whether the education which it provided for boys was more of an asset than a liability.

It was my hope that I would be able to remain impartial about this question, as it seemed to me that I was evenly divided in my heart as to whether my own education had done me more good or harm. But I was perfectly clear that, to balance existing trends of thought, defense would be more needed than attack. To hit the Groton of my day would be to beat a dead horse. The educational concept of secluding a group of boys from the temptations of the world while they are inculcated with physical and mental disciplines in the ambience of a single faith has become hopelessly unfashionable. Regardless of what I felt about my own school, I would have to do a good bit of explaining of any similar institution if I did not want its goals to seem merely foolish to contemporary readers.

Similarly, with my headmaster, I would have to explain the value of his inspirational qualities to some boys as well as their almost murderous effect on others. When the book was ultimately published, I ran into a good deal of comment in the press as to whether or not I "approved" of my headmaster. I don't know. Certainly I considered him a great man, and I meant that his faith should be as much the core of the novel as the faithlessness of Saul Bellow's protagonist is that of *Herzog*. Surely, it is as valid to study faith as to study its absence, particularly in delineating institutions founded on it. But I suppose there is no getting away from the old business of "taking sides." There are still people who claim that Shylock is a hero and others who maintain him to be a villain. In our era, it may be permissible for a novelist to be neutral about an alienated character or a non-hero, but if he introduces the values of yesteryear, he is expected to show where he stands. However, in this respect, as in many others, the Goncourt brothers remain my models. I am neither a satirist nor a cheerleader. I am strictly an observer.

My next problem was how to tell my story. It would have to cover a considerable lifetime, for reading through all the biographies that I could find of New England headmasters (a dreary task), I was struck by how many had attained longevity. Furthermore, there seemed to be one generation that had obviously been the "great" generation, that of Peabody, Drury, Thayer and Mather, a generation of thunderous idealists and of long reigns; and it was clearly among this little group of splendid contemporaries that I would have to place my protagonist if my story was to achieve the proper verisimilitude. The only way I could see to deal with the problem of a long-lived character was to cast the novel in the form of a biography, or even of an autobiography.

I rejected the idea of autobiography, for the simple reason that one of the most important aspects of any headmaster is his effect, presumably powerful, on other people. This even a fictional autobiographer cannot very well describe without seeming fatuous. Then I was afraid that doing the book in the form of a biography would limit me to the point of view of my fictional biographer, but I found that I could get around this by the expedient of introducing the reader to my biographer's source material, so that he would be constantly looking over the latter's shoulder as he put together his book. This opened up a wide field for the proliferation of points of view. My biographer would be able to ask people who had known the headmaster to write up for him some particular period of the headmaster's life. He could find letters and diaries which would be set forth in full in the manuscript, or he could record his own conversations with persons who had interesting memories of his subject. Of course, I ran here into the danger of having the finished book seem artificial. There are some critics who will always attack a literary device of this sort, whether or not it be successfully executed. They will arbitrarily refuse to understand why any character who is telling them a story should be telling them that particular story and should be telling it to them in those words. But to me it always seemed that to tell a tale through an "I" is one of the most basic and natural forms of storytelling, and the gulf between myself and the critics who feel it must be apologized for is an unbridgeable one.

Actually, even from a strictly factual point of view, I discovered, after finishing *The Rector of Justin,* that nothing which my fictional biographer had turned up could not have been turned up by a true biographer writing a book about a true headmaster. One friend sent me a privately published diary, several hundred pages in length, that had been kept by a master at a boys' boarding school for the purpose of recording, over the decades, his secret but never-diminishing detestation of a very famous headmaster.

But my fictional biographer, what sort of a man was he to be? I was caught up for a while by a fancy theory which intrigued and later almost obsessed me of a man who would be convinced that the headmaster had been a saint, a true saint in the orthodox Christian sense. As one read his book, however, it would somehow have to become clear to the reader, in Jamesian fashion, that the saint was not, indeed, the headmaster, whose worldliness and occasional cruelty barred him from any such category, but the biographer himself. This was not only a theme that I found I could not handle; it turned out to be a theme that had no true relation to my point of departure. It was another book altogether. I then decided that my biographer should be an early graduate of the school, a poor boy who later made a fortune and became Chairman of its Board of Trustees. He would raise the huge sums needed for the school's endowment and bring Mammon onto the hitherto innocent campus. Needless to say, he would be loathed by the headmaster. I eventually did put such a character into the book, and he played a leading role as David Griscam; but the first version of the novel, in which he appeared as the headmaster's biographer, had to be scrapped entirely when his personality got out of hand.

A week after giving up this first draft, when I was absolutely discouraged, I had a sudden inspiration of how the book should be done.

My biographer would be a man two generations younger than the headmaster, who would make his first appearance at the end of the old man's life. The headmaster would be attracted to him by the one quality that they had in common: their religious faith. To make this stronger I would define my biographer in terms of opposites to the headmaster. He would be unhealthy, irresolute, untidy, utterly devoid of "command presence." He would be sensitive and emotional, yet redeemed by integrity and courage. He would become the intimate of the headmaster because they would both come to realize that the faith which was the bond between them was almost totally lacking in the school, the faculty, the parents and the trustees. These latter all would care only about the appearance of faith. Indeed, they would often be actually antagonistic to anything *but* this appearance. As Brian Aspinwall (which was my biographer's name) and Dr. Prescott would come to recognize what they had in common and its tragic uniqueness in the world about them, they would be drawn together in love and in despair. Brian, after the death of Dr. Prescott, would be able to live only in his planned biography.

The form of the book, then, was not going to be a biography but a preparation for a biography. It would be cast in the form of Brian Aspinwall's journal starting in 1939 with his first meeting of Dr. Prescott, and ending in 1946 just after the latter's death, when Brian decides to start his book about him. At each point in the journal where he comes upon material shedding light on the life of Dr. Prescott, that material is included in chronological order. On the last page Brian has completed his researches and, as the reader closes the book, Brian is picking up his pencil to start his biography. We never know, therefore, what he writes or even if he succeeds in writing it. Personally, I doubt if Brian would have been able to finish it. As I see him, he is the kind of perfectionist who would be constantly tearing up each page that he had written.

Besides Brian Aspinwall, I decided to add, in the form of material he discovers or collects, the points of view of five other observers. An old expatriate dandy, an epicure and lifelong friend of Dr. Prescott, gives Brian three unpublished chapters of his never-to-be-published memoir, "The Art of Friendship," dealing with Dr. Prescott's youth. Brian then gets his material for the early years of the school through the notes supplied him by Mr. Griscam, the embittered would-be biographer of Dr. Prescott, who has abandoned his project because of the headmaster's hostility. He learns of the domestic side of the headmaster's life through his talks with Dr. Prescott's daughter and through reading a chapter of a novel written by her lover who has died of World War I injuries. And finally, Brian sees the memoir written by Mr. Griscam's son, who has committed suicide, as an exercise for a French psychiatrist who was attempting to exorcise from his patient's soul the ghost of the headmaster whom he had hated in his boyhood.

Once I had my scheme, after so much floundering, the book was speedily written. It still seems to me that the shifting points of view are successful in keeping constantly open the question of good or evil in the headmaster's relationships. What to me is not meant to be open is the central fact of his faith and sincerity. And so, in the end, perhaps I did what I had first had in mind: to write a work of hagiography, to study a saint, and to leave it up to the reader whether saints are good or bad.

WRIGHT MORRIS

One Day

One Day:
November 22, 1963–November 22, 1967

THAT FRIDAY IN November it drizzled all morning: a good day
for work. Under the cat in the wire basket on my desk was an
inch or so of uncounted pages, the rough draft of three or four
months' work. A final page inclined on him, rippling as he
breathed, shielding him from the light. I had paused at that
point in my story where Harold Cowie, absent-mindedly day-
dreaming while out for a drive, had driven through a stop sign
and found himself in the hands of a local cop, Patrolman
Closkey. A chronic daydreamer, Cowie had been in the midst of
recalling an experience central to his life—and quite possibly to
my novel. I didn't want to rush him, but I did want to distract
him. It was the author who needed a break, not Cowie. The
appearance of Patrolman Closkey provided the author with time
out, for lunch, and an opportunity to reflect on *what next.*

In those novels I seem to like, as well as those I write, an
accumulating backlog of hints and complications provides the
motivations for what comes next. It is a matter of feeling: hopefully, it is also a matter of chance. The imagination is seldom at
its best when toeing the line. A novel's *line,* like a political party
line, inhibits what originally set the writer to writing. Toeing the

line produces the necessary prose but depresses poetry. There is no supporting structure without lines to follow, but there is little of interest with too many of them. The furniture of the scene may or may not be given, the action undetermined or carefully plotted, but if chance is excluded from *what next,* the scene is deprived of imagination. To that extent it is also deprived of truth. Unavoidably, many scenes are. The novelist cultivates the pedestrian while he waits for the gift of relevation, the line, paragraph, or scene that generates spontaneous illumination. This both involves and displays the writer's awareness of the element of chance. It is crucial to the craft of fiction. At the unexpected moment of this confrontation he is "free." If he has wings, he can do a bit of flying. If a walker, he can walk on water. In whatever medium that is congenial to his talent, his imagination, at this moment of chance he effortlessly *takes off,* he painlessly cracks through how things *were,* to how things *are.* It would not be for long, of course, but this is his moment of truth. Something that has served its purpose is displaced with something that serves.

I was slow to learn this simple fact because it went against my admirable working habits. I sit down and work. I have sometimes worked too hard. Quite by accident, quite, that is, by chance, I once gave up trying to force a difficult scene—and paused to shave. Midway through the shave, my face puckered with lather, the scene arranged itself to the imagination's dictates. Half-shaved I rushed back to work. I had my moment of flight. In this instance it was the *break,* the recess from forced effort, that released the imagination from the will's constraint. The tumblers fell into place. Chance had played its role in the imaginative act. The writer who stops to smoke, pare his nails, abuse his wife, or just pace up and down the creaking floor of the kitchen, is wooing the bird of flight to sing and the chances are that song, not a singing commercial, will be his reward.

That Friday in November I was four months into a novel I might have entitled *How Things Are.* I wanted to know. Writing a novel is one way of finding out. I wanted answers more complex, and more gratifying, than previous novels had been able to supply me. I was ambitious, that is. I wanted to put up, or shut up. With this in mind I had set up the scene, and carefully screened the characters. They would have to tell me, not I them, how things were. If I judge myself a novelist, if I accept it as a calling, if I might, like James, refer to it privately as "my dear genius," it is because my talent, such as it is, finds its realization in the creation of *characters*. The refinements and complexities of the novel are introduced to stimulate and gratify the demands of the characters, and to involve them, along with the author, in the bizarre, horrifying, and fascinating details that make up what we call the immediate present. They have their true existence in the world of fiction: they are imaginative facts. Readers with a taste for the other kind would be wise not to read novels. The abuse would be mutual: the use of both book and reader a waste of time.

My shaping novel featured seven characters, and one of them was Harold Cowie. Thanks to his temperament, and his past, he had a special feeling for "accidents." Indeed, until accidents could be "explained"—and ceased to be accidental—Cowie questioned the value of all explanations. He put it like this:

> . . . the word accident was his baptism under fire. Every day there were thousands. Every day they cost money, limbs and lives. An accident took the life of the child in the home, the driver on the highway, the traveler on the airplane, and the poor devil idly passing the building going up, or the one coming down. The man in the street—perhaps the worst place to be—mortgaged away his peace to appease this monster, as men in the past sacrificed maidens to appease their Gods. And those appeasable Gods had disappeared to be replaced by a new one. The accident. The meaningless event . . . what other word so empty of meaning seemed so full of it?

It was such an event—his traffic violation—that had given Cowie the time and the excuse to switch on the car radio and listen to the news. That was where the author left him when he stopped for lunch. The manuscript reads:

> He tipped forward and switched on the news. A nameless boy, thought to be brown-haired, had been bitten by a squirrel thought to have rabies. An infant (unidentified) had been left in a basket at the local Pound. Luigi Boni, a local artist and barber, had been struck by a truck backing out of an alley. His condition reported as fair.

These last two lines were pencilled in (after the sheet had been taken from the roller) as a final hint to the author of what might be next.

Along with lunch, I had a bad cold. I worked less on what next than on my wife's sympathy. The scratch pad (and useless ballpoint pen) beside my plate were not used. Because of my cold, and the drizzly weather, my wife Jo went for the mail. It's a five minute walk from the door to the mailbox, but she was gone longer than usual. In time I heard the clack of her heels in the drive, and as the door opened she cried, "They shot him! They shot him!"

What did I say? Perhaps nothing.

"He's been shot!" she cried, and crossed the room to stare with fury at the machinery in the hi-fi corner. It takes an engineer to find the right button. She is not an engineer. "Will you turn it on!" I turned it on. In silence we waited for the tubes to warm up. Her breathing was hoarse, her face flushed, the drizzle had jeweled her hair with sequins, and the novelist she married would recall it was his wife—not the hi-fi—that brought him the news on the hour. Someone not yet identified had shot the President of the United States.

Several days passed before I got back to the sheet I had left in the typewriter. The news on the hour had proved to be different than Cowie had reported. Its impact, among other things, had overpowered my fiction and paralyzed my imagination. How could the writer match the news on the hour? While he stood waiting for the tubes to warm up, the world passed him by, or bulldozed him under. "Typographic man" might not be quite dead, but there was no question he felt himself threatened: that with each news on the hour he felt the chill in his extremities.

At that point of stoppage, a traumatic block, I had thought myself abreast of *how things were,* with a fair chance of a fresh report on my findings. I had my scene, a large cast that featured seven contrasting yet representative people, and a theme that audaciously (I thought) reconsidered man's inhumanity to man, his fall, and his second chance. I am inclined to feel—and have somewhere said—that this country is the country of the second chance. It makes it tick. It also makes it difficult to read the time. To catch the tick and the time I had this idea of a young woman, a reluctant beatnik, educated and committed to concepts of justice, a Civil Rights rebel and civil wrongs corrector, who leaves the child of her brief affair with a young Negro protester in a Bon Voyage basket at the local Pound. This bizarre event would provide the novel with its appropriate motivation. It would be that occasion, apparently fortuitous, that would shape the events of the day to its meaning, and leave its impact on the characters. It seemed to me, at the time, sufficient. My problem was to make it acceptable and convincing. That was what I was doing before the news from Dallas disrupted the lines of force between the book and its author, rearranged the scenery and reconsidered the events, and reduced Alec Cartwright's act of audacity to an impulsive prank.

What next? Not a few modern writers of fiction have been unhinged by daily events. It is how things are. Nor was it the first time that I had been faced with the decision of including the world in, or phasing it out. Once before the news on the hour had brought a novel of mine to a halt. Charles Starkweather, one of the first of the new breed of cold-blooded assassins, and like the author, a native of Nebraska, had occupied the news spotlight for a week. Starkweather's shooting preserve happened to include the landscape of my novel. In his flight to escape he might have passed through the fiction of Lone Tree. When the novel had recovered, which took some time, it incorporated much of Starkweather's impact on both the author and the characters. One might say the *ceremony*, in *Ceremony in Lone Tree*, owed its recovery and something of its quality to repeated transfusions of cold blood.

Was it in the writer's power, and the tolerance of fiction, to somehow incorporate what he habitually excluded—the omnipresent and distracting world of the immediate present? I had been stopped in my tracks by the march of events—why shouldn't they also stop my fiction? Instead of fighting them, why not join them? Alec Cartwright's story, in the novel I was writing, had been shaped by the potter's hands of daily events: and now a further, more formidable event had fallen across it like a roadblock. How—within the structure of the novel—admit it? Appropriately enough, both character and author would suffer the same trauma. Both would have to recover. Disrupted lines of force would have to be reestablished. Incredibly enough, the novel I had been writing concerned itself, specifically, with fortuitous events. Its theme was nothing less than how things are. From such events, in their respective pasts, the characters had found their motivations. If this latest event seemed to trivialize the very theme of the novel—then let the novel admit it. Let it begin, precisely at that point, with what was not trivial. To make such a beginning I had to do no more than confront the page before me in the typewriter. I had left Cowie sitting there, stopped by Patrolman Closkey, listening to the news on the hour. How prepare a scene better for the anticipated occurrence? A novelist can try. It came on too fast—Cowie needed preparation that would be familiar to the novel's reader. So I first filtered the news through Closkey—as my wife had filtered it to me.

Pulling on his gloves (Closkey) said, "He must think I'll believe everything he tells me. How you like that?"
"Like what?"
"There's a report out they shot at him."
"Shot at who?" Closkey seemed to have forgotten he had a point to settle with Cowie. He got into his car, switched off the blinker, and swung it around in an illegal manner: the spin of his wheels threw gravel on Cowie's window. For the time, Cowie switched the radio on. The voice of the announcer . . . went on to say that a bulletin, as yet unconfirmed, had just come in from Dallas. . . . We have a bulletin from Dallas, the voice continued, we have confirmation on the word from Dallas, an attempt has been made to assassinate the President of the United States.

Few novels would tolerate such a bizarre and horrifying intrusion, but the one I was writing seemed structured for it. Its theme was how things are. This was how they were. It was up to the fiction to accommodate the facts.

Respect for the facts breeds a reliance on the facts that is seldom good for the novel. But such respect has a long history. It is involved with our concepts of the growth of the novel. Currently—and for reasons easily and fashionably exploited—it is assumed the novelist's purpose is to grasp *the facts*. The fictive elements in his performance are considered unfortunate and secondary. Mr. Capote gave these notions fresh currency in his comments on *In Cold Blood*. Since facts speak louder than fiction, why not stick to the facts? Writers as various as James Jones, Norman Mailer, and Saul Bellow are open to this persuasion. With his narrative skill the writer of fiction gives us the facts in the guise of a novel. The reader—who prefers the facts—is spared the embarrassment of taking fiction seriously. The Great American Novel, in this view, is the most complex of all How-To-Do-It books. How to make love, make murder, make hay, and above all make time, based on a bona fide personal experience. What we like best about Walden Pond is that bit about the low cost of living—

House	$28.12½
Farm one year	14.72½
Food, eight months	8.74
Clothing, etc., eight months	8.40¾
Oil, etc., 8 months	2.00
In all	61.99¾

That's living. In terms of the bare facts, that's what it cost.

In my novel concerned with a single day's happenings in the lives of a generous assortment of people, the one assured, bona fide *fact* is the news on the hour from Dallas. No reader known to me, seeking *further* facts, was long fooled. In remaining a book of fiction, *One Day* also remained *au-dessus la mêlée* for the reader who heard the news from Dallas, and wanted the facts.

In four years numberless books of contradictory facts, most of them to be classified as bad fictions, seek to persuade the reader with what actually happened in Dallas—what happened in the reader is judged of little interest. What happened in the reader is the subject of *One Day*.

The characters in my novels—now that I can appraise them after more than twenty years of screening—prove to emerge from abiding preoccupations. Archetypal figures (reasonably clear in a montage of sixteen novels) have the final say as to *who* will appear as a character in my fiction. They may bear a close resemblance to an actual person (as such persons resemble archetypal humors) or they may be assembled, whole cloth, from my imaginings and the needs of the novel. *One Day* has both. Harold Cowie, for example, is a contemporary mask on a personality I consider unchanging—the decent, sympathetic, reflective dropout who does not have (or does not *choose* to have) what it takes to make the scene. He is both the square and the square peg, sympathetic to his own predictable failure. He keeps in touch with life, and what he values, through children, eccentrics, dogs and cats. He turns up in my life and in my fiction. He relates to Will Brady in *The Works of Love* and to Peter Foley in *The Huge Season*. He receives something of a trial run as William Bryan Jennings in *Ceremony in Lone Tree*. But something still remained to be said, and in *One Day* he says it.

Alec Cartwright, the first of her breed, the preview and trial run for the beat generation, I met in the flesh in 1945. At that time she suffered the frustration and familiar eclipse of having a talent too far ahead of her time. Her acute sense of rebellion had no focus. By the time suitable cause had been determined (in the mid-fifties) she was the mother of pre-hippie children. My belated tribute required no pre-dating, since the times had finally merged with her image. That she seems on the *square* side, intellectually speaking, is *how things were* in the mid-forties: a decade would pass before the rebel would throw in the intellectual sponge.

Alec's mother, Evelina, made a brief appearance in *Man and Boy* (written in 1947) and again in *The Deep Sleep* five years later, where her hoarse voice and baying laugh contribute their touch to the Porter wake. Among other attributes, I see that Evelina comes to my mind when I'm confronted with death, her *ewig Weiblich* vitality surviving her own mound of collapsing flesh. Her role in *One Day* is aided and abetted by the perceptibly dissolving Adele Skopje, the concrete embodiment of Evelina's inexhaustible passion for the orphic, the mysterious, and the occult. They make a fine pair. Adele Skopje I first saw, happily just in passing, in the weedy shade of her beach umbrella just off Sunset Boulevard where it twists and turns through the sacred grove that divides Beverly Hills from the gates to Bel Air. From the rim of her umbrella suspended a STAR MAP, a guide to the homes of the Hollywood stars. An unforgettable sight. At last glimpse (winter 1967) one of her kind is still doing business at the old stand.

Most of my life, or so it seems, Wendell Horlick has been a neighbor, his son Irving going through the trash before the Goodwill people got around to it. Horlick is "hard of hearing"—the first and most successful of his many withdrawal symptoms. Horlick knows that "people are no dam good," and reserves his affection for the hound Larkspur. With the disappearance of Larkspur, the humane sentiments go out of Horlick's life.

The original of Larkspur, a police dog on loan from neighbors who were spending a year in Europe, occupied the rumble seat of a Model A coupe I drove from Los Angeles to Cleveland in 1938. This experience waited twenty-five years for its cue. He wore goggles. Like Larkspur, he was destined for better things. Until the rigors of travel wore him out and he dropped out of the wind to sleep on the luggage, he deflected traffic (especially that approaching) and attracted enthusiastic crowds who had never seen a dog sporting fur-lined goggles. I had never forgotten this adventure, but it waited a quarter of a century for Horlick and *One Day*.

In a bookstore we still frequent I once watched a plump, teenage boy with a skillfully bold but infectious manner con my wife into giving him 17 cents toward the 40-cent volume he was dying to buy. Who would deprive a child of his love of books? Not my wife: nor many book browsers. He had a profitable venture going. Even better—he actually read the books. That incident is the seed for Irving Horlick, Wendell Horlick's precocious offspring, who gets through to his father without the need of a hearing aid.

If *One Day* is concerned with the past of its characters, something of my own is revealed in their selection. The Yucatanian Chavez, and his wife, Conchita, date from a few weeks I spent in Acapulco in 1955. He and his family "occupied" the shell of a resort cottage that would one day, hopefully, have windows and plumbing. In exchange for this shelter, he saw to it that others did not dismantle and walk off with what existed—an old Mexican custom. This scene figured prominently in the Acapulco rendezvous of Horter, Mac, and their chicks in *Love Among the Cannibals*. Chavez himself, however, Chavez as a *persona*, a long suffering piece of baked Mexican earth, had little representation in *The Cannibals* and stayed in the wings until *One Day*.

Luigi Boni, and his childhood in Venice, is a souvenir of our first extended stay in Venice in 1959. The cats were first my wife's problem—then Luigi's. From the window of our apartment we watched the cats and the children that provide Luigi Boni with his Venetian childhood. The gentle-tempered Luigi, one of those hairy, masculine Italians with the temperament of a Botticelli maiden, I saw every day, several times a day, on the Italian liner westbound from Genoa to New York. With his wife, a corseted, creamy-skinned, hairy-legged Amazon, and *her* two pasta-stuffed offspring, he sat subordinate and silent, passing trays of food, or wagging his huge head in approval. Having once caught his eye, and in a glance shared his life, I was at pains *not* to observe him. He rose early and often stood alone at the front of the boat.

To this group (including Horlick's wife Miriam) only one voice was added by the event that changed the course of the novel. Holmes, the mortician, provides the twelve o'clock news that serves as the watershed of the story. His between-the-acts appearance, his "sermon" on Death, reveal my long admiration for the *Devotions* of John Donne, and the Knights who speak out in Eliot's verse dramas. The effect achieved by the tone of these statements (the Knights at the front of the stage, having completed the murder) seems to me masterly. My idea of Holmes, the tone and style of his delivery, came to me one of the nights I lay awake pondering *what next*. That night I got up, about an hour before dawn, to catch the tone and rhythm of a few memorized lines, then I held on, with this start, to write four or five pages. In the morning I finished it off. The manuscript indicates it required very little rewriting. It is one of those pieces in which a writer takes more than a grudging pride. It is at one stroke the sign and the proof of being possessed by his subject, and responsive to its revelations. Not many readers, from the reviews I have read, were able to share this release with the author. The irony of the statement, the refusal of Holmes to show his hand in a conventional manner, was lost on the reader who anticipated an elegy on the death of a hero—rather than a devotion on the larger subject of Death itself.

Evelina and Alec Cartwright, Wendell and Miriam Horlick, Harold Cowie, Luigi Boni, Ignacio Chavez, and Holmes, the mortician, report on the events of one day in Escondido as seen through their eyes, and in their own voices. This makes for the complexity of how things *really* are. But it also makes extra demands on the reader. No single narrative line or voice guides him through the apparent incoherence of events. In placing Chickpea's story (another name for Alec Cartwright) at the end of the day, I intended that the unity of her experience would provide the catalyst for the reader: through Alec's experience he would reappraise the day as a whole. There were those who did. Others abandoned the project before Alec was there to reassure them. From the writer's point of view, implicit guidance is offered, and available, in the omniscient voice of the author,

sometimes well-, sometimes ill-concealed, in the voice of each
character. This authorial and omnipresent persona, no matter
who is observing or speaking, provides the ideal reader the author has in mind with the clues and hints necessary—but no
more. To my mind, the craft of fiction is to hold the reader
against all persuasion to turn off, tune in on something else, and
drop out. Only such a reader is actually worth the incalculable
effort to win him over. The rest is cinema, in which the craft of
reading plays no part.

In the writers I admire there are moments (Joyce supplied the
word epiphanal) when the reader and the writer share a more
than customary empathy. On these occasions more than either
bargained for, or anticipated, is revealed. It is, in truth, a bonus,
a whisper of "well done," mutually achieved between the reader
and writer. Communication on this level gives rise to the notion
that the writer is involved in a serious calling, and that a
humane life among human beings should be possible. Because of
him life is at once more acceptable, promising, and intolerable.

I have sometimes felt that it is at such moments, and they
illuminate all good fiction, that what is unique and impalpable
in personal experience finds its appropriate and intimate revelation—rather than merely embarrassing public exposure. An example would be Gabriel Conroy's ascendant moment of insight
at the close of "The Dead." We feel with a certainty greater than
usual that this scene parallels Joyce's actual experience, and
that the memorable details—"One boot stood upright, its limp
upper fallen down: the fellow of it lay upon its side"—were
observed and recorded on the spot. But the craft of fiction lies in
their use, not their observation. Thomas Mann's memorable and
poignant adolescents, little Hans in *Buddenbrooks,* Tadziu in
Death in Venice, and Nepomuk in *Dr. Faustus,* have their origin
in Mann's special sympathy and eye for the expressive, evocative
gesture of children. This would seem to release in both the writer
and the subject the same unearthly, unheard music: the "in-
eluctable modality of the visible" made visible. Facts presented in
this manner—or more accurately, apprehended in this manner—
once seemed to me sufficient to explain the special quality of the
epiphanal moment. But my experience departed from such a
persuasive and sensible text. I have repeatedly noted that the

scene most convincing in its use of *things seen* owes the telling details to the imagination. An example of this, in *One Day,* is the caged bird observed by Cowie during his recovery in Matamoros.

> *. . . This object, cleverly made of wire and daubed with splatters of dung-colored paint, was obviously a cage, a cage for several birds. And the birds? Two days passed before Cowie saw the bird that was in it. . . . A species of canary, Cowie's first impression had been that it was an object, made of cork and pipe cleaners. Artful, perhaps. No question it was horrible. There were quills, but no feathers, below the neck. The head with its lidded eyes was elevated on the neck like a lampshade. The legs and claws were twisted bits of wire. Cowie took it as an example of the Mexican taste for the macabre: the skull-and-bone cookies eaten by children, the fantastic birds and animals made out of paper. When he glanced up to see it headless, he simply thought the head had dropped off. But no. Nothing lay in the bottom of the cage. The head, with its knife-like beak, had been tucked under the quills of one wing. Fly it could not, lacking the feathers. Sing it would not. But on occasion it hopped.*

This object, like the car stripped down to its essentials in *Love Among the Cannibals,* serves the same suggestive purpose, and like the car, is imaginary. I had not thought so when I wrote it. I felt myself to be describing a bird closely and intimately observed. Later, it occurred to me that the actual cage in question had been empty: the bird had already died. It had not been hard for me, at the time or later, to imagine why. And this doomed bird was the one I conjured up.

What I wanted was an event that would provide a *public* shock, followed by a private, and anguishing, reappraisal. While I was brooding on this topic my wife and I went to see the movie *Mondo Cane.* We were not prepared for what we saw. Later in the evening we reconsidered what we had seen. My wife was particularly sensitive to the plight and abuse of the animals. One could, in her opinion, do very little about people, but there should be bigger and better refuges for animals of all kinds—encampments, that is, where they could find escape from human beings. I cited Whitman's lines—

> I think I could turn and live with animals, they're so placid and self-contain'd
> I stand and look at them long and long.

and they reminded me of something, recently noted, that seemed more to *my* purpose.

> While I was a man I liked my condition well enough, and had a very low opinion of beasts, but now that I have tried their way of living I am resolved to live and die as they do.

This seemed to me both grist to my mill, and something new in the way of Edens—birds, beasts, flowers, and a smattering of God's *little* chillun. Some children, as one reads every day, would surely be more at home in the Pound than with their parents, and would perhaps grow up to be more humane human beings. Or so my wife felt. I spent most of the night trying this new Eden on for size. By morning it had become largely a question of how I could make such a place, and such an event, seem plausible. What sort of a mother would be capable of such an act (whether in jest or in earnest) and more important, would her action be understood? It seemed to me that Alec Cartwright, in so far as I knew her, might come to such a conclusion about society and be capable of acting in such a manner. She was a strange, unpredictable girl, but I wanted her unpredictably *human:* shockingly human. This aspect of her personality was so unusual I felt it required a suggestive model—a similar horrifying and shocking action out of love of life, rather than a distaste for it. I found this in the story of Ruth, Alec's college roommate, who managed to bear her unwanted child in a Pullman compartment, alone, and then destroy it. This horrifying action was made possible by her love for the young man who fathered the child. A more than human act (one we describe as inhuman) to preserve a human value. In her shock at such a deed, Alec sensed in her horror a secret admiration. Ruth had been capable of an action that surpassed respectable understanding. But Alec understood it. Was she capable of such an action herself? This is the core of her unresolve as a young woman in love, and in profound rebellion with how things are. The time will come for her to act in some appropriately "absurd" manner. It comes soon enough, but the shock she had planned is lost in the day's larger vibrations. Her private act is made trivial, and she is involved—as are all the others—in an effort to come to terms with the world they have all made.

The first draft of the novel was completed three to four months after the President's assassination. It closed with the fulfillment of Adele Skopje's prophecy, Under Scorpio, that Friday, the 22nd of November, was not a good day for travel. Evelina's car, with Adele Skopje captive and dying in the front seat, runs away from the platform of the ice machine to crash into and partially demolish the front of the Pound. The dogcatcher, Chavez, as in his Mexican past, sits as a caretaker in the half-ruined structure, his mind on Death, the night full of the baying of the distracted Pound dogs.

> *Death was a weightless phantom, or a distant music, or feathers plucked from a lifeless bird, but the word* dead *was like a stone, and as heavy.* Dead. Dead. Dead. *The weight of it might be said to be the measure of the missing life . . . To live but an hour, or a day, entitled that person to be dead forever. In their eyes to have lived must seem a small thing. A mortal moment among the immortal dead. All day Chavez had not shed one tear, dry-eyed and dry-lipped he had stuck to his business, but now strange winds blew in the wings of his mind. A halo surrounded the lamp on the corner, scalding tears doused his dangling cigarette, leaving salt and the taste of ashes in his mouth. In this manner, Ignacio Chavez, dogcatcher, kept the night watch.*

On this elegiac note the first draft of the novel ended. It seemed to me, at the time, the appropriate finale to such a day. As I began the rewriting, however, Alec's long story, coming early in the novel, seemed to unbalance the events of the morning. It had much to do with Alec Cartwright, but insufficient to do with Escondido. In length, and in narrative interest, it overshadowed what preceded and what followed. If left at the front, too much of the long day would seem an anticlimax insufficiently related to the story of Alec. In a book conceived with many centers and competing voices in mind, each indispensable to the day's happenings, a single penetrating and insistent voice confronts the writer with a dilemma. It *will* be heard. It speaks with an authority that is superior to his concept of the book's organization. It is precisely such a voice that is necessary to the novel's life. If there are changes, it must be with this voice in mind.

As I neared the end of the second draft, Chavez seemed to speak from the bottom of an incline that had been too long in the making. It was right as rain for Chavez, but the trough of a wave for the reader. I felt, at that point, the need of the story to relate itself with its beginning—but the reader should experience this about-face through fresh eyes. The freshest eyes were those of Alec. At the end of this day—not at its beginning—the length and import of her story were justified. Through her still fresh and committed eyes we would re-experience and comprehend events that had seemed incomprehensible. Many months had passed since the news from Dallas, and the realignments caused by this tremor had finally persuaded the author and the novel to settle on this new foundation.

This realignment led to minor alterations in Cowie's past. In the place of a successfully seduced, ghostly lover, we have an unravished, artful dodger—and a buffoon. This is the term applied to him by Concepción Lopez when it is clear that Cowie misunderstands her attentions. This conformed more closely to the Cowie of the novel who somehow managed to elude all confrontations, but endlessly broods on the meaning of events.

The opening, scene-setting chapter of the novel was modified to present the day at its close, the local events summarized by Cowie as he sits at the window of the Escondido diner. The time is passing on the clock, the day is passing into history, and the community, at the stroke of midnight, will return to what passes for normal in an abnormal world.

> "Well," says the cook, "I guess that ends it."
> "Ends what?" Cowie mutters.
> The cook makes no comment. He knows better than Cowie that this day had a beginning, but who could say that it would ever end?

This questions hangs in the air as the novel begins, and it is still in the air as it ends with Alec.

> Her mission was accomplished, as Jackson would say, and if her eyes were wide as those of the oracle at Delphi it was because she, too, held the future in her hands.

One Day was published in the early spring of 1965. In the two and one-half years since its publication I have heard from readers who like it very much, others who like it very little, and a few who hope to read it—if and when they find the time. I am in that category. The time necessary to read my own novels I shall never have. Even the first, published twenty-five years ago, has not receded to the point where I can read it. I'm good for eight or ten lines—then the ghost who wrote it intervenes. He wrote the book, but he will never recognize it with the shock of recognition. The most casual, indifferent reader will know it in a way that will forever escape him: the whole of it, the novelty of it, the unique surprises and pratfalls of it! The book for which I am solely and uniquely responsible I will never know as well as those I can read, remember, and forget.

An author is still entitled to his impressions, however, and they are complex. I am able to see the justice of many honest complaints. Why do I write such *complicated* books? Like the reader, I would much *prefer* they were simple. But my preferences have little or nothing to do with my preoccupations. As a reader I too dream of the book that flows like the mountain water in the beer signs, clean, cool and clear as the trout-haunted shallows of Hemingway's Big Two-Hearted River. I like them—but they are not the books I am bidden to write. My feelings and my thoughts do not lend themselves to recommended practices of simplification. Since I find nothing simple, why should I simplify? The releases I need, and sometimes get, are at the heart of the maze, not at its exit. Above all else, that to me is *how things are*. To the extent that I am able to grasp how they are, I can live with them.

It seems to me now that the news from Dallas distracted the reader more than it distracted the novel. Preconceptions on the part of the reader, a year and a half later, made it virtually impossible for such a reader to accept a piece of fiction. My concern proved to be that of Holmes, the mortician, brooding on the role of Death in a deathless culture. The reader's concern was with the assassin, and the assassination, of John F. Kennedy. The reader still in shock from the event, or persuaded that the event was an experience of shock, was of little mind to reconsider the nature of the happening. I believe this is still true. The death of the President is now secondary to *who* killed the President. Books on this fictive topic will prove to be inexhaustible.

The novels I write, if the writing is good, resist the well-intentioned tampering of the author. How do I know when the writing is good? When I fear for my life. I feel an impersonal and transcendent obligation to finish what I am doing. I hate distractions, believe in vitamins and omens, dread the possibility of untoward events. I would never, no never, have left the house on hearing the word from Adele Skopje. When the writing is good I am always Under Scorpio.

Like the reader, I would have preferred such a tale as that recounted by Alec Cartwright, at once simple, complex, and inevitable. Such a tale would comprehend the *gist* of *One Day*, but the gist was not what I was after. I do not write like James, nor think like James, but I have his endless, parenthetical impressions of reality. The impression I wanted is one that I experience in the presence of a jeweled Medieval landscape, at once panoramic and minutely detailed, a scene that comprehends the lived quality of life and presents it in the necessary perspective. This parallel has been meaningful to me since *The Field of Vision* and *Ceremony in Lone Tree,* where the multiple aspects of a single scene—the bull ring in Mexico, the hotel in Lone Tree—are intended to reveal, layer upon layer, a single moment in time and space. My feeling is that such obsessions produce writers, and that is my obsession. No reader is required to share it.

I am of the opinion that the reader each writer wants is part and parcel of the novel's conception. His special presence is evoked in the style and texture of each line. What we call style is the explicit inclusion of some readers in, and all other readers out. For all those included in, the writer is beside himself to delight and charm to his own persuasions. Above all, he wants to *hold* them. He wants to hold them against their desire to escape. If he so manages a pact is formed. A "public" can be said to exist where such pacts are observed. It may number a few hundred or a few tens of thousands but it has little to do with the selling, the merchandising, or the distribution of books. In this pact writer and reader are committed not to crack-throughs, crack-downs or crack-ups, but a show of how things are in a fiction based on mutual respect.

ANTHONY BURGESS

Nothing Like the Sun

Genesis and Headache

FOR MANY YEARS I had had the intention of writing a novel about William Shakespeare, but the prospective difficulties seemed so immense that I was glad to keep putting it off. In January, 1963, however, I saw that the ghastly but fascinating task couldn't be delayed any longer. The quatercentenary of Shakespeare's birth would be celebrated on April 23rd, 1964, and I would never find a more appropriate publishing date. Moreover, there was a duty that only a novelist could fulfil—that of qualifying the quasi-religious attitudes of the impending festival and showing what the man, not the bard, may have been like. I had had my title ready a long time. *Nothing Like the Sun*—a phrase from one of his sonnets—meant primarily that the human reality of the artist bore no resemblance to the shining golden image that time had made. But the phrase couldn't be separated from its context, nor did I wish it to be. "My mistress' eyes are nothing like the sun": the sonnet is about a dark woman whose hair is black and springy and whose body is more brown than white. Who was this woman? Scholarly conjectures have turned her into a dark-tressed Anglo-Saxon lady of the court; only Professor G. B. Harrison, I think, ever suggested that she might be Negroid. I wanted to write about Shakespeare's relations with a fair woman—his wife Anne—and a woman far more exotic. I knew that in Shakespeare's London there were brothels with Negresses in them (was there not a brothel-madam whom the law students called Lucy Negro?), but I wanted a dark woman who came from the East—a woman like one of the Malays or Achinese or Bugis I had been hotly attracted to during my time as a colonial civil servant. I knew nothing about black women but plenty about brown.

But this would be mere conjectural biography, of superficial interest only. Since long before reading Thomas Mann's novel *Doctor Faustus,* I had pondered on the relationship between genius and disease. Why had so many poets been tubercular? Was it possible that the tubercle actually promoted inspiration and stoked the creative fires? But there was a bigger disease than that—the great aristocrat, syphilis. I noticed that Shakespeare's most superb creations came during a time when, to judge from the imagery of his plays, he was preoccupied with disease—disease in the body, in the spirit, and in the State. It seemed at least possible that he was drawing his most powerful metaphors from his own morbid condition, and that this had something to do with physical love: the revulsion of that sonnet beginning "Th' expense of spirit in a waste of shame /Is lust in action" and King Lear's terrible outcry at lechery pointed to some personal experience of such ghastliness that it could only be purged in art.

Speculation only, but Shakespeare's love-life begged to be probed with the novelist's instruments. He had married, a boy in his teens, a woman in her late twenties; the first child was born a mere six months after the wedding. Who married whom? The poem *Venus and Adonis* presented a mature goddess trying to seduce a boy not yet interested in love. Shakespeare left Stratford, his wife and his three children, to seek his fortune in London: he never asked his wife, even in the time of his affluence, to follow him thither. The marriage was perhaps not a happy one, and I imagined quarrels, taunts, allegations of an ageing woman trapping a young man into a state that had nothing to do with love or "true minds." I found, in my reading, certain documentary evidence of a shotgun wedding. In London, it seemed that Shakespeare turned for a time against women and formed an emotional attachment, and probably also a physical one, to a young man of great beauty, considerable intelligence, and high rank—the Earl of Southampton, who became Shakespeare's patron. Then there is the dark woman, the loss of her to a friend (all set down in the sonnets), the bitterness and the nausea. There was, I saw, plenty of material for a novel.

I had been reading pretty widely, ever since my student days, in books about Shakespeare, in Elizabethan documents, in close scholarly background history. I had taken a lot of notes, and, in early 1963, I took notes feverishly, making a chronological table which related the known facts of Shakespearian biography to the wider events of the time; covering page after page with clinical data about the *morbus Gallicus*—the French pox, or syphilis; reading the plays and annotating them. But much of this work proved to be an excuse for not doing any work. I dreaded actually starting the novel. But at least I planned it. I find it helpful to imagine what a projected book will actually look like when printed and bound: there it is, published; all you have to do now is to get those printed words back into typescript. The length I was sure of: about eighty thousand words. This, I felt, would be enough if I left out that period of Shakespeare's life (say, from 1600 to 1616) when there is little of biographical interest to report, though it is also the period of the greatest plays—*Hamlet, Macbeth,* and so on. Most of the story I wished to tell belonged strictly to the Elizabethan, not the Jacobean, age. The accession of James I genuinely marks a new period, with no more worry about the dynastic succession, with a lot of new-type courtiers, an attempt to make peace with Spain through a royal marriage, and (I get this from *1066 and All That*) the execution of Sir Walter Raleigh chiefly because he was left over from the last reign. Shakespeare in James I's reign asked for a different sort of novel.

I planned *Nothing Like the Sun* as a binary movement with a brief epilogue. Part I was to deal with Shakespeare's puberty and end with his departure for London. Part II, the more complex and the longer, would be about the mature, but not senescent, Shakespeare and end with the shock of syphilis (in other words, it would deal only with the "sweet Master Shakespeare" who was the darling of the Inns of Court and merely, in a single paragraph perhaps, foreshadow the bitter and misanthropic tragedian). Rather arbitrarily, I decided that Part I and Part II should each have ten chapters, and that a chapter of Part II should be about twice the length of the corresponding chapter in Part I. This has been, I think, pretty accurately fulfilled. I look now and find that I.1 goes from page 3 to page 10, while II.1 takes from page 79 to page 94 (the proportion is 7:14=1.2). I.7 is from 46 to 53; II.7 from 160 to 175 (7:15—near enough). And so on. The epilogue was also to have ten chapters, very brief, each of them *half* the length of the corresponding chapter in Part I. This didn't work out. It made the epilogue seem too contrived.

But, on the whole, this sort of arithmetical proportioning is not so cold-blooded as it appears. Nobody regards the sonnet-form as too artificial to express passion, and it was the shape of a poem—monstrously enlarged—that I wanted for my novel. A lot of contemporary fiction would be better for the constrictions of a mould, however artificial: there's too much reliance placed on publisher's editors, whose job is mainly to stem the Thomas Wolfean flow. I was also thinking subconsciously, probably, of Ben Jonson's dictum about Shakespeare: *"Sufflaminandus erat."* This was a kind of sufflamination.

But I was still not far advanced along the line of actually producing a novel. The characters were there waiting—ready equipped with names, if not all with rôles. For one character, though, there was as yet no name: I mean the dark lady. But, reading one of those sonnets which express disquiet about love, I found her name acrostically presented, or very nearly:

> Feeding on that which doth preserve the ill,
> Th' uncertain sickly appetite to please.
> My reason, the physician to my love,
> Angry that his prescriptions are not kept,
> Hath left me . . .

There it is: FTMAH. That is an almost pedantic transliteration of the Arabic spelling of the name Fatimah (all the vowels missing except one). To amuse myself, I tried writing a rather jejune but still Shakespearian sonnet that acrosticised the name in full, backwards as well as forwards:

> *Fair is as fair as fair itself allows,*
> *And hiding in the dark is not less fair.*

The married blackness of my mistress' brows
Is thus fair's home, for fair abideth there.
My love being black, her beauty may not shine
And light so foiled to heat alone may turn.
Heat is my heart, my hearth, all earth is mine;
Heaven do I scorn when in such hell I burn.
All other beauty's light I lightly rate.
My love is as my love is, for the dark.
In night enthroned, I ask no better state
Than thus to range, nor seek a guiding spark.
And, childish, I am put to school of night
For to seek light beyond the reach of light.

FATIMAH—HAMITAF—Roman and Semitic letter-orders. No critic noticed the acrostic, which was, anyway, meant to be a secret between myself and myself. A mere whimsy, but it started the novel for me. I saw, fairly early in Part I, the seventeen-year-old Shakespeare writing this sonnet at home, surrounded by a family quarrel. I caught a clear enough image of his parents, his brothers and his one surviving sister Joan, and the youth himself trying to make a sonnet for a dark-haired girl he was to meet at the May-night junketings just outside Stratford. Shakespeare was unaware of the acrostic in his poem; this gave me a sense of power over him. I could at last conquer my diffidence in his presence and start to get him down on paper.

And yet the problem of an appropriate style stood in the way. Obviously the language had to be an approximation to Elizabethan English, but behind me lay the horrible examples of Wardour-street, the Sir Walter Scotteries of *gadzooks,* the embarrassment of *thou* and *thee.* Unlike the Englishmen of the South, however, I belong to a dialectal tradition that still uses the *tutoyer* long abandoned by the Queen's English. In Lancashire we say "Where's tha going, lad?" and get the reply "I'm coming back with thee to thy place." If I used *tha* in my novel, that would be close to a living tradition and far enough from the artificialities of Wardour-street.

First I wrote a whole chapter in fair Elizabethan, and I put it in the mouth of Shakespeare himself. The novel, then, was to be a first-person narrative. I read this chapter over the BBC's Third Programme in a series about novelistic work in progress. I was shocked to hear the playback. It didn't sound like a real person, a possible young Shakespeare; it sounded like an impersonation and hence insincere. Very well, then: it must be a third-person narrative, and it must be in a kind of Elizabethan protected from sneerers and carpers by a sort of built-in irony. Let (it was really coming now) the whole thing be a kind of story delivered by a college lecturer. The lecturer should not be altogether sober. I myself had lectured on Shakespeare in the Far East, sometimes when not altogether sober. Make this a farewell session to special students and (delightful: the engine was starting to throb) make it a means of bringing West and East together—a Western poet and an Eastern lady; a West that was drawing jewels and spices from the East; a West, moreover, that had something to give to the East, even if that something was only its greatest poet. I scrapped everything I had so far written and produced the following exordium:

> *Mr. Burgess's farewell lecture to his* special *students, who complained that Shakespeare had nothing to give to the East. (Thanks for the farewell gift of three bottles of* samsu. *I will take a swig now. Delicious.) The text being the acrostical significance of the following lines . . .*

The "following lines" were the ones that said FTMAH. (*Samsu*, incidentally, is a very potent Chinese rice spirit.) I felt I might now get the reader into a relaxed mood, prepared for irony, drunkenness, parody, even the breakdown of the mock-Elizabethan vernacular. And I myself could be somehow involved in the narrative—not myself as I think I know myself, but as somebody on the borderlines of fiction, a character vaguely play-acting because partly drunk on *samsu*. Eventually, I thought, I could make a comic self-identification with Shakespeare: I could foresee that, if things worked out as I planned, it might be technically very useful.

And so with a better heart to the writing of Chapter One in something approaching a final version. What did I want to say? That Shakespeare in his teens, eldest of a moderately sized family, was dissatisfied with the life of the son of an impoverished butcher-glover and yearned towards something better. But what? Something best expressed as a compound image—the riches of the wide world beyond Stratford; the love of a superior woman, not a mere country hilding; the status of a gentleman. One man from Stratford did, as we all know, make good long before Shakespeare himself: this was Clopton, after whom a bridge over the Avon was named. So it seemed reasonable to me to present the young Shakespeare walking with his sister and brothers on the Avon's banks, Shakespeare "marking with storing-up eye the spurgeoning of the back-eddy under the Clopton Bridge." This word *spurgeoning* is the first of my literary tricks. It's derived from the name of Caroline Spurgeon, a modern scholar, who, in her work on Shakespeare's imagery, noted that he introduced the peculiar behaviour of the Avon under that bridge as a simile in *The Rape of Lucrece.* Few reviewers noticed this, even though I gave them another chance by repeating the trick later. The day is Good Friday: Shakespeare has not yet reached his East or Easter. Still, it is spring, and it is the spring of England's Renaissance.

After a draft page, I decided that Shakespeare must be called WS. Too many connotations cluster round the full name; it needs to be purged of all the harmonics of greatness in a novel which has no concern with that greatness. WS—it seemed to me sufficiently neutral. So then WS walks on a spring holiday through Stratford grass, accompanied by his sister Anne and his brothers Richard and Gilbert. Anne and Richard—the associations with *Richard III* were hard to resist. I made Richard chase Anne and Anne cry (in allusion to the arms of the Duke of Gloucester): "Bristly boar!" I distinctly saw young Richard limp, like his usurping namesake, and this gave me the idea of making him lame—one leg shorter than the other. Needless to say, there is no documentary justification for this, any more than there is for making young Gilbert Shakespeare epileptic, moronic, and afflicted with religious mania. What I have to do is to wait until somebody can prove that he was *not* these things. I will have to wait a long time.

I made the object of WS's vague longings into a sort of goddess, summing up the Muse, sexual gratification of a patrician and yet exotic order, the spirit of adventure—what you will. Later, I knew, she had to change into something more deadly. But it seemed necessary to present in more naturalistic form these aspects of the bigger world that would, separately or together, quench an adolescent's vague discontent. I brought in a lying "inland mariner" (one who boasted much but might never have actually been to sea) to spout the usual nonsense about gold and silver growing on trees in the Indies (I got all this stuff from the travellers' tales so popular in Elizabeth I's day). I brought in WS's own erotic vision of coition with a lady to whom he had been sent by his father to deliver a pair of gloves. And I also introduced the smarts and pricks of Shakespeare's own mother's disdain for her failure of a husband. After all, she was an Arden, one of a once wealthy and still revered family: the Shakespeares, despite their aggressive name, were nothing.

It struck me, in writing this chapter, that nowhere in his poems or plays does Shakespeare ever mention the craft of glove-making or, in poetic images, use the technical terms he must have known well—*trank, gusset, fourchette.* And it seems to me that he deliberately missed, when writing his sonnets, mentioning that he had exchanged the art of clothing five fingers in kidskin for the one of clothing five feet in words. His shame at having been a glovemaker's son is always there. He desperately wanted to be a gentleman. He was a bit of a snob.

I rewrote Chapter One so often that I despaired of ever finishing the whole book, let alone getting it ready for April 23rd, 1964. But, from the next chapter on, things flowed a little more easily. I began to enjoy using Elizabethan English (an encouraging sign: one *must* take pleasure in one's medium), but I found difficulty in moving towards the first major event in WS's young life—his affair with Anne Hathaway and his subsequent marriage to her. I felt, and still feel, a certain shame at the presentation of a young country woman as a sort of sexual monster, but I needed a WS very heavily seduced and, eventually, rendered sick—for a time anyway—of the varied patterns of heterosexual lust. But a good deal of this hot imaginative overlaying was cooled by an awareness that I was, in respect of the history of WS's courtship, following documentary evidence pretty closely. WS and Anne Hathaway slept together (probably lying, along with other pretty country folk, between the acres of the rye), but WS then seems (I refer to history now, not fiction) to have fallen in love with a certain Anne Whateley. We know that he, or somebody on his behalf, went to Worcester to procure a marriage licence—both names are set down fair in the bishop's register— but that two men, Fulk Sandells and John Richardson, relatives of Anne Hathaway, forestalled him by getting the banns of a marriage between "Wm Shagspere and Anne Hathaway, maiden" read in the same diocese and by paying forty pounds for a bond to indemnify the bishop against consanguinity (thus only one reading of the banns was needed, instead of the three that— unless WS himself could find forty pounds, no mean sum—were necessary in the case of himself and the other Anne). It was satisfying to know that I was dealing with real history here, and not dull history either.

What should be the next stage after the shotgun wedding? He must become sick of sex with a fair woman (I made Anne very fair, gingery almost) and achieve contact with a black one (totally black; why not?). I had to get him somehow to the West Country and close to Bristol, where, so far as I knew, there were Negresses in brothels. Now, a Warwickshire legend still has it that Shakespeare spent some time as a schoolmaster, and his knowledge of the details of Berkeley Castle, which comes out in *Richard II,* seems to show that he had been to Gloucestershire. I decided to send him to work as a tutor in a fictitious justice of the peace's household near Berkeley. I had no history to guide me now, and I didn't wish to spend too long in the world of conjecture. So, in the space of a couple of chapters, I made the following happen:

(a) WS teaches Latin to the five sons of Master Quedgeley, J.P. (I derive the name from the nearby small town, still there) in Berkeley, Gloucestershire. Two of these sons are twins, fore-shadowing the twins his own wife will give birth to.

(b) The troupe of actors known as Lord Berkeley's Men give a performance at Berkeley Castle, playing a comedy of Plautus in an English translation (the troupe actually existed; the per-formance of Plautus is, I think, very doubtful). Quedgeley thinks his sons might learn Latin more quickly if they acted Plautus themselves, though in Latin.

(c) WS rides to Bristol to buy copies of the *Menaechmi*—in which there are parts for twins. In Bristol a black prostitute calls to him: "What cheer, bully! Dost dou seek a bert?" He falls for this promise of an exotic experience, enters the brothel whence she calls, finds he hasn't enough money, is beaten and driven out, leaving his copies of the Plautus play behind. He daren't go back for them.

(d) Back at Berkeley, he cannot admit his loss, so he has to pretend that his pupils are translating the *Menaechmi,* with his help, and, as if they were "My Lord Quedgeley's Men," are proposing to act it as an English play at Christmas. This means that WS has, from his school memories, to compose a play of his own based roughly on the *Menaechmi:* "WS must be Plautus, not Ovid. That was a part of life's irony." This is a means of anticipating WS's later position—the journeyman-playwright who would rather be a gentleman-poet. It is also a device for making him write, against his will, *The Comedy of Errors*—little more than a pastiche of the *Menaechmi.*

(e) Excited and frustrated by his non-Anne sexual experience, he falls into the only other non-Anne sexual experience available —pederasty with one of the Quedgeley twins. Later failure to recognize which twin is which (the wrong twin howling outrage) leads to his dismissal and return to Stratford. But three kinds of WS, not before known, are now ready for my future development: 1. The playwright. 2. The homosexual. 3. The man haunted by a dark woman: ". . . that vision of the golden trull, the black nipples, the flash of breast-muscle, even the fierce small fists upraised, haunted his sleep and oft, in the dawn, lashed his seed to cold and queasy pumping out."

What remained to be done in the first part of the novel was to get him a law job with Henry Rogers, the Town Clerk of Stratford and a true historical figure, burden him with twins in addition to the daughter who was the true occasion of his marriage, and then send him off to London. It was necessary that he get his legal knowledge somewhere (his works are crammed with legal imagery) and also that he learn some French (with Rogers willing to oblige with the teaching). There was a tortuous reason for the latter. Why were Shakespeare's three children named Susanna, Judith, and Hamnet? Susanna seemed explicable enough: "his purity, pharos in lust's sea." Judith? He has been reading Rabelais, wherein a sophist called Holofernes is tutor to Gargantua. He himself has been a sort of Holofernes, and I will make him act another tutor of that name in *Love's Labour's Lost.* Holofernes suggests Judith. We now have an S and a J. Gilbert, announcing the birth of the twins on a rainy February day, suggests that his brother is like "Noah in all this

flood-water with three childer." Noah's sons had names beginning respectively with S, J, and H. WS needs his own Ham and
hits on *Hamnet*. Fanciful? The naming of children is often fanciful.

It is a historical fact that the acting troupe known as the
Queen's Men visited Stratford in midsummer, 1587. Why
shouldn't Shakespeare, sickened by Anne, by the responsibility of
working for her and three children, by no prospect except that of
scratching at law parchments in a provincial town hall, go to
them, show them his unfinished play (that mock *Menaechmi*),
and be accepted as an apprentice actor and copier-out of parts,
perhaps even a sort of play-doctor? I had to contrive a suitable
climactic melodrama here—the drought, the whipping of a
woman suspected of witchcraft, the sado-masochism of Anne
Shakespeare, the sick determination of her husband to get out.
The novelist has to try to excite (one says it sighing); the forcing
of a climax is part of his shameful skill; even Shakespeare had to
be made to submit to a manifest contrivance. End, thank God, of
Part I.

This Part I was extremely difficult to write. At one stage I
doubted if I could, at my snail's pace, get the whole novel finished by, say, early autumn. I thought I might publish Part I as a
novella, with the promise of a novel of Shakespeare's maturity yet
to come. But I then felt that, so agonising had been the work so
far, I would never fulfil that promise. I got drunk and then back
to the story of WS in the years 1592–1599.

*

Part II was, on the whole, a good deal easier to write than its
younger (and half-sized) brother. This was because WS was in
London, in the middle of public events, and I could build a
framework of historical data to support the structures of fancy.
But there is probably less fancy in this part of the novel than
critics assumed. What I had to do—and this required craft,
craftiness even—was to relate documented events to the conjectural *development* of WS's character.

In the beginning, in 1592, he is a member of the troupe known
as My Lord Strange's Men, along with William Kemp—the
comedian who came to Stratford with the Queen's Men in the
fateful (my fateful: fateful to WS) midsummer of 1587. We can-

not be quite sure of this membership, but it seems likely. Certainly Strange's Men were at the Rose playhouse, under the aegis of grasping Henslowe. The chief actor was Edward Alleyn, creator of Marlowe's Faustus, and Heminges—eventually to give, with Condell, the First Folio to the world—was one of the subsidiary players. Now, I have to make WS *unhappy* in this first London rôle of his: he is a playwright, but he wishes to make money and become a gentleman. He needs patronage, and the best way for him to secure this is to dedicate a poem (with permission) to some noble lord. What public events can best serve to stress his discontent? First, the vulgarity of the playhouse, with that apprentice riot in the summer of 1592 which had to be quelled—and bloodily—by the Marshal's Men. This shut the playhouses down for a season, and the troupe had to go on tour, glad enough to leave plague-hit London. Then Robert Greene dies—a drunkard and whoremaster but a master of arts, a *gentleman*—and leaves behind a repentant pamphlet attacking the upstart playwrights who are *not* gentlemen. WS is one of these: "in his own conceit the only Shake-scene in a country." Well, it's a kind of tribute: a dying gentleman was evidently jealous of a Stratford glover's son. But WS is determined to make himself into a gentleman, which means first a poet—as learned as Greene.

And so *Venus and Adonis*—erudition and conceits overlaying the tale of his own seduction by a country wench much his senior. A dedication? I make the Earl of Southampton, accompanied by the Earl of Essex, visit the Rose the following January. WS, author of *Titus Andronicus,* is summoned to their presence: they are interested to see what manner of man could write so bloodthirsty a play—"the one with the black Machiavel and the boys baked in a pie." WS's chance: he asks the Earl if he may dedicate his poem to him. The Earl carelessly says yes. WS is on the way up.

It was time for me, the teller of the story growing bolder, perhaps drunker, to make the style itself do more work. A mild beginning was the juxtaposition of WS's high-flown dedication to the earl and the realities of filthy London: "and vow to take advantage of all idle hours . . . ," *Pickpurses strolled among the gawping country cousins;* "till I have honoured you with some grave labour . . . ," *A limping child with a pig's head leered out from an alleyway*. So much of what now followed was common enough biographical knowledge: WS and the Earl close friends, the hint of a homosexual relationship, the sonnets on marriage (commissioned by the Earl's mother?), a kind of honeyed imprisonment among the nobility, the odd trip home to Stratford with gold in his purse. Describing the first of these trips, I incorporated a long poem I had written years before—one that dealt with the mystery of fatherhood (Hamnet is growing): I set this as prose, obviously. My aim was to start thickening the texture of the novel, implying the growth of complexity in WS's own imagination. But I also had to get ready for a piece of naturalism whose prospect sickened me—the description of the hanging, drawing, and quartering for high treason of the Jewish doctor Lopez and his associates. This was not just gratuitous sensationalism: it was meant to represent the high world of plotting and politics, a world in which WS was a shy intruder. Perhaps he might be better off back in the playhouse? After the publication of the anonymous book *Willobie his Avisa* (in which "HW" —evidently Henry Wriothesly, the Earl of Southampton—and "WS"—we know who that is—are presented in a rather sordid story about the attempted seduction of an innkeeper's wife), the two friends are somewhat estranged: it is time for WS to go back to the playhouse as a possible shareholder of the Lord Chamberlain's Men.

And then, with WS comfortably settled in lodgings in Bishopsgate, the first appearance of Fatimah, the dark lady, one of his near neighbours. "Let me take breath, let me take a swig, for, my heart, she is coming." That is myself, story-teller, speaking: I need a thin protective film of irony. The development of the affair between her and WS, the losing of her to the Earl, in whose orbit WS is once again soon spinning—these I thought it best to present in the immediate form of a diary. Then a sermon (very much a mock and mocking one) in which WS could nurse his *tristitia*. From then on the novel ran very smoothly—so smoothly that I began to fear something was wrong somewhere. Of course, much of the material was authentic history and biography—the death of young Hamnet Shakespeare (and the need to re-create him in an ideal image in the play *Hamlet*), playhouse trouble, the grant of a coat of arms with the motto *Non Sanz Droict* (which Ben Jonson mocked as "Not Without Mustard"), the achievement at last for WS of the status of moneyed gentleman.

It is one of my quirks or faults as a novelist (it has been pointed out to me often enough) that I can allow no character, however untouched by gross sin or great *hubris,* to dwell long in triumph. Having raised WS high and allowed him (or rather history allowed him) to purchase New Place in Stratford—Clopton's own house—I had to start kicking him down. He visits New Place and finds his wife Anne in bed with his brother Richard. This, of course, was a thesis first presented by young Stephen Dedalus in *Ulysses.* It is a useful and suggestive notion: it gives Hamnet-Hamlet a sinful mother and turns WS himself into a kind of deposed or murdered king. For my purpose, it served as a device inducing melancholy, adumbrating the new Shakespeare of the bitter comedies and, soon, the tragedies. The shock had to appear great, and I tried the technical device of making the real world—the one that goes on busily spinning outside the private tortured mind—seem suddenly unreal: I put the events of the real word in blank verse, leaving the personal agony in prose. What next? After the defection of a wife, the defection of a friend. The Earl of Southampton is a supporter of the treacherous Essex; he comes to WS, asking that he write a play or poem showing the wretchedness of a community ruled by a senile queen, the succession unsure, the need for the usurpation of a strong man. But WS is sick of real, as opposed to imagined, events. He wearily warns the Earl of the dangers of high politics but is sneered at as a scared paunchy burger, then laughed at as a man cuckolded by his own brother. Can his state sink much lower?

But he gains his comfort, his promise of new life, from two new things—the building of the Globe theatre and the reappearance of Fatimah, his dark lady. She brings a renewal of love, but also the aristocrat of diseases—the *morbus Gallicus;* the Globe is to see the distillations of ultimate disillusion in the great tragedies. WS, with the red plaque of the primary sore on his penis, approaches the playhouse entrance and has "to stand aside an instant to let a bowing smiling wraith come out—sweet Master Shakespeare."

And so to the brief Epilogue. This was murderously difficult. I gave it a first-person narrator, but I wanted his identity to be not directly that of my hero—rather my hero trying to speak through the mediumistic "control" of the story-teller or lecturer, who was myself. The following was deliberately ambiguous: "I see you have your pennies ready, ladies. Twitch not, hop not about nor writhe so: I shall not be long now." This could be a dying man talking to his wife and daughters, who have pennies ready to lay on his eyelids. It could also be a lecturer telling his girl students that they must wait a little longer before they can go to the john (for the use of which they must spend a penny). "I am near the end of the wine." This means what it says (the three bottles of *samsu* are nearly finished) and it means also "I am near the end of life." What I wanted to present, as economically as possible, was the steady worsening of WS's disease—which he sees as a figure of the decay of the State and ultimately as a symbol of the inborn rottenness of the human condition—and its culmination in the dream-appearance of a goddess (in the form of the dark lady, but really a fusion of the final stage of the disease and the tragic muse herself). She allows him to smell the very essence of evil.

To bring any novel to an end is most difficult and, ultimately, a falsification, for actions have no end. My last few paragraphs rushed over the years to April, 1616, WS on his deathbed, but also the lecturer–story-teller dead drunk. "I am sick and tired and long for my East. Take off at." My own desire to fly back to Malaysia, as well as the poet's desire to leave the body. Then, after the question *Subject-matter?*, a mad catalogue of nonsensical subjects for art (*the sigmoid curve, cardinals, touchability*). The dying brain cracks, but its last words are "My Lord." Whether this means Jesus Christ or the Earl of Southampton I am not prepared to say.

I was disappointed that the novel's first reviewers failed to notice the author's personal monograms sewn into the fabric of the work or to understand the technique of narration, which was a highly subjective one. Anachronisms of language were gleefully pointed out, but I did not reply that these were intentional. On the other hand, I was accused of inventing words when all I had done was to steal from Elizabethan chapbooks, pamphlets, and Shakespeare's own plays. Where I was most serious I was supposed to be most facetious; where I merely transcribed documentary truth I was said to be wildly and implausibly inventing. Any author must expect this sort of insensitivity, but it still hurts.

And it hurts, of course, when one's most carefully contrived artificiality is dismissed as something unlicked and crude: one feels like a hostess who has painfully stuffed individual spaghetti strips with a complex forcemeat, only to have the dish shovelled down without comment, much less with thanks. *Nothing Like the Sun* was, I know, a literary task almost haemorrhoidally agonising, and it must have consumed yards of paper and thousands of cigarettes. Nevertheless, looking back to 1963, I wonder when precisely I wrote it. I know that the year began with the decision to begin it, but it seems that I was finishing a book on linguistics at that time (a book which was published about the same time as *Nothing Like the Sun*). I know I was in Tangier in April, 1963, for I remember reading a review of my *Honey for the Bears* on a Tangerine boulevard, and I remember also reading a review of my *Inside Mr Enderby*—published pseudonymously—at Gibraltar airport the following week, on the way back to London. Why was I taking a holiday? Had I temporarily abandoned *Nothing Like the Sun?* I certainly shouldn't have been able to spare the time for a holiday, especially as I seem to have been in Tangier again later that same year, arriving back in England in time for the news of the assassination at Dallas. I remember also reviewing hard and doing a regular weekly television feature. Of the actual sweating over *Nothing Like the Sun* I can recall very little. But in a notebook I certainly recorded the following bits of information:

Drake returned from circumnavigation 1581. Could bring back Malay girl (Philippines?). When WS meets her she is, say, 19 yrs old.

Syphilis: *Incubation: 4 weeks, then primary sore or chancre. After 2 months fever, loss of appetite, vague pains, faint red rash on chest, hair falls out (cf. Shakespeare portrait), sores, enlargement of lymphatic glands.*

Sample dialogue:

"Who is she?"

"She? One of the Queen's Glories. A heathen born, now a Christian. When Sir Francis Drake returned from round the world in '81 he brought her from the Indies, an orphan, her parents being killed by Sir Francis' own men."

Shakespeare appraised her wide nose, the big lips, the bare brown bosom that showed her, in the fashion, a virgin still. (This will not bloody do at all. Far too pedestrian.)

The floor was littered with fallen chestnut-leaves, like over-fried fillets of fish.

The shadow of fern in the vase passed over his hand, giving it the look of a skin disease.

Their garden was verminous with fallen apples.

PART II

1. *First meeting with Southampton.*
2. *Friendship?*
3. *Friendship!*
4. *Friendship!!*
5. *First sight of Dark L.*
6. *Love affair. She goes to Southampton (Earl not place).*
7. *WS in Stratford. Anne's adultery.*

Andrew Boorde 1575 in Breviarie of Health *states: "In English Morbus Gallicus is call'd the French pocks, and when that I was young they were named the Spanish pocks."*

1592 March 3: Harry the 6th Part I
　　Sept. 2: Greene died.
　　Oct. 22: Alleyn married Joan Woodward, Henslowe's step-
　　　　　　daughter.
　　Dec.: "Kindhart's Dream."
1594 Strange's Men became Lord Chamberlain's Men.
　　Oct.: Theatre, Shoreditch.
　　"Willobie his Avisa."
1596 Friendship between S. and Southampton cools.
　　Oct. 29: Shakes. Coat of Arms.
　　Lease of Theatre one year to run.

I can find little else. There are, I confess, one or two sample cover-designs, very crude, but carrying the name ANTHONY BURGESS very large. This must have been whistling in the dark.

One thing I can remember, and that is that nearly every page of typescript was commenced at least six times. I would write a sentence, even a paragraph, and then tear up the sheet it was on and start again. I was not correcting so much as enriching. Here is one extant example. It comes in the chapter where WS, on May Eve, gets drunk in a tavern in Shottery (Anne Hathaway's village):

1. Drink, then. Down it among the country copulatives, O London-Will-to-be, gentleman-in-waiting, scrike thy laughter with Hodge and Tom and Black Jack.

2. Drink, then. Down it among the titbrained country copulatives, of a beastly sort, all. Swill thou then among them, O etc.

3. Drink, then. Down it among the titbrained molligolliards of country copulatives, of a beastly sort, all, their brown fambles a-clutch of their pots, filthy from spade and harrow. Swill thou then among them, O etc., scrike thine ale's laughter with Hodge and Tom and Dick and Black Jack the outlander.

4. Drink, then. Down it among the etc., their browned pickers a-clutch of their spilliwilly potkins, filthy from handling of spade and harrow, cheesy from udder new-milked. Swill thou then etc.

5. Drink, then. Down it etc. etc. udder new-milked, slash mouths agape at some merry tale. Swill thou etc. etc. Black Jack the outlander from Long Compton.

6. Drink, then. Down it etc. etc. some merry tale from that rogue with ratskins about his middle. Swill etc. etc.

7. Drink etc. etc. etc. about his middle, coneyskin cap on's sconce. . . .

8. Drink etc. etc. etc. sconce. Robustious rothers in rural rivo rhapsodic. Swill thou etc. etc. etc.

The beauties of the plain style are often urged on me, the duty of excising rather than adding. But the Elizabethan spirit doesn't take kindly to the Hemingwayesque, the spare and laconic, nor does my own spirit. I don't think that *Nothing Like the Sun* has too many words; I think perhaps it has too few. One has to be true to one's own temperament, and mine is closer to that of the baroque writers than that of the stark toughies. To hell with cheeseparing and verbal meanness: it all reeks of Banbury puritanism.

One final point. I expected that, after all the careful work of building and encrusting, I should end with something like an acceptable portrait of William Shakespeare, Mr. WS. But he remains elusive: he can't be defined in terms of his human appetites, his petty ambitions, his clownish sufferings, his diseased imaginings. There's something beyond all these, and we can't reach them. I don't mean the genius, which was only an immense parcel strapped to his back; I mean that human essence which is more than the sum of its parts. In writing *Nothing Like the Sun* I thought I might get closer to Shakespeare, but, at the end of the book, I found myself as far away from him as ever. "We ask and ask: thou smilest and art still." But perhaps there's really nothing behind the smile except this huge and ghastly talent. On his tomb in Stratford church one can read the following doggerel:

> Good friend, for Jesus' sake forbear
> To dig the dust enclosed here.
> Blest be the man that spares these stones
> But curst be he who moves my bones.

Something like that; I quote from memory. Perhaps the curse is the curse of finding nothing but bones. Thank God I shan't see a quincentenary—either of his birth or death—and be faced with another agony of trying to make these bones live.

ROBERT CRICHTON

The Secret of Santa Vittoria

Preface

THE ONLY THING I ever wanted to accomplish in life was to write a good novel. I wanted this so much that I came to think of myself as being a novelist even though I had never written one. Despite this little failing I was quite convinced that were I to die right then my obituary would read Crichton, Novelist, Writes Last Chapter because everyone would know how much it meant to me. And it would only be fair; I had all the novels in my head. All that was lacking was the technical formality of transferring them to paper.

This state of affairs went on until I was past thirty. When no novel had appeared, in order to account for the void and save my self-respect, I was driven to conclude that I was a classic example of the pitfalls of Grub Street. I was a free-lance magazine writer then, living from one assignment to the next, always one advance behind, and I saw myself as a victim of the literary sharecropper system, as hopelessly snared in my web of circumstances as those wretched cotton farmers James Agee described in *Let Us Now Praise Famous Men*.

The matter was out of my hands. I was a victim and I was quite happy that way until the spring of 1962 when a magazine publisher named Henry Steeger came back from a lunch he had with some Italian wine growers and told me the story of a small Italian hill town where the people had hidden 1,000,000 bottles of wine from the Germans and how they managed to keep their enormous secret.

"Someone should write that," Mr. Steeger said. "It has the quality of legend and yet it happened in our own time."

I could recognize that much. I was astonished in fact that this fat plum of a story, swelling with possibilities, was still unplucked. By this time, however, I had so perfected my defenses to repel anything that even hinted at the potential of becoming a novel that I was able to tell myself that it actually wasn't a very good story at all. I increasingly found it more desirable to apologize for a book I hadn't written (but which just might be great) than to apologize for one I had written.

Camus has written that ultimately all men are prey to their truths, even in the act of denying them, and Santa Vittoria became one of mine. Even while denying it I knew the story of this town was the basis for a big grab bag of a novel, a *bildungsroman*, in which, because of the sprawling framework of the story, almost anything goes and anything works. Against my will the story preyed upon me, fermenting in my doughy spirit, fizzing there like a cake of yeast in a wine vat.

I woke one morning in March, there was snow and thunder in the morning, very rare and very strange, with the line "In dreams begin responsibilities" running in my mind. It is a line from Yeats (borrowed, I have since found out, from some obscure Indian poet) that I used to write in all my notebooks when I was in college. It is a line that has been the subject of profound scrutiny and some subtle interpretations have resulted from it. But on this morning the line was very clear to me: If you dream about something all the time you have a responsibility to do something about it. I apologize to William Butler Yeats. I began going around New York that morning trying to raise enough money to take me to Italy. I felt the least I could do was look at this place which had become my responsibility. When I accumulated $800 beyond the cost of a round-trip air fare I set out for Santa Vittoria.

The trip to Italy, which by any other terms than those of a writer would have to be classed as a continuous disaster, I include here because it illustrates something important about the craft, namely, anything that happens to a writer can, with good fortune, be turned into something of value. In a matter of weeks I was run down by a car in Rome, robbed in a country inn, and managed to make a profound fool of myself in Santa Vittoria, and each incident turned out to be more fortunate than the one before it.

The car incident is a good example. I was in a pedestrian crosswalk which guaranteed me the right of way when the car bore down on me. I, an American and a believer in the sanctity of signs, couldn't believe he was going to keep on coming. He couldn't believe I wasn't going to jump out of the way. He must have been a good driver because he only drove halfway over my body before managing to stop. I had my first intimation of the way things were going to go when a man helped me out from under the car.

"You're very lucky," he said. "You didn't dent the fender."

My last intimation, or my first revelation, of truth came in the police station. I was talking about justice and my rights and I could see that they felt I was not well balanced. I didn't get the idea, they assured me. The car was bigger and faster and stronger than me and therefore the car had the right of way. Couldn't I see that much?

So on only my second day in Italy I was privileged to begin to understand the basic fact of Italian life which is that power, the balance of it, the having and not having it, is the key to all life. Survival depends on a respect for it. The possession or lack of it determines the course of a man's existence. Success depends on how well you learn to manipulate it. I was never able to get anyone in Italy to be sympathetic about being run down in a safety zone. They would listen to the story and they would nod and then they would always say: "Yes, but why *didn't* you jump out of the way?"

These people, then, who pass themselves off to the world and to themselves as romantics are the most realistic of people. Two broken fingers and the knees gone from the pants of my one good suit was a small price to pay for such knowledge. I might have spent months in Italy before learning what I did.

The robbery was a very Italian kind of crime. I was headed north to Santa Vittoria, taking all the back roads available so I would have a feel of the country before getting there, and I took a room in a country inn on the second floor with a terrace. Few Italians would have taken that room. It faced away from the inn and not in toward the courtyard. Italians like to be with people. Americans, who have allowed the North European psyche to inflict itself upon our national soul, prefer privacy. Even if he took the room no Italian would have then opened the window on to the terrace. They don't trust the night air and what might come in with it. Americans like to clean the portals of the mind with fresh night air and they like to be trusting and believe in the possibilities for humankind to be good.

It must have looked like a ritual scene from some old Italian *novella*. The thief came up the stone wall at night and onto the terrace and into the room and through my pockets. I should still be angry with him but the thief did one marvelous thing; he left me half of my money. I picture him working swiftly and dangerously in the dark to leave me my share and I warm to him. He was a humanist and a man generous to strangers which is as good a definition of a gentleman as any. So another factor; Life is a matter of power tempered by an incorruptible humanity, which in itself is a kind of power. I was a more tolerant man after that and I was also one long step down toward poverty and my ultimate entry into the Italian lower depths where few outsiders are allowed to go.

In Santa Vittoria, on my first day, I was invited to a luncheon at the winery held for some American wine buyers and I proceeded first to praise and then to rave about one particular wine which I assured those present made all the rest taste like scented toilet water. Certainly someone should have warned me that the wine I was praising was a comparison wine, designed to make the local wines taste good by comparison. It was suggested by a company official after the lunch that I didn't seem to be the right man to tell the story of the great thing they did in Santa Vittoria. I left the town the same day I arrived in it.

And this was fortunate, too. Fearful of attempting a novel I had determined to write a non-fiction book but now I had no alternative. I also thought that I would be able to live off the generosity of the people I was writing about and now I was condemned to live off the land. I headed south, down the spine of the Apennines, in search of my own Santa Vittoria. In all I stayed in twenty hill towns, each one separate in my mind and yet all of them finally merging into one conglomerate city, richer than the sum of its parts. I learned some things of value along the way.

In the beginning I had the belief that people would resent my intrusion and I sat at solitary tables in the cafe in the piazza and sat like Proust at a party, *"J'observe, j'observe."* It took me time to learn that my discretion only bred suspicion. No one told me anything honest. At last I fell back on the tactic of simple honesty. On arriving in a new town I learned to approach the first person who seemed to command respect and tell him exactly what I was doing in his town. I was an American, a writer, I was planning a book on just such a town as this one, but not this one, and I wanted to know everything good and everything bad about life in a hill town that anyone wanted to tell me. Very often the man would take me to the mayor who would tell me everything good about the town and then the people would come and tell me everything bad about it.

Every day I grew poorer and this was good since it put me into the hands and then the homes of people I couldn't have met otherwise. Toward the end of my stay I was reduced to knocking on stranger's doors and asking if they would like to sell me a plate of peas and rice or some soup and bread and wine for 100 *lire.* They were always happy to do it. Someone could always go without a meal but where could they get an extra 100 *lire?* I learned a great many things with my soup.

The trouble with poverty as a tactic is that you can't fake it. I don't think you can plan to be poor and in this way get to meet what are always referred to as the people. I tried it afterwards in Appalachia and in the coal fields of Scotland and it was no good. Peasants smell the poverty in you. When you pay the 100 *lire* you have to feel the sweat on your forehead as you count the money out. And you have to do sneaky little things to save little sums of money that peasants recognize but which the bourgeoisie never even notice.

There is little to do in hill towns after dark and because of it, the loneliness, I developed a system of information gathering that has proved invaluable to me since. From a simple need to communicate, with no specific purpose in mind, I began to write long rambling letters home, putting down everything that interested me or puzzled me during the day. Months later, when I sat down to start on the first draft of *Santa Vittoria,* it was the letters that turned out to be filled with the kind of information I needed. My notes were mostly useless.

The reason for this, I think, is that a letter is an inclusive thing. Notes tend to be selective and therefore exclusive. When a person is taking notes he generally has some idea of what he is looking for. The haphazard, the irrelevant, the unexpected, since it doesn't fit the pattern is ignored or not even seen. I suppose it is possible to do as well by keeping a diary as writing a letter but most people tend to cheat in diaries. As time passes entries tend to become more terse and cryptic, the diary becomes filled with one-line notations the writer is sure he will be able to re-create later, with all the emotion and sounds and smells. In a letter, since it is going to someone else, the effort to re-create has to be made right then if the letter is going to make any sense at all. It's more interesting to write to someone else than oneself anyway. The only people who write good diaries are people who know their logs will be part of history and egoists who hope theirs will be.

When I returned from Italy I attempted to organize my notes because this is what I felt writers did. The notes were so meagre and pointless, however, I began making notes from the letters. These I put in a large shoebox because I couldn't think of any sensible way to file them. It was sloppy and disorganized and yet the system had an unexpected virtue to it. In order to find out something I was compelled to flip through as many as a hundred notes and while doing this I was reminded of all kinds of facets of Italian life that I wouldn't have remembered if I had been able to go to the source at once. Some of this haphazard extraneous information was bound to seep into the scene I was working on and the scene would be a little richer for it. In time I came to think of the shoebox as my compost pile, a dung heap for potential fertility, and the leaping from note to note as an act of cross-fertilization. Marianne Moore once wrote something close to "Thank God for the privilege of disorganized things" and in this case she is right.

54

I kept making notes because I was afraid to actually start the book. For the same reason, to avoid starting, I began to read a great deal about Italy, hill towns, wine making, despite the fact that I had been led to believe that it wasn't a good idea for a novelist to read too much about the subject he would be writing about. The idea was that the reading tended to rob the writer of his individuality and that he would be exposed to material similar to his own and would not want to use it although he might actually handle it in quite a different fashion. There is also always the danger of reading something so superlative that the writer will be smothered by it. Who wants to write a novel about the War of 1812 after reading *War and Peace?* In my case, while admittedly stalling, the reading turned out to be enormously rewarding. Everything I read seemed to trigger some kind of creative response in me. It didn't matter very much what the subject was or whether the writing was good or bad, anything at all I read had the potential to give birth to an idea, often one that had no relationship with the reading at all. Some African tribes believe that energy creates energy and it got this way with my reading; every response seemed to create a climate for a heightened response. One of what I will boldly call the more effective scenes in *Santa Vittoria,* a competitive dance in a wine press, was suggested to me by a series of letters from an Edwardian schoolteacher to her class while on vacation in Sicily. She thought the wine pressers were ugly because they looked like hairy pagan goats. One incident, which plays an important part in the book, occurred to me while reading the financial statement of a modern wine company. When the barometer of the creative nature is set for a spell of writing, evidently anything can excite it and in my experience, and to my surprise, reading had the strongest potential of all.

There finally came a time when I could no longer find a believable excuse not to begin. I even announced the fact to my family and friends. "Tomorrow, I begin." I made it easy on myself. I vowed I would write exactly one page and write just one page for a week. This shouldn't frighten anyone and at the end of the week I would be like a colt let out to his first pasture.

But I couldn't do it. All day I sat at my desk and I wrote one word. "If." Toward evening I wrote the word in pencil so that it covered the entire page. The next day I wrote "So now I begin" and never got further than that. The day after that I tried the reliable weather and date technique. "On a cold blustery morning in May, 1943, on the sunless eastern slopes of the Apennines, spring was coming hard. . . ."

After that I quit. I rented an office away from home not to inspire creativity but to hide me from those who could see me doing nothing for hours on end. I gave up the idea of one page; this goal seemed insurmountable. I came under the idea that if I could get one good opening sentence, the keynote, and get it down right, the rest of the book would unravel itself from there. I was very conscious of the fact that I was like the man in Camus' *The Plague* who spends thirty years on *his* opening sentence, honing it, pruning it, polishing it, but it didn't matter. Who was to say if he got his sentence right the rest of his book wouldn't have inevitably followed. It was all I had to hang on to.

"How did it go today?" my wife would ask.

"It's coming; it's coming," followed by several very strong drinks.

One afternoon I realized I was never going to write the sentence and once I understood that I arrived at the idea of disowning art. I had become so self-conscious about style and craft that I had become incapable of reading or hearing words any longer. When I said them they sounded strange and when I put them down on paper they looked strange. I recall writing "This book begins" and then stopping because the word book looked wrong. What kind of word was book. An indefinite word. It could be a checkbook or the Bible. Volume was better. Journal even better. "This journal begins. . . ." Too pompous. But I couldn't go back to book. Novel, that was the real, precise word I wanted. But what kind of novel? The reader had a right to know.

In this way the day went. It was possible to fill a wastebasket in a day and never write over four different words. I always used a clean fresh sheet for a clean fresh start. With every empty sheet there was hope, and failure. On this afternoon, however, I began to write the story of Santa Vittoria in the form and style of a Dick and Jane first reader.

"There is a little town on a hill called Santa Vittoria. It is in Italy. The people in the town grow grapes and make wine. A great thing took place in the town. One day, not too long ago. . . ."

It astonishes me now that I was able to keep this up for several weeks. Because the words didn't count the words poured out. And I was happy about the sound of my typewriter because I had grown embarrassed by the silence from my cubicle.

"What's he do?"

"He's a writer."

"Oh. What's he write?"

"I don't know. I never heard him write."

I heard that. Now the pages were piling up and I felt good. It was silly, considering the manuscript was one that I would have shot someone over, before allowing him to see it, and yet the feeling was real. In the end I had several hundred pages filled with one-syllable words and while I pretended to disown the pile of paper it meant a great deal to me. It was no good but at last I had *something* which was no good. All kinds of things were missing but now they were missing from something. I was conscious that through Dick and Jane I had outflanked art.

A week later I cut the manuscript down to 125 pages and in the process something strange happened to it. In the starkness of its naked simplicity the book became mysterious in tone. In the cutting the manuscript had become fragmented into a series of pared-to-the-bone pastiches and I was faced with the realization that somehow, inadvertently, I seemed to have written A New Novel. I had the wild thought that Alain Robbe-Grillet would discover me. The book would be published by Grove Press and reviewed by *The New York Review of Books,* perhaps (who could tell how far it might go) by Susan Sontag, favorably, of course, thereby immortalizing me to my peer group; and then the thought passed. I was a fraud and what could be more fraudulent among the grapes and stones and lives of Santa Vittoria than a novel Alain Robbe-Grillet could approve of? Marienbad, *oui,* Santa Vittoria, *non.*

I had the bones of a book. The problem now was to flesh out the skeleton. I was still afraid to begin but not as much as before. The first act of creation is the terrifying thing and once this is done, it now seems to me, no matter how badly, something menacing has been overcome. I wasn't swimming yet but I was in the water.

I began by putting *place* in the book. I wanted a sense of the town to permeate the book because place plays such an important part in the book. What happened could only happen in an isolated hill town. Whenever there was a change of scene I began to describe in detail what the new place would look like, whether it was a room, the piazza, the entire town itself. In this process of supplying place the absence of people to the place made itself evident. Almost in spite of myself I began to people the places and in this way the book began to get itself written.

I have never had any idea about character. It is one reason I don't think I could teach literature. I only seem to see what people do. I don't recognize an evil man until he does something evil and then I'm not sure that he meant it to be evil. The same goes for good people. There is no good or evil in itself, as Camus has pointed out, but only the consequences of acts. All things are in all people at all times. So I couldn't plot out a character or even conceive of one, they simply happen, and from day to day, capable of a ridiculous, mean action one day and something generous the very next day.

"The character lacks unity." What nonsense. "He wouldn't have done that." What nonsense. He *did* it. Everyone is ultimately capable of almost everything which is after all the fascination and horror of life.

In his book *Individuals,* P. F. Strawson has written that "the primary conceptual scheme must be one that puts people in the world. A conceptual scheme which puts a world in each person must be, at least, a secondary product."

This idea is one of the few dogmas about writing that I am conscious of holding. I didn't want my characters to stand for anything, to explain, to symbolize, to account for anything but simply, in the words of Denis Donaghue when describing what a novel should be, possessed of life to a degree of irrelevance . . . all carelessness and luck, who, when given their first push, would leap on their way.

My final concern was style, although I didn't know it then. I am ashamed to admit that I thought of style as a mannerism, the decor of a book. I learned later that this is a technique, an artifice, not a style. The best description of style I have ever read and one of the most valuable lines about writing is by the same Donaghue who says: Style is the right feeling animating the voice.

I had no voice. I didn't know who was telling the story and why he was telling it. If I chose a Santa Vittorian I would be compelled to accept the limitations of a peasant's vision of life. I could choose to be the author as God, omniscient, wilful, intolerant, irrational, as gods tend to be, but I knew I didn't function well as God. It's not my type. One day I thought of an Italian writing a novel about life in Conway, Arkansas, and I almost fell apart. The opportunities for error were endless. As a result my decision was made for me. I was forced into what might be called a literary cop-out but which became inevitable. To account for my ignorance I invented as narrator an Italian-American airman, a deserter who parachutes from his plane after a pointless bombing of a nearby hill town and who has remained in Santa Vittoria after the war because of his fear of returning and a misguided sense of shame about what he did. He hopes that by telling this story he can earn some money and by explaining why he deserted in one part of the book, in exchange for telling the greater story, perhaps redeem himself.

Was it the proper voice? Does it meet Donaghue's criteria? Probably not. In the long haul the narrator is not truly a voice but a device and not a character (he mercifully almost never appears in the book) but a sound. The worst part of it for me was that I didn't commit the errors that I was certain I would. So I didn't need Robert Abruzzi after all but I didn't know it then and that was important. He served me well but let him know this: If Abruzzi were to come back to Santa Vittoria again I would have him lined up against a wall and edited to death.

When I had written 150 pages through the eyes of Abruzzi I sent what I had done to my publisher, Simon and Schuster, in the hope of getting an advance. Unfinished manuscripts tend to seem more promising to editors, I was told. Also, if the publisher gives an advance he now has a vested interest in the final product. An advance tends to blind an editor's judgement of a manuscript since the house is already committed. Finally the advance is supposed to bolster the unsure writer's confidence.

"They really *want* me. They *believe* in me."

None of it worked this way for me. I did nothing until I got the advance and when I did it had the effect of stopping me altogether. Now there was no way out. I had taken the money and I was the one who was committed. I had a contract. They could take me to court if I didn't produce a novel. But perhaps it was all to the best. I determined not to spend the money, but I did, and it was finally my fear of having to pay the money back, which grew stronger than my fear of failure, which led me to finish the book. It was this version the publisher bought.

I felt they were wrong to buy it. I knew the book was all wrong. I had the place I wanted in the book and the people and the story but each of these elements stood in its own place, one immovable chunk of writing hard by another. The novel seemed to me like a freshly blasted quarry with no one to pick up the pieces. By chance I saw an editor's note about the book that said: "This is really very good you know" and I felt the note was a plant, a kind of editor's waterwings designed to buoy me up for the sea of revisions ahead.

They asked for very few revisions and this I took as a very bad sign. If they were really interested in the book they would want all kinds of changes. I figured they had given up on the book but would go ahead and print it in the hopes of recovering their advance. They gave me two weeks to make the revisions we agreed to. One of them was on page one, a four letter word which wasn't called for but which I had included to show right off that I wasn't afraid to use four letter words. I scratched the word out and the page looked messy and so I retyped it and it came out a line short so I retyped the second page and it came out wrong so I went on to the third page. I began cutting some paragraphs and then an entire scene and to add dialogue and change dialogue and somewhere along the way that morning a new character entered the story. I had meant to work until lunch but when I stopped I was surprised to find that it was five o'clock in the afternoon and I had written 42 pages. I had no sensation of having worked hard. I intended to stop the next day but I didn't. I wrote 35 pages that day, much of it a complete re-working and I knew that evening I was going to do the whole book. There was no question that it was exciting to me and that I knew I was doing something good because, for no reason I could explain, the immovable blocks were beginning to join one another in a way I had never been able to make them do.

The word I have found for the experience was immersion. It is something I intend to work to find again. Previously I had worked on the book and at the book but all at once I was immersed in the book. The book seemed to be carrying me instead of me pushing it. It was a very rare sensation. The book was much more real than anything else in my life then. As I went into the second week I had the sensation of being drawn very fine, as if I could thread myself through a needle. I seemed to have my own sense of the way things were while before I had always been listening over my shoulder to see if I could get a lead on the way things should go. I was out of life, under water, immersed.

I was, of course, making mistakes but they were my own mistakes and because of this they at least had the virtue of a certain consistency about them. I told no one what I was doing for fear of breaking the spell. Physically I must have shown it. In three and a half weeks' immersion I lost 20 pounds. One night my wife said "Bob, you seem so small" but the only physical effect I experienced was the phenomenon of the missing drinks. In the evening I would pour myself a drink and when I looked for it it would be empty. Evidently I was masking fatigue with alcohol and I must have drunk a great deal to sustain myself but I had no conscious desire to do this and never got drunk. At the end of 23 days I finished a manuscript which, when published, occupied 447 reasonably tightly printed pages. The following day, while walking down Madison Avenue, I collapsed in the street. It was, I tried to tell the doctor, a case of the bends, coming up too quick after my immersion, but he didn't understand.

What were the mistakes? I think I know most of them now. Most of them were the products of a lack of self-confidence caused by a lack of experience. Partially they were the results of waiting too long so that the assurance of youth, when one trusts one's judgement even if one has no reason to do so, gave way to the doubts of middle age, which is far more dangerous. I couldn't imagine who would be listening to me and who would want to read anything I wrote. As a consequence I determined to make them hear if I could. I overloaded scenes that were loaded enough as they were. If there was a legitimate chance to grab the reader by the lapels, I took it. I left nothing to trust and I presumed my potential reader was half deaf and half blind. I even worried about Marshall McLuhan and tried to make everything as visual as possible so I couldn't be accused of being a disciple of Gutenberg. The result is that there is too much muscle in the prose. I could see none of this then. When I turned in the book I thought it was thin and reedy and hollow and that wind could blow right through it. I now know that it is actually a rather dense book (in the best sense of that word), too dense, but I didn't know. Now perhaps I will.

Out of the whole experience I developed one tactic about writing that other writers might be able to profit from. I call it across the river and into the prose. During the Second World War a friend of mine serving in the Alaska Scouts noticed that when an American squad came to a river near the end of the day the squad would ford the river so they could build fires and dry their equipment and be dry when starting out in the morning. The squads with Indians always stopped on the near shore. The reason for this was another facet of immersion. In the morning the Americans, comfortable, warm and dry would tend to move very carefully and slowly across the tundra to avoid getting wet. They would detour for miles to avoid crossing a stream. The Indians on the other hand would start the day by fording the river and they didn't give a damn what happened to them after that. The worst had already been done.

I felt this could be applied to writing. There is a desire to finish a paragraph or chapter and enjoy the satisfaction of finishing. It is a good feeling. But in the morning there now is only that empty white blank sheet of paper to be filled. I have wasted days trying to regain a momentum I have lost. Now I don't allow myself the luxury of finishing, of getting dry and comfortable. When I am going good but have worked enough for the day I stop before finishing a paragraph I am anxious to finish and then I stop in the middle of a sentence. It is irritating and frustrating but also effective. There is nothing in writing harder to do than to start. But in the morning I finish the sentence that has been left unfinished and then I finish the paragraph and all at once I am in the river again.

Now I intend to write the book I intended to write all along, the one I used to think I had written, the one they would mention in the first paragraph of the obituary. There is a saying attributed to the French that no man should write his first novel until he is forty. This is the age when most Americans cease writing their last novels. I do hope the French are right.

MARK HARRIS

Trumpet to the World

How to Write

THE FIRST REAL writer I ever knew was a man named Robert Marks, who lived on the top floor of a small apartment dwelling at 520 Madison Avenue, and who lives there yet, for his name is on the bell, and the lady who answered the door told me so. I had not seen him in twenty years, and I must have been uncertain whether I wanted to see him now, for when she told me he was out I received the news with something like relief, and turned, and went back down the stairs, leaving the name of my hotel.

He flattered me by telephoning me, though when I had known him, twenty years before, it had been a part of his sublime sophistication never to return my calls. And now, when he called, and left a message, I was unable to reply. Why? Out of what? The student who, by some standard, approaches his teacher, promises humility; the teacher is determined to be graceful and generous and accept the young man as an equal. But I did not think that either of us could play those roles, and I went about my business.

And who was the lady who answered the door? Twenty years before, there had been several ladies, and that too was a part of his sublime worldliness; ladies came, ladies went, sometimes speaking with slight foreign accents, now Viennese, now French. He was a tall, handsome man, he smoked Pall Mall cigarettes with devastating nonchalance and the deepest inhalation, and he too had a touch of accent up from Charleston, South Carolina. His perfect choice in all things was awesome to me. He sold articles to *Esquire* and *Coronet,* and he was the ghost who wrote the columns of Elsa Maxwell, now herself a ghost. It was I who carried the "copy" from him in his surroundings of sophistication to her in her apartment in the Waldorf, and then back to the office of the newspaper syndicate for which we all worked, where I typed the columns onto mimeograph sheets, ran them off on an inky machine, and mailed them to newspapers all over the United States, who seemed to desire them, and so gave me the sense of being engaged in work of importance.

I wanted to be a writer like him. I dreamed that I had written a book and that he had praised me. Actually, when I showed him my writings he said, "You have a talent for the writing, but you won't really write very well until you have something to say." I had no idea what he meant by that; it was a mystery, like his ladies.

The war began January 12, 1943, and ended April 7, 1944, the dates of my induction and discharge. From its first hour it was a revelation, and it gave me something to say. On the train from Manhattan to Fort Dix a military policeman, bearing a large basket, passed down the aisle, instructing us to deposit in his basket all guns and knives. Owning neither, I could not imagine that others did, but the basket was quickly filled with a wicked collection.

I remember next the inexpressible suddenness of spring that year. After Dix, and two months in Virginia, where it was very cold, I was suddenly transferred to a specialist school at Athens, Georgia. Winter in Virginia on Friday, it was spring the next day in Georgia, the dogwood bloomed and my heart burst. It was on that morning—Saturday, March 27, 1943, shortly after seven o'clock—that I decided, in gratitude for this most sensational spring, that I simply did not intend to die in this war.

I had not known that such a matter permitted choice, and I was not even sure of it yet, but I meant to explore the possibility. As quickly as I decided this I must also have decided to find for myself special and acceptable reasons why I should receive the privileges of salvation: why should I live while others died? With that determination I soon found them, and one principally—that the cause was not good enough to die for; and to find fault with the cause I had only to allow to develop freely within me certain notions gathering down there in the sunny South. I was soon able to declare that the segregation of the Negro was as immoral as the depredations of Nazism.

It was a poor argument, but I had a poor mind. Had my mind been better I would have clung to the argument that my reasons to live were purely personal, that I desired it, and that my desire was reason enough. All young men should declare that they are opposed to all wars, and will refuse to fight any, only because they are not prepared to die. But my poor argument was all I then had, and I came to believe in it as fiercely and as deeply as I believed in my own life, and it was my belief which saved me, for the promise I made to myself that morning in Athens I kept, and escaped, and so lived, and became a writer like Robert Marks, as we shall see.

My Diary tells of a journey to Clemson College, in South Carolina, but I think I have no memory of the journey itself. In a life of motion, travel, and disconnection, my Diary was the line of continuity framing and enclosing all chaos, and serving at last (now) as a true record of who I was and what I thought. At Clemson I soon discovered a house of girls of all ages named Fendley, and their mother. I loved the girls and their mother.

Mrs. Fendley valued me at a moment when I had serious doubts about myself. Did I show her any of my little writings? I must have. Regardless, she declared that I was a writer, because she knew that that was what I had in mind, and one way she knew it was that I put *her* in mind of Ben Robertson, who was a local hero thereabouts, having written a book called *Red Hills and Cotton* and been killed in the war.

Of course I promptly read *Red Hills and Cotton,* but I have no memory of the book, only of the circumstance, and of Mrs.

Fendley, who saw in me one whom God had blessed with the gift of words (I am paraphrasing from her most recent letter, twenty years afterward) and Who would spare me to express things good, kind, helpful, and uplifting to mankind.

The Army's plan for me was different. I was to study scientific subjects and be good at them, or else go back "to the troops"— that is to say, active service, live ammunition, and death. My Diary is filled with resolutions to study hard, buckle down, apply myself, keep at it, persevere, consider the consequences, but clearly I failed of all resolutions. Day by day I surrendered. I could not keep awake. The heat was awful. I failed every course but English. I swam, I pursued the Fendley girls, I played baseball, I rode bicycles, I walked the roads with fellow-soldiers, failing like me, living for several autumn weeks wholly in health and joy.

How significant it is that a little book I wrote in the midst of my darkening prospects was entirely comic! It contains (I mean the treasured, traveled manuscript) not a single word about my true fears. I now had something to say, but I did not know that a book was the place to say it. I was filled with hatred, but I did not yet know that a book was the place to put it. I sent it to a literary agent (that is to say, an agent for literary work) who circulated it for some months and returned it to me, by which time I had deeply entered another, but truer; not much true, but somewhat true; a disguise, yet a beginning. The new book begun would be the book which even Robert Marks would hold in his hand. As for me, it would teach me how to write.

Now I was sent from Clemson College to Camp Wheeler— guns, infantry, marching—groping there for a means to save myself. At some moments the popular means struck me as logical, and there were days of doing as others did, learning guns, learning bayonets, learning gas, learning dying. But such days decreased. *November 15, 1943:* "Took to the woods in the afternoon, slept there awhile, finally fled at the approach of a soldier," and below, same day, "Trying to think of a book idea." Half-crazed with the idea of Negro segregation, I had no idea that *that* would soon be my book, for I had yet to learn for myself that books absorbed obsessions. I played poker, I played Ping-pong, and I hitchhiked often to Macon to a girl named

Josephine (not my wife, whose name is also Josephine) whose job
it was at a place called The Amus-u to lie upon a bed and be
knocked to the floor by soldiers throwing baseballs at a target
rigged to springs beneath Josephine's bed. I thought it humiliat-
ing work for a girl, though she seemed to like it; she was unable
to understand my objections to it.

December 1, 1943: "Don't know what's going to be done with
me." Listless, lethargic, distressed, unable to learn even those
bloody skills which might some day save my life or the lives of my
mates, I came to conflict with *them,* my peers. They began to see
in me a liability. One of them was a rough man named Lemuel
Ponkus (Ponkis?), who owned a gun and a large collection of
women's clothing mysteriously obtained. Ponkus threatened that
when we were aboard ship on our way to the battlefield he would
throw me overboard, shooting me in the back as I was sailing
down. I betrayed myself by my clear belief that he was capable of
such an act, that it would be a pleasure to him, if only for the
amusement of it during those humdrum days at sea.

One night, as I was writing, Ponkus asked me what it was, and
I told him it was a novel about Negroes. He congratulated me,
saying it was time someone wrote such a book, believing in the
chaos of his mind that the book I was writing would disvalue
Negroes, put them down. I could not resist correcting him,
whereupon he who a moment before had loved me, now hated me
again. He accused me of crimes it never occurred to me to be
guilty of. For example, he accused me of smothering the fires in
the stoves. Why should I have done such a thing, who loved
warmth as well as anyone? But, after repeated accusations, our
Captain Banister must have concluded some truth lurked there,
and he took me (this occurs again much later in my novel *Something About a Soldier*) twice in a single day to the station hospital, with the intention of causing me to be committed to a mental ward.

The poor Captain met frustration there, finding himself unable to describe to the physicians the specific manifestations of
my insanity. I was none of the things you needed to be to gain
admission—not disorderly, not given to weeping, not given to fist
fights, not given to AWOL or bedwetting, thievery, homosexu-
ality, or hallucinations. In short, I was merely inadmissible,

unqualified for medical treatment, and my Captain Banister was forced to find another way. One night soon afterward I was suddenly informed that I was to be transferred to the station hospital, not as a patient but as a worker. The next morning I was gone, returning only once, to retrieve my "garrison hat," which I had loaned to the baker. I never saw Captain Banister again, nor Lemuel Ponkus, each of whom has reappeared time and again as fragments of my fiction. I am convinced that they and all that Company are dead.

At the hospital I worked in the supply room, I mopped the ramps, and I was a medical clerk. When I discovered that nobody was keeping track of me I quit both jobs and spent the days writing my novel, leaving for Macon at nightfall, my Josephine at The Amus-u.

It was there, then, early 1944, that I discovered how a book might contain my feelings, my hatred, my obsessions, my indignation. With something to say at last, and the desire to write a book besides, I discovered that the two could be one, that a book was *personal*. My earlier writing had been rather denial than feeling, and my models were chosen from conventional literature: when I was not imitating Howard Spring I was imitating Marion Hargrove. But this new *personal* writing was a new life for me, and it was interesting and exciting to me in a way my writing had never before excited or interested me. As I wrote, I was headlong, eager to get on with it and find out who these people were and how they would come out. I had no idea where the story was going. I had no plot. I had no plan.

Now I had something to write about, not only the Negro race I had just now personally discovered, but also myself, my own fear of death, my own hatred of guns and violence, my own isolation and unhappiness. I had no idea what I was actually writing about: I knew only that I felt better for writing it, life quickened for me, all things became more interesting to me, many things clarified themselves for me, and at nightfall, when I went to my girl on her bed of springs, I was purged, empty, clean, and newly informed by things I was discovering every day in rapid abundance. In my daily writing I killed my enemies. For example, Miss Dodge, a medical secretary, argued the biological inferiority of Negroes. I incorporated her into my book, and had my revenge upon her there, battering her there, for custom and society prevented me from battering her direct.

February 5, 1944: "Book is progressing. Over 10,000 words." Newly questioning the logic of things, I refused to salute officers. I wanted to translate all thought to action. I could abide no contradictions. Therefore, taking my pay (it occurs to me now that I must have saluted to do so), I left Camp Wheeler without permission on a day no doubt chosen for its meaning—Lincoln's Birthday—carrying with me Marguerite Steen's *The Sun Is My Undoing* and only one handkerchief, which I washed as I traveled, and dried upon steam radiators.

I left behind both my manuscript and a letter to one Captain Albin. I felt that he would help me. I had worked briefly for him at simple labor—sorting the records of sick soldiers into categories according to their afflictions. Their two principal afflictions were "undescended testicles" and "psychoneurosis," and I knew which it was I had. To call myself to Captain Albin's attention I told him in my letter of the contradiction between America's war aims and its domestic behavior. I cited specifically anti-Negro and anti-Semitic attitudes among soldiers of the armed forces. I declined to serve our country until those situations were corrected. I mailed my letter as I left Camp Wheeler—and in the act of leaving committed, of course, the overt act qualifying me for mental help.

I hitchhiked to Cordele, to Perry, to Sylvester, to Thomasville—all those lovely Georgia towns—reading *The Sun Is My Undoing* in one-night stands in rented rooms, and attending the motion pictures: in Sylvester I saw a movie called *Hitler's Children,* in Thomasville a movie called *Dixie.* My plan was to travel from Thomasville to Albany to see the movie *My Son, My Son,* taken from the novel of Howard Spring which had given me utmost pleasure, but it was a movie I was destined never to see, for on the morning of February 16 I was apprehended by military police on the main street of Moultrie—"taken," says my Diary, "to Spence Field, where I was made a member of the guardhouse squadron."

One of my fellow-prisoners was an engaging fellow who presented himself to me as a lieutenant. I disbelieved him. He declined to argue the matter. But he behaved with such gentlemanly dignity that after five days I believed him, learning only in my final minutes at that prison that he was but a private like me, and his handsome face has appeared to me again and again over the years, as I write, reminding me—*show*, don't tell; *dramatize*, don't argue; *be*, don't say. One Sergeant Dycka took me by bus to Camp Wheeler, where Major Samuel Hibbs committed me to the ward maintained for non-violent psychoneurotics.

In my private room I completed my novel, maintained my Diary, and tended my vast correspondence with friends and relations. Summarizing for March, I wrote, "More writing this month than ever before. Some of it good." I went to the Red Cross for free cigarettes, I played Ping-pong, I telephoned Josephine in Macon, and I saw boys returning from the war all shot to pieces.

I offered my novel for criticism to several persons. Major Hibbs asked to see it, but after keeping it for some time he returned it without comment. I gave the manuscript to a Negro psychoneurotic named Joe Simms, who occupied the room next to mine, offering me my first opportunity to know a Negro socially. He disappointed me by returning my manuscript to me with little comment, although I had expected him to recognize it as a document which would shake the world loose from its prejudices. Weeks passed. Now and then I was called for an X ray. Now and then I was weighed. I was "under observation," but although there was a little window in my door nobody ever seemed to observe me through it, and upon my chart the constant entry was made, "worked typewriter all day," several times repeated, and finally reduced to ditto marks.

On Friday, April 7, 1944, I was discharged from the army, given $159.02 in pay, and sent upon my way. On my route through Camp Wheeler I met the sergeant for whom I had worked in the supply room. "Now you got what you wanted," he said, not with bitterness. I felt that he was mistaken, and I denied what he had said. Only as the years passed could I begin to know the real state of my mind in those days, and then only by continuing to write as I had first learned down there to do—by flailing, planless, using my writing to discharge my furies.

The manuscript I carried north with me contained somewhere

within it the novel I would have written had I been able then or ever to go straight from start to finish. But the straight way is probably impossible, and the mass of papers I carried with me was a weight I would afterward recognize as the inevitable first phase, the chaos of options, a document of meanderings seeking one firm beginnning.

My father, who thought it as finished as I, for he had no more experience as writer's father than I as writer, carried the manuscript on Memorial Day to the offices of Reynal & Hitchcock, now defunct. They were on that day merely closed. Therefore, he carried it to an agent for literary work, whom he and I would innocently have called a literary agent, and we waited. The agent—Mary Abbott of McIntosh & Otis—soon carried the manuscript back to Reynal & Hitchcock.

In those days almost any young man eager to be a writer thought of his home-town newspaper as a place to begin, and I thought of mine, which, having no place for me, sent me up the line of the New Haven Railroad to Port Chester, New York, where I was engaged as a reporter at thirty dollars a week. Later, when my editor saw me reading the classified section of the *New York Times,* he raised me to thirty-five. I paid four dollars a week for a little room on Poningo Street near the firehouse, and I learned so much in one year of newspapering that I would advise young men to go into it if they were sure they could get out.

When I received from Reynal & Hitchcock an "advance" of five hundred dollars against potential royalties I was stunned. The idea that my novel would gain money for me had never entered my thoughts, and I had no special plan for the money when it came. Unaware how swiftly a large sum can grow into a small sum and disappear, I did what appeared logical: I quit my job and settled down in my little room on Poningo Street to do the revisions I was told I must.

Who told me? Reynal & Hitchcock told me. My editor there was Frank Taylor, who soon passed me along to Walter Pistole, and whereas they were correct in believing the book needed revision they had no idea how a book was revised, for they had never done it, and neither did I, for the same reason.

Of course the first refuge of ignorance is authority, and almost all authority believes that the reason a book needs "revision" is that it wasn't rightly done in the first place. Since I was young I assumed I was guilty. Yes, I confess, I had written the book without Plan, without Outline, just jumping in every day and battering at it and following it wherever it went, and all this in spite of my conventional training in conventional public schools, where I had been taught to love my country and Plan Ahead. Consider the poor teacher, burdened by her Supervisor, hearing night and day that she must prepare a Lesson Plan. To keep her job she believes in the Lesson Plan, it becomes a point of philosophy with her, and she passes her philosophy to her pupils, telling them in all earnestness that they, too, must Plan, whether they are Taking A Trip or Building A House or writing. Luckily for me, something in me never learned that lesson, and I could see now, as I undertook my "revisions," that there was nothing *wrong* with the draft I had written in the army; there was simply something necessary and inevitable about it; I had done the right thing blindly.

Somewhere inside those pages was a book, and my eye began to see it. Where my reading of my pages flagged I cut; into the basket went all that hot "prose poetry" children love so much, all that precious language I'd wept over. From what was left I built upward, as much as possible in a straight line.

My mind often darts back to that room on Poningo Street, for it was there that I learned, or taught myself, the uses of revision, which meant, as well, by implication, the uses of the first draft, too. Knowing that, I knew the value of speed, of writing fast and planless, even as I had done, but which I could now do with confidence, guiltless, in spite of all I had been taught. I think it was in that room, too, that I discovered the sensation of writing around in a circle, not from beginning to end, but round and round, keeping going, never stopping, so long as things needed doing. Part informed part, something discovered here illuminated something over there, occurring by faith and by process as it could never occur by plan. Until the writer has experienced that process and acquired that faith he will have a hard time going on, and I am thankful I learned it very young, and knew it when I saw it, and trusted it, and have tried to tell other people about it ever since, for it is the only way to live. Really, too, it was the primary profit of that first book.

On Poningo Street, near the firehouse, where writing so much began for me, I learned also to live with my daily dose of hatred, born of isolation. The moment is dismal before work begins. I hear automobiles passing. I know that people are at play. I see from the window a lady pass by. To blind myself from the view, and to protect my eyes from glare, I draw the shade, darken my room, and now my isolation is not only dismal but also dark. Who is doing this to me, and why am I doing it to myself? I think of someone I know who is outside my window right now, enjoying himself. He is not always the same person, from year to year he changes, and I hate him because I know that he is at cocktail parties criticizing with all the juices of his envy a number of books he has never read, nor means to, or which he has read while tieing his tie for the party. My hatred generates me, and I work. The pattern is often unpleasant, but the way was set on Poningo Street, and I have lived with it, having learned by accident, as I learned the magic of revision, the uses of hatred.

In May, 1945, I moved from Port Chester to New York City, to work for the newspaper *PM*. I lived in another small room, this one at 40 West Twelfth Street, in a house, someone told me, once occupied by Mark Twain, though whether that is true I never knew, and at the time it would have been meaningless to me: I saw no connection between myself and the past. The house was now a rooming house, and my room was rather longer than it was wide; as for height, it had none. I was perfectly comfortable sitting or lying, and there was a trick to closing the door: you entered, you backed yourself against the wall, you reached out, you swung the door, and you leaped out of its path while it closed itself. To open it, you reversed the process. My room had no plumbing. The bathtub was in the public hall, with a screen around it. In short, it was a heavenly place, and I wrote well. Suddenly, June 3, 1945, about eighteen months after beginning, I came to the end of my book. I had not expected it to end that day, but it did, crying to quit on a high note, with the bad result that we never know how the Negro came out at his trial. My editors complained of that blemish in my story, but they had lived long enough with the work, and knew that I could go no farther.

In *Trumpet to the World* (1946) I am disguised as a powerful black man determined to smash the heads of certain white bastards in Athens, Georgia, who refuse to permit me to attend the University.

I am a great reader of books, the names of which are never specified, and I write poetry, none of which is displayed within the novel.

One day Willie Jim (for that is the name I assume) is walking along the highway when he is picked up by a white girl named Eddie Mae, who is singing as she drives. She takes him home and shelters him in the house of her father, who is a professor at Midfield College (Clemson College). Willie Jim works in the college kitchen, and Eddie Mae becomes his tutor.

In the kitchen Willie Jim tries to organize the workers. The truest moment of the book—that is to say, the moment at which probability firmly conquers fantasy—occurs when the Negro workers, after a moment of daring, resume submissiveness.

Sometimes Eddie Mae entertains people at her father's house, and Willie Jim is their social equal. But who were those people? We shall never know; the author did not know.

Eddie Mae becomes pregnant and goes to New York to have her baby. Willie Jim, practically with his bare hands, fixes up an old house near Good Hope, Georgia (a town which reappears in my fiction eleven years later), intending to live there with his bride and baby, apparently unaware that interracial marriage is frowned upon even in a place with such a name. His house is burned down (he saves his manuscripts), and he flees naked through the woods, like Emperor Jones. A fairly nice little sentence appears here: "The ground was white with the thin filigree of frost."

By good fortune, he is rescued by a Negro family and returned to health. He makes his way to Atlanta, where he refuses to accept the segregation of the railroad station, and he is next seen in the army, apparently having been drafted as a punishment in lieu of prison.

For a while he is a good soldier—"a soldier with a belief"—his larger intelligence enabling him to see the war's purpose in spite of the cruel treatment he has personally known. *He was eager for battle!* However, when he sees that Negro soldiers are not to be permitted to enter combat his spirit breaks.

He never sees Eddie Mae, but he keeps in touch with her by mail, sending her installments of his book, which she reads while airing the baby in the integrated park. Willie Jim, anxious to complete his book, leaves the army without permission, rents a little room, completes his book, and returns to the army, where he is sentenced to sixty days in the guardhouse. One sympathetic member of his trial board says, "This man ought to be reclassified—properly."

Soon he gets an army job—teaching illiterate soldiers to read and write. He is a very good and informal teacher and is soon promoted to sergeant. He arranges a Christmas party for his students, but the party is disrupted by a villainous major (a professional soldier, a racist) whom Willie Jim hits with a left hand and a right hand, after which—another fairly nice little sentence —"He lighted a cigarette with steady hands and carefully pocketed the burnt match." He runs away and never comes back, as far as we know. His legal defense is organized by his publisher, and we end with the feeling that men of good will can succeed if only they write down their feelings and publish them: as the book ends, Willie Jim is preparing a book of his feelings.

Ten months were to pass between the day I completed the book and the day it was published. That is to say, in ten months I would become myself complete, published, finished and begun, a writer like Robert Marks, infinitely happy, king of the world. Who were all these peasants? Off with their heads. And the world itself would be different, for my book would make it so. Ten months to racial harmony!

Fired from *PM,* I was assigned by International News Service to its St. Louis bureau. One of my last errands in New York, before leaving for the west, was to sit for a photographer engaged by Reynal & Hitchcock. I wanted to co-operate with her, but I did not know what I wanted to look like. She must have said, "Just be yourself," and I tried. I wore a clean white shirt and a dark, knitted tie, and round eyeglasses with silver frames. I was twenty-two years old and I had just had a bath behind the screen in the public hall on West Twelfth Street. The walls at Reynal & Hitchcock were painted lemon. One day, at a cocktail party there, I was introduced to Mr. Reynal himself, who shook my hand and held his smile long enough for someone to flash our picture. He said nothing to me. With the explosion of the bulb he turned back to someone else. I may have been rather a sensation among my friends, but to Eugene Reynal I was only an inconvenient young man who was going to cost him money before earning him any (if ever). I went to St. Louis.

I arrived in July, the bomb went off in August, and in all the middle west of America I met only one person who thought the dropping of the atomic bomb on Hiroshima a more critical event in human history than my forthcoming novel. Her name was Josephine, like the girl on the bed so long ago and far away, and I went to her in Springfield, Illinois, wearing a dirty raincoat she would always remember as emblematic of my life and my mind in that year.

Since St. Louis was filled with charming girls I don't know why I went time and again a hundred miles to Springfield. It must have been that I was unable to impress her. I thought she should love me because, as soon as Publication Day arrived, I would be revealed as Great Emancipator II, and I imagine now that what she was telling me, and I too simple to grasp, was that the richest part of the experience was behind me, the joy of writing was private, that nothing lay ahead worth happening except other writing, for Publication Day would change neither the world nor me.

That was the real state of things. *January 14, 1946:* "In letter Frank [Taylor] says book will be published March 25. Am in poor spirits when my spirits should be good. It's probably the prospect of the 70-day wait." Waiting for who? Six days later appeared a little "plug" for my book in the St. Louis *Globe Democrat.* Imagine my sitting there that morning, reading the *Globe,* and seeing my own name rise from the pages as if I were somebody else! I was real because the newspaper said so. Why were my spirits poor when they should have been good? On January 25 I won a prize of money from International News for the excellence of my writing, a full-page advertisement for my book appeared (in a trade magazine), and I was beginning to observe in myself, as one observes any dangerous disorder, sudden swellings of elation at the sight of my own name, followed by swift deflation and mild depression. That night: "Supper at Union Station & proceeded to sink into low spirits. To library and was reminded of my lack of knowledge. . . ."

Can you imagine that instead of an orthodox marriage announcement I distributed an imitation of a newspaper notice? Religiously atheistic, we were married March 17, 1946, "according to the laws of God and the ordinances of the State of Illinois," and I returned to St. Louis that very night alone. In St. Louis I had happily begun to permit myself to attend many little parties celebrating my forthcoming book: to that I was married.

Now I was coming to the end of my lesson, for the test of the writer may be whether he ever writes another word beyond New York and Publication Day, whether the writing serves him apart from all rewards of egoism, whether he requires it for the ease of his spirit; or whether something else will do. We flew from Chicago: the flight required five hours in those primitive days.

Monday, April 1, 1946: "Today TRUMPET TO THE WORLD, my first novel, officially came out." The entry has a certain confidence about it; plainly I expected to follow this book with others, one began and one went on, inspired by the excitement of the day: we had lunch at the Algonquin with an editor, we were received by Roy Wilkins of the N.A.A.C.P., we dined with Robert Marks, we were guests on radio shows, we were interviewed by the press. We went to Harlem, but the part we saw was still slums in spite of the appearance of my book.

The point was lost. I too, swept up in the excitement, forgot for the moment that the roots of the book lay deep in distress and indignation, but I think I began sluggishly to know during one week in New York that the reward of the work had passed me by, that the pleasure of writing was emotion and craft—Camp Wheeler, Poningo Street, Twelfth Street—and I'd know where and when to look for it next time; that all else was irrelevance. That, too, was the lesson my first book taught me, the learning happening without plan, for which no substitute exists. Now I knew something about how writing happened, and when to turn my face away.

MARY RENAULT

The King Must Die

Notes on *The King Must Die*

OFTEN I HAVE found that the germ of a novel has emerged, in what has seemed an entirely accidental way, from some secondary theme, or bit of background material, made use of for purely functional reasons in some previous book. The selection of a theme, of course, is never an accident with any writer; its provenance, however, does sometimes seem to be thrown in one's way like a coin in the sand, which catches the light when one walks past at a certain angle.

A passage of dialogue and discussion among the characters of an earlier novel set in 1940, *The Charioteer*, gave the starting-point to my first historical novel, *The Last of the Wine;* and from this in turn grew *The King Must Die.*

The Last of the Wine is about civilised, highly educated Greeks of the fifth century, who lived much with the legends of their founding heroes, but had not, any more than had Shakespeare when he clothed Caesar in a doublet, knowledge enough to picture them in their real contemporary context. Between these Athenians and the Bronze Age, Homer with his mixture of authentic tradition, Dark Age accretions, and eighth-century personal genius, was the only link.

In classical Athens, Theseus was a household word. He was the first High King of all Attica, saviour of the land from tribal anarchy, establisher of Athenian pre-eminence, and founder, by tradition, of the rule of law; a just and strong ruler, upholding the Virgilian precept, *"parcere subjectis et debellare superbos,"* to whose sanctuary, for centuries after, maltreated slaves could fly for refuge. His shrines were dominant, his images were everywhere; but all, of course, in the visual idiom of the sculptors' own day; a young athlete with the proud unconcern at nakedness which marked out the "civilised" Hellene from the white-skinned, over-clad, pudent "barbarians" who had been stripped and mocked when they struggled ashore from their rammed ships at Salamis. Had these fifth-century sculptors been offered as their model a real Bronze Age warrior, in a helmet of hide stitched with boars' teeth, wearing embroidered *lederhosen* and massive jewels, no doubt they would have recoiled. Yet their idealised, nude victor still wielded in battle the weapon which had come down to them in his living tradition, the immemorially ancient Minoan-Helladic double axe, cult-object and royal mace of Crete.

Theseus had no place in *The Last of the Wine,* except as part of the stuff with which one had learned, in one's reading, that the characters' minds were furnished, as their rooms were furnished with supper-couches, red-figure rhytons, and household shrines. Sometimes they had occasion to remember him: "There is a labyrinth," says the Priest of Apollo to Alexias, "in the heart of every man, and to each comes the time when he must reach its centre, and meet the Minotaur." But while writing this, I still saw only the Theseus whom the priest and Alexias would know.

I cannot remember exactly when, or how, this face in the crowd came forward to take the stage. But about this time, the first Linear B decipherments were appearing, with their glimpses of feudal Mycenaean kingdoms; along with some dramatic discoveries of royal tombs. There began to be descried a mainland culture different from the mannered elegance of the Minoan. Here with their skeleton hands still folded over their long goldpommeled swords, lay the tall princes whose descendants took Troy; beside their domed tombs had stood the great stone walls of their fortress-palaces, the gates with their huge lintels, lifted no one knows how, and their lion-carved capstones. The written tablets shadowed a warlike society, well organised, aristocratic and art-loving, but primitive and barbaric by the standards of Crete's millennial sophistication.

At some stage of these thoughts, I began to picture the young Theseus, a product of this environment, making his appearance at Knossos as hostage, athlete or invader. But the moment of cross-fertilisation, when I first knew what the book would be about and why, happened when after reading, if I remember rightly, Robert Graves's *The Greek Myths,* I was reflecting on the concept of the Royal Sacrifice. Clearly it had been sometimes enforced; just as clearly, it seemed to me, it must have been sometimes voluntary. When, and why?

Suddenly, everything fell into place. I could begin to guess at the way Theseus' mind was furnished, the kind of beliefs and aspirations and responsibilities which might have determined his actions; the tensions between victorious patriarchy and lately defeated, still powerful matriarchy, which could have underlain the love-conflict element in his legendary relations with women. The story became self-propelling in my mind and I started serious reading, in order to check errors before it ran away with me. But everything I read went along with the tale as I had conceived it, nothing against.

There was one more crucial turning-point, however, after the novel was actually in progress. I had written several chapters, presenting Theseus in the Greek heroic image; that is, the Homeric, with the build of the tall princes in the tholos tombs; adding, since he was a hero, a few extra inches for good measure. Somehow, I couldn't tell how or why, I found the story resisting me. Something was dragging, something stuck. I went on, with an increasing instinct that I was going to fetch up against some block or other which would refuse to be side-stepped and would make me a lot of work. I was, and it did. I had already accepted fully the view now held by most scholars that the tribute of youths and maids from Athens, prey of the Minotaur (which just means "Bull of Minos"), the doomed company which Theseus joined as a volunteer, must in fact have been conscripts for the bull game, whose astonishing athletics are so dominant a theme of Minoan art. Two discrepant images had thus been wrestling in my subconscious imagination. Among these light, slender, wiry young acrobats, who possessed the only possible physique for the bull dance, what on earth was this six-foot-three warrior doing?

Here it was. He had dragged on me because, though orthodox, he was unreal. Suddenly I saw Theseus as the kind of man his conditioning might produce, if his mind and aspirations had been those of a Helladic prince, but his body that of a bull-leaper; a body not of his own conquering race (and there was a mystery about his birth) but of the conquered Pelasgians. A constant element of the Theseus legend, I remembered, was that he had invented the science of wrestling. Why should a big man need to do that? It would much likelier be the resource of an intelligent lightweight.

I remembered Alexander; a man of just such slight limber build and lightning reflexes, with a face of striking beauty, of whom a contemporary would none the less record for later historians that his limbs were remarkable for strength rather than good looks, "for he was not tall." Height was, to the Greek, a *sine qua non* of physical prestige, even in women; a prestige perhaps historic and racial, as well as aesthetic, and having its origins in a day not far antecedent to Theseus' own. Legend was bound to confer this quality on a founder-hero; nothing else would be conceivable. But the real Theseus was a man who had made an asset of his liabilities, as so many real-life heroes do.

Obviously, there was now no alternative but to re-write from the beginning. But from this decision on, I started to enjoy myself. Nothing is more exciting, when one explores the past, than the sense of having, perhaps, found a new lead into truth. Some day, no doubt, new documents will be deciphered, which will restore the lost history of the Helladic age, and some or all of my guesses will be disproved. Never mind; it is better for us all, including me, that more truth be known.

I have never, for any reason, in any historical book of mine, falsified anything deliberately which I knew or believed to be true. Often of course I must have done through ignorance what would horrify me if I could revisit the past; at the best one is in

84

the position of, say, an Indonesian resident who has never met an Englishman, trying to write a novel set in London from documentary evidence, pictures, and maps. But one can at least desire the truth; and it is inconceivable to me how anyone can decide deliberately to betray it; to alter some fact which was central to the life of a real human being, however long it is since he ceased to live, in order to make a smoother story, or to exploit him as propaganda for some cause. I have yet to be persuaded that the word "committed," if analysis is pressed home, will ever be found to mean anything which does not boil down to, "a state in which something else matters more than truth."

There is nothing amusing about committal; the victims of that slaughter lie strewn around. But exhortations to be contemporary always strike me as irresistibly comic. When a lady blue-stocking announced in the presence of Carlyle that she accepted the universe, he remarked aside, "By God, she'd better." If one could, even for an instant, be anything but contemporary, one would have achieved omniscience. What a triumph of the historical imagination! Anyone now alive is contemporary whether he likes it or not, and any kind of creative work he does will show it. Kipling is wholly a man of his own world situation, while doing a first-class job of reconstruction on the life of a Roman-British centurion manning Hadrian's Wall; Spenser, painstakingly archaising Prince Arthur in Fairyland, is quintessentially Elizabethan. Thackeray's characters listening to the cannon of Waterloo are all mid-Victorians; we are far nearer while Jane Austen's shore-leave naval officers chat about their prizes in an English parlour.

We all bring to the past our own temperament, our own preoccupations, to limit the reach of our insight; our visual field at its widest will be small enough. It seems to me that it is in the struggle to stretch these bonds, to see the universals of human nature adapting to, or intractably resisting, the pressure of life's changing accidents, that the excitement of writing historical novels lies.

You cannot step twice into the same river, said Herakleitos. People in the past were not just like us; to pretend so is an evasion and a betrayal, turning our back on them so as to be easy among familiar things. This is why the matter of dialogue is so crucial. No word in our language comes to us sterile and aseptic, free of associations. If it was coined yesterday, it tastes of that, and a single sentence of modern-colloquial slang, a turn of phrase which evokes specifically our own society, can destroy for me, at any rate, the whole suspension of disbelief. Yet phony archaism merely suggests the nineteenth century instead, and actors in ill-fitting tights. If I wrote about the England of any earlier century, I should want to use, as far as it is still understandable, the actual speech of that day. That this can be done, is proved by Rose Macaulay's magnificent *They Were Defeated*. whose smell of authenticity quite goes to one's head. However, I was writing about people who spoke Greek. In such a case all one can hope for is to be, as far as possible, transparent, not to intrude.

Greek is a highly polysyllabic language. Yet when writing dialogue for my Greeks I have found myself, by instinct, avoiding the polysyllables of the English language, and using, as far as they are still in the living language, the older and shorter words. This is not because the style parallels Greek style; it is entirely a matter of association and ambience. In Greek, polysyllables are old; in English, mostly Latinised and largely modern. They have acquired their own aura, which they will bring along with them. Their stare, like that of the basilisk, is killing. Take the following sentence, which I have just picked at random from a magazine: "High priority is to be given to training in the skills of community organizing and conflict resolution." It contains no concept which Plato did not know, or, indeed, did not in fact deal with. But it comes to us steeped in notions of the company report, the social survey, and so forth. When I see writing like this in a historical novel I know what the author is after. He wants us to identify with the situation of his characters as if it were our own. But it isn't, and identification thus achieved is a cheat. You cannot, as an advertising copywriter would say, enjoy a trip to fifth-century Athens, or Minoan Crete, in the comfort of your own home. You have, as far as your mind will take you, to leave home and go to them.

Does all this really matter? Yes, I think so; and not just aesthetically. Every era of man's development, from the palaeolithic upwards, is still in living existence somewhere on earth. Indeed, the metropolitan technocrats whom self-centred intellectuals glibly call Twentieth Century Man, are as few today in relation to all humanity, as the spores in a mould-spot on a grape where it has scarcely begun to spread. We live in blindness if we forget that history is not only vertical; it is also horizontal.

However, one does not go to the past as a public utility. So why? One can say, "Because it is there." But unlike Everest, not only is it there, but we are its products. We go, perhaps, to find ourselves; perhaps to free ourselves. It is certain we shall never know ourselves, till we have broken out from the brittle capsule of Megalopolis, and taken a long look back along the rocky road which brought us where we are.

WILLIAM GASS

Omensetter's Luck

A Letter to the Editor

I suppose I could have redrawn this letter—rubbed out an eye, shortened a nose—so my portrait should not show me quite so clearly a fool (though unyoung, yet a young fool!), but a letter is no longer genuine when it abandons the moment that made it, when it no longer moves toward its recipient as though hurled by feeling from a bow. Letters which have been repaired become merely literature; they lose the man; so I have not made this letter's rough places plain, but have left its obscurities obscure, its inanities inane, its loose ends loose, and its impoverished arguments poor. Mr. Segal had called me simply to ask for suggestions concerning jacket copy. He could not know that he was talking to a madman. I had suffered so much over this book already (it had been years in the writing, the manuscript had been stolen, rewritten it had been rejected and rejected) that it seemed natural—inevitable—that I should suffer further, and that the editor who had championed it at last should prove now not to understand a word of it, to be indifferent to my aims as an artist, and in this final stage to want to argue. These were delu-

sions only one who was half unhinged could have had under the circumstances, but I had them, and they account, in part, for this letter's angry, hurt, defensive tone. I have not altered it for another reason. We like to think we grow, improve, replace our fears and rages with maturities, when we weaken rather—weary, age. Alas and hurray: I am just as mad a man now as I was then, or have been ever.

June 26, 1965

Dear Mr. Segal:

I cannot see that this is going to do either of us any good. My only feeling is one of dismay. It would be so much better for you if you could publish my book with confidence, because you are going to need some inner support. People are going to wonder at your judgment. It appears you have begun to have doubts already. Or maybe you had them all along, and my changes have simply underlined them. Under such circumstances, if I say—hang on, this book will make you famous—you will put it down to the vanity of authors. What passes for vanity, however, is often knowledge. Ford used to say that Conrad had been sent to him because Ford knew more about writing than anyone in England. Had he set down vanity beside his lie? When he was so completely and demonstrably right?

Furthermore, I shall have to telegraph everything; tell you things you already know; and appear dogmatic. I hate to write sloppily of matters about which I feel strongly, not because I desire to persuade (the reverse is more nearly the case), but because the ideas involved (and I did not discover them) are, like all true ideas, noble in themselves, and worthy of reverence.

You are, of course, surrounded by immeasurably ignorant people—charlatans and salesmen, the cheap, the vulgar, and the noisy. If you can hear a true sound through that din . . . Well, there is no god to come to strike them dead. They know commodities. They will continue to blat. And they will confuse writing and politics, writing and religion, writing and philosophy, writing and sociology, writing and history, writing and life. They know sales and reputations, awards and prizes, puffs and personalities. They trade in slogans and clichés, fads and whims, the slippery and easy, the smart and the latest. They are fond of the negro question, the drug question, the jewish question, the catholic question—of communism, poverty, population, sex . . . Where does this group come from; why is there so much commerce in it; so much frantic sloshing about; so much fear? Philosophy, for example, is a noble and arduous discipline. Fiction is equally severe. But literary philosophy is shit. Literary sociology is shit. Literary psychology is shit. What would literary physics be? There is a loss, in these things, of discipline and order, severity and control, purity and clarity. And so you phone me to ask what the hell I am doing, what my book is about. And all I can feel, at such a question, is dismay. But I shall try. First of all I tried to write a book that would not be like all the books I despise. I would hope it had these negative qualities.

Arnold Bennett (strange advocate!) long ago observed that the reader and his responses are not the test of a classic. The classic, rather, is the judge of him. Ortega made a similar point. *Melanctha, Happy Days, Under the Volcano, Ficcones, The Good Soldier, Moby Dick, Words for Music Perhaps, Eupalinos, The Duino Elegies, The Golden Bowl, The Sot-Weed Factor*, etcetera —as different as they are—are examinations. They measure the emptiness of their readers, for these books completely and absolutely *are*. Many times I have had the experience of holding in my hand a book that was more real, more alive, more sensitive than I was. I know that a sentence can contain more Being than a town, and I know that I would sell my soul for such a sentence; I would sell the town. Now if we were to imagine this kind of test in moral terms rather than in esthetic ones, then we would have to imagine people responding to a Socrates or Jesus—some similar somebody or other—feeling them to possess electrifying moral force. At first I thought of Omensetter in this way. There were two obvious things the matter with that. I didn't want to get involved in another allegory of the Second Coming. Furthermore, it is no longer possible to represent moral qualities unambiguously, inasmuch as there aren't any unambiguous moral qualities. Omensetter had to be conceived as an "illusory Christ." Three figures immediately grouped themselves around him . . . but of that, more in a moment. You must not be spared a few additional yards of theory.

First: the difference between literary writing and other kinds.

A sign like GENTS tells me where to pee. It conveys information; it produces feelings of glad relief. I use the sign, but I don't dawdle under it. The sign could have said MEN. It could have been replaced by a moustache. The sign passes out of consciousness, is extinguished, by its use. To the degree a sign grows literary, it does not have a "use." The meaning is not extinguished. I return to it again and again. The secrets of literature lie in that magnetism. (Valéry is wonderful on this point.) There are some people who have no sense for instrinsic value. They use their knives and forks. They use their wives and friends. It is immoral to treat people as mere means. The same sorts want to know what poems and paintings are good for. Watch out for them.

Second: the difference between poetry and literary prose.

1. Fiction has to do, primarily, with the strategies of middle and long distances. It is no accident that the epic poem is dead. It died of printing. Homer's devices (his looser form) were contrived for the ear. The condensations, the small close formalities of lyric poetry, meant as they are now for a reader who may ponder them as long as he likes, are not suited for big bounds. Distance makes a difference. Poe was right.

2. By and large, fiction is a three dimensional medium, poetry a two dimensional one. Fiction is more complex, more inherently tense, but poetry is purer.

Third: the nature of the medium.

1. Fiction, first of all, involves the invention of a world. Here the writer needs, not the gift of writing, but the ability to create scenes, particulars, and persons—to make imaginary lives and objects. When this ability is lacking, it is often replaced by observed scenes and persons, who are then falsified in some way, or simply regarded, by convention and in the context, as imaginary. It is a rare gift—this inventive ability—and a misunderstood one. It is a test of beautifully imagined persons that they escape their representations. Ford and Tolstoy—both could do it. It is obvious, however, that this ability is not linguistic.

History is the description of real things and people. Fiction requires their creation. But why create them? So as to arrange them esthetically, rather than as chance and natural law contrive. The natural sciences discover an order in these events if they can, but it is not an artistic order, and the obvious advantage of fiction is its freedom from the *esthetically* senseless. Psychology is esthetically senseless, and whenever I observe an author *motivating* a character, I observe a journalist. Hamlet has no unconscious. Hamlet is a mouth, a vocabulary. Children fire cap guns at movie bandits, and critics explain Hamlet's vacillation as if he were someone they'd met yesterday. One might as well wonder why imaginary steak does not nourish. Remember all those clods who complained that the beacon could not possibly flash the news of Troy's fall to Clytemnestra? It can if I say so, said Humpty Dumpty. Again: the advantage a painted table has over a real one is that you can put the legs where they will look well. Rubens painted belly buttons nicely and he spotted them about for painterly reasons, not anatomical ones. Most writers—incompetent stupid lazy wretches—bind their meager imaginings together—give them what sense they have—by leaning on what they conceive the actual laws to be: the laws of mind or body, sex, society or money. And then these change, and their laws have to be regarded as esthetical conventions like Jonson's humours.

This dimension of fiction is not, as I've mentioned, linguistic at all. It is common to the movie maker, the jokesmith—to all kinds of repugnant people—and in the form of the daydream, it is common to all of us. Consequently it is the least important dimension—poets tend to back off from it. Shakespeare had no time for it at all. He borrowed his plots and his people. He then gave them immortal poetry to speak. Joyce leaned on Dublin data. The gift of creative imagination, when it is the kind that parallels history, is so rarely found in writers that they either (a) steal plots, etc., or (b) eliminate them, or (c) use autobiographical material. The danger in *a* and *c* is that the material does not come esthetically composed. It must be altered. This is also difficult, and seldom performed.

When a writer is dealing with *naturally* strong situations (sex, violence, etc.), the first thing he must do is disarm them, otherwise these natural responses will interfere with the esthetic ones he is supposed to want. A good deal of power is achieved by frankness, these days, but there is nothing artistic about frankness.

93

Some people want the illusion of life. Let them have it. Pornography is easy to write, and there are many who will be happy to provide it. Let them hide their heads in books. They would rather read about living than live. My blessing.

2. Concepts constitute the second, and the fundamental dimension of literature. As history, etc., describes the actual order of events, and psychology, etc., accounts for their connection, so logic and mathematics account for and arrange concepts according to law. But history is simple happening, is esthetically confused. So logic and mathematics are involved only in the rational order of ideas, not in their esthetic exploitation. Degas wondered why his poems weren't better. He had many ideas, he said. But poetry is made of words, Mallarmé is supposed to have replied. It's just as simple as that. A poet makes things of words. So does the writer of fiction, for that's his medium. Consequently he must know all of the ways whereby concepts may be organized. He must be as at home with Forms as Plato was.

What logic is to science and philosophy, metaphor is to poetry. It is the central gift. All walls fall to it. Only a word about it: a metaphor may be regarded as a verbal context in which one system of meanings is interpreted, reorganized, and perceived, through another system. A metaphor need not be stated to be present. In *Omensetter's Luck,* the idea of grace (never directly discussed) is ironically represented by the idea of luck. Metaphor need not be verbal. If I imagine the movement of my arms (or someone's arms) to represent the movement of my feet, I have made a metaphor. Most often, however, metaphors are constructed out of interacting systems of ideas. The first overt metaphor in *Omensetter's Luck* is "he'd see the summer under"— appropriate, I think, for Tott (tod). The interpretation of a metaphor must always yield more metaphors. The moment you get literal results, the image has been *translated* (i.e., destroyed). If, in calling Charlie a fox, you mean he's sly, then you should have said so. If I call Charlie a fox, I mean he is one—he has, for example, a tail. A metaphorical system can itself be interpreted metaphorically, and that one again in terms of another, and another, on and on until positive wonders have been constructed. A simple scene, a sudden flash, can be used metaphorically, to represent a whole—and there are simply a million possibilities.

94

3. Sound is the third dimension. It is, in itself, meaningless. But it is necessary. Something must carry the concept. In non-literary uses of language, the sound (or shape) carries the concept to its grave. In poetry, it makes us return to the word; it is our only hold on the physical; it makes of the word a thing. The musically minded among poets will often allow the sound to lead the sense, but of course the secret lies in the inevitability of the union between the meaningful and the meaningless—and in fiction, between things, sounds, and ideas. A novelist, for example, must unite gesture, concept, and noise, not only so that they seem one, but also so that each level seems to flow inevitably. Valéry said he could not write: the marquis went out at five. He could not bring himself to perform such a prosaic act. The novelist must either satisfy the requirements of his art *and* get the marquis out at five, or he must forget about it. What cannot be esthetically assimilated must go. Valéry also remarked that he found it difficult to read fiction because he began, immediately, to imagine alternatives. The marquis could have been a comte. He might have stayed home. Or he might have gone out at five fifteen. Or his departure might have been expressed: the marquis left his house at five. Etc. The more you tie things together, the more you wed the event to its expression, and when this is understood, it is no longer possible to regard the events in a novel as anything other than linguistic events. A man either jumps, descends, or alights from a carriage. One may say that there is a difference in idea as well as act. Yes. But there is also a difference in sound. X jumped from his carriage and stumped off to the inn. In such a sentence we know one of the reasons why he jumped from his carriage—because he was going to stump off to his inn. This is as good a reason as any other . . . rather—better than most, because it's relevant. I remember once, in a class, John Crowe Ransom asking us why a particular word concluded a line in a sonnet of Wordsworth's. We racked our brains for nothing. Because it rhymes, he finally said—and taught me an everlasting lesson.

OMENSETTER'S LUCK

Three figures grouped themselves around Omensetter: the devoted chronicler, the worshipper, the opponent. All must see an extraordinary power in him, otherwise they would not stop to chronicle, worship, or oppose. Then I began to consider how the illusion might wrap itself like a sheet around its occupant, so that Omensetter might become a ghost even to himself. So we have:

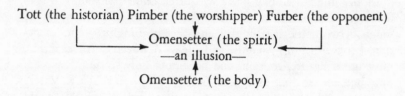

Omensetter, conceived as a moral touchstone at the level of story, and esthetic touchstone at the level of language, must not only affect these people morally, then, but esthetically. Therefore, Tott took on the responsibilities of narrative, Pimber the responsibilities and problems of the lyric, Furber those of rhetoric, and finally, since he is pivotal, the dramatic as well. This formula gave me a chance to move through all styles. One needs to practice, after all. The book's progression does not square with history. It goes epic, lyric, dramatic, with the rhetorical as decay. Mine is more positive and ends on an objective note.

Part One: The Triumph of Israbestis Tott
    Tott has seen the summer under. He's still alive. A relic, he is surrounded by relics—each being sold into indifference. He's as ill as the "things" are; barely held together. Tott knows these objects; they remind him of his history; their sale upsets him. He is upset still further by his inability to find an auditor. Only children will listen to him. They are egoists like himself. All these things, and the events and people of which these things remind him, are dear to Tott only as objects of the narrator's art. Kick's cat is beloved as Kick's cat in the story of Kick's cat. Tott isn't interested in other people—in what they are or what they have to say. To the degree we have a positive feeling for Tott, to that degree we have been sucked in—are like him. Tott loves Omensetter as a figure in a story. Lots love Jesus for no other reason. We should grow a bit uncomfortable with our impression of Tott as the book goes on. So Tott is tod, certainly, because, by

putting people in stories he destroys them as people; but he also preserves something—he preserves history—a record of what is no longer alive. One incident especially disturbs him. He discovers that a cradle belonging to Omensetter is being sold along with Mrs. Pimber's things. This doesn't fit in the life he remembers. An important detail is the sale of the plates, etc., which Mrs. Pimber has painted. Later we learn that Furber has made the suggestion cynically; we can surmise that she took up the suggestion desperately—for therapy. Tott as a story comes first so that we'll know how to evaluate the rest. The coolness of the ultimate conclusion echoes this. We observe Tott, finally, a worn pathetic figure, pursuing a spider with his thumb. This is scarcely an eloquent gesture. It is a child's game and has a child's heartlessness . . . killing ants, swatting flies, capturing bugs and butterflies. It has something, too, of the child's innocent indifference. I have tried to make the suggestion, too, that in a weird way, he is the narrator of all that follows. So he is the muse of storyteller. You are right. And yet what follows is not a story. It's merely that I have an unpleasant sense of humor. Spiders are honest artists, by the way. Tott is the first of the three people in this book who are shut in by language. Chief triumph of this section: the life in the wall, where I think I manage some eloquence about a theory of art I detest. Best stanza: little one on fishing.

Part Two: The Love and Sorrow of Henry Pimber
    Henry Pimber, like a character in Alice, lives in a well. He lives on treacle, too, for that matter. His life is over, if it ever began. Omensetter, arriving suddenly, as if out of nowhere, creating omens, smashes Henry's meager values to pieces. Still, Pimber takes advantage of Omensetter from the first by charging him for an unlivable house. Omensetter seems to be free of Henry Pimber's burdens. He possesses what Pimber has always desired: a gargantuan capacity for life. He seems, like an animal, without guilt or anxiety. He has received grace (has luck). This part begins with words spoken by Tott (a frequent device). A catalogue aria follows—the contents of Omensetter's house. This is a musical parallel with the auction objects in Tott, with the garden catalogue in Furber—all occur in similar places. Henry's later identification with Omensetter is made easier by

97

the fact that both wives share the same name. Dialogues between Henry and his wife will later be paralleled by dialogue between Omensetter and his Lucy. Section two develops the image of the fox in the well. The reasoning here is as follows:

> I am in this well like the fox is.
> Only Omensetter can save me.
> Omensetter won't save the fox.
> _____
> Omensetter won't save me either.

This is a metaphorical conclusion to a metaphorical argument. But I think it "follows" nonetheless. Henry is disturbed by Omensetter's indifference to the fate of the fox because of the simple callousness it seems to imply, and because of his own symbolic identification. He reasons, however, that this ruthlessness is perhaps a weakness in him, and he hopes Omensetter will not be callous with him. In any case, the fox cannot be allowed to suffer. His shooting the fox prefigures his own suicide.

> If Omensetter won't rescue the fox,
>   then I shall kill it.
> "If Omensetter won't rescue me,
>   I shall kill myself."
> Omensetter won't rescue the fox.
> _____
> I shall kill the fox.

> Will he rescue me?

Additional complexities: The fox has fallen in the well because Henry has failed to have it properly covered. This has made it dangerous for Omensetter's daughters, too. The fox *out* of the well is identified with Omensetter. The fox *in* the well with Henry. Later on, in part because of Henry's inversion of the image, Omensetter will be in the well. Henry notes that foxes do not recognize time, whereas he counts the hours (tick-tick theme throughout book), and Henry thinks this about the fox: "But now, thrown down so deeply in himself, into the darkness of the well, surprised by pain and hunger, might he not revert to an earlier condition, regain capacities which formerly were useless to him, pass from animal to Henry, become human in his prison, x his days, count, wait, listen for another—another—another—another?'' It is appropriate that his own illness should stem from shooting the fox—an act against Omensetter.

Henry's illness is attended by Doctor Orcutt (science), Jethro Furber (religion), and Omensetter (nature-as-magic). Pimber seems to have been saved by Omensetter. He also, during his illness, sees the world independently of language and emotions etc. (Lockjaw.) He sees as a stone sees. The world is beautiful and terrifying in its indifference (as Omensetter was indifferent). As Henry recovers, while of course he begins to slide back to his old self again, he believes and hopes for a new life for himself. He has been brought back. I kept Lazarus out. Things were obvious enough as it was. But how would Lazarus have felt if he had been restored to a life he didn't want? (Nice story for Borges.) There are other things here—passages to be paralleled later, of dialogue about having babies etc. Stoning motif. Naturally, in this book, the stones are words. These exchanges work on Omensetter and his belief in himself. Now when Omensetter and Pimber walk to the hilltop, Pimber discovers (or thinks he does) that Omensetter is really indifferent to him (as he was to the fox), and that he is indifferent because *either* (a) he has changed, believes in his luck, and so attempts to remain lucky—i.e., is no longer natural, or (b) never was anything special in the first place. Buttons are on, teeth are clean, nails are trimmed, shoes are shined. He is concerned for his baby and his wife. The money makes a convenient symbol for the change, for Henry does not deserve to be saved—he has exploited his savior, and he knows it. Omensetter ignores his illness, does as he pleases. This is entirely in character, but no longer seems so charming. Now it is Henry's hope (and belief) that Omensetter has changed; that he has been corrupted; that he has become like Henry himself. But the reader must not accept this conclusion without reservation. For one thing—there is the whole of Furber to get through. I want a certain amount of ambiguity. Pimber is unable to see Omensetter (trees in the way, wind waters his eyes); he can't hear him (wind again); he can't talk to him. They don't *touch*. Henry falls down the hill as the fox fell down the well—with the hen in his mouth. I.E., just when he thought he might be made a new man. So he completes the syllogism. And since I inverted the well image (darkness of well becomes darkness of sky), I invert his manner of death. (Many other symbol patterns satisfied by this act as well.)

Henry's errors are based upon a romantic view of life—an emotional view—which wrongly identifies the good of man with a life without responsibility, anxiety, or guilt—and without reason. To the degree Omensetter represents this sort of promise, he is evil (as Furber says, for Furber is right about everything). This romantic view is represented by a lyrical style and extravagant images.

This explanation is very tedious and wooden, and certainly unconvincing. But Henry's suicide remains convincing to me because it is esthetically necessary. Given the character of the image system of which he is a part, his death and the exact manner of it, are inevitable.

Chief triumph of this section: the revisions of the fox-well scene. Best stanza: naming the trees.

Part Three: The Reverend Jethro Furber's Change of Heart

We now come to the hero of our story. First of all, what is Furber's change of heart? Furber is a rhetorician. He makes speeches. He dramatizes. He likes to imagine that reality is nothing more than a series of symbols. But because he dramatizes, playacts, etc., so continuously; because he is so acutely aware of the distance between his feelings and his actions, of the contrast between his inner and outer life; he cannot believe that what he says (orates) is true. He is a person, further, whose feelings can express themselves only in an appropriate disguise—verbal formulas, symbolic gestures. No act is genuine, or exists in its own right. His feelings circle endlessly inside him, therefore, and when he is faced with a situation which posturing won't help him overcome, he goes to pieces. He loves what sounds well, not what is true. This is esssential to the artist, but is disastrous in a preacher, for Furber literally has no real beliefs. This accounts for his anomalous doctrinal position, the contradictions, etc. found in it. Furber regards himself as a liar. Actually Furber's heart is extraordinarily complex, and section 1 of part 3 is devoted to establishing it. By book's end, Furber has come to regard the view of the world he has offered as a rhetorician in sec. 1, and hasn't really believed in, as true. It is true, that is, substantially —emotionally. The main flaw in the book, as I see, lies in the space taken to establish Furber's full condition. I took too long, yet I did not feel I could take less.

Section One. The most experimental part of the book, it is composed of a series of stanzas in different tempos, styles, and orders, arranged to reveal (by means of ordinary time shifts) the nature of Furber's consciousness and character, and at the same time to establish the factual continuity necessary to hold what little plot there is together. Furber has been sent to Gilean by his church for unspecified but guessable misdemeanors. He is bitter and revengeful to begin with. His memories include flashes of his early life, his parents, etc., as well. He arrives during a dry spell, preaches an inflammatory and misguided and confused sermon, antagonizes everybody. Over the years, however, though he's never liked, he does gain a certain ascendency over the people. This he attributes to a series of confessional sermons (I have done wrong) which he preaches following a "religious experience" he has in the garden of his church. His success is far less than he imagines, and when Omensetter arrives on the scene, his belief that Omensetter is undermining his position is largely imaginary. He destroys his own position with his increasingly insane efforts to discredit Omensetter. This section opens with Furber listening to the laughter of the people playing along the river. They have just come from church. This reminds Furber of the time when Omensetter's dog nearly drowned chasing Omensetter's hat, of the time (the same) when he scolded the people for their light-hearted behaviour on the sabbath. Then one thing leads to another.

Composition is the chief thing. For example: catalogue of the contents of the garden parallels contents of Omensetter's wagon. It is also the catalogue of his childhood dream—his neighbor's garden. Style changes with: Rancorous ivy. Changes more severely in the heya-heya-heya passages. This foreshadows increasing use of sheer noises, etc.

I play around with point-of-view and tense shift. In one sentence I'll shift from the direct interior monologue to the I-report to the 3rd person to plain omnipotent author. Like a camera moving in and out of someone's head. Then a series of speeches—Hamletish—which, while they are made up as exercises by Furber, carry forward and finally present one of the book's essential syllogisms: God is omnipotent and omnipresent; He made and is in all things. What, of all these things, shows him to us best? He cannot display his power best in making good, because he is good. Only by making evil. God is evident most in the Devil. And the Devil, being a master of deceit, hides himself in the Good. So what appears good is evil, and what is evil is most like God. This kind of dialectial nonsense governs the movement of the images throughout.

Furber remembers principally, here, a luncheon he has when he first arrives in Gilean. A number of "characters" are introduced. There are a great many, but for Furber they are merely faces. So many heads. He visits the church. Sees the graves of the other ministers in the corners—there is a place left for him, but as we eventually learn, he escapes this fate. The garden has been run down, but Furber restores it. He makes a walk—circular and symbolizing a clock—and when he moves around it, he imagines he is moving time along with him.

If-I-played-the-banjo section reminds us of earlier sessions with the good citizens of Gilean (in Pimber) and foreshadows the later ones. This one is, of course, imaginary. The construction of these paras entirely musical. This passage is followed at once by a passage in sober formal convoluted prose. Different style for a different feeling. Vary the pace so that poetic intensity can be sustained. Vary form for the same reasons. Vary syntax. Vary diction. Furber has trouble with names. This section is pretty obvious. Furber is attracted by the legend of Rev. Andrew Pike, the church's first minister. It is Pike who "appears" to him during his "religious experience." He supposes some romantic legend about Pike and only learns at the last, quite by the way, that Pike was scalped by the indians.

The rhymes, which are designed to resemble a depraved mother goose, reflect Furber's infantilism, his incipient madness, his love of word-play and tendency to determine matters through verbal resemblances. They show his education, too, and his vulgarity. He is sexually timid. But he is linguistically brave. They frequently are quite formal. The Nell poem is. Willie the whiny is an Eliz. dirge. Incidentally, just as I invent all my poems, with two exceptions chosen on purpose, I invent all my own "jokes" too.

A number of paras in still another style on the Bible. All the corpses lie. These Biblical paragraphs I regard as the best writing I've ever done.

Symbolic act idea worked out in Aunt Janet sections. This is followed by the seven sentences of wisdom, and the revelation scene. Then back to that luncheon—page after page on that—that—that. Then a passage of pure image—resting places. (Isn't this informative.) This section, more than any other perhaps, symbolizes Furber's inability to reach people. He makes love to a girl on the train with his shadow.

If one follows the construction of stanzas like the name-his-name passages, one will see how I work. I am particularly pleased with that one, especially the suggestion of the "social notes" style in part of it.

In the remainder I'll only point to some constructional principles, esp. concerning the chapter you don't like. (That is, the one you said you didn't like on the phone.) This has gone on and on, and though you deserve it, I'm getting tired. And the information has dwindled to zero.

Section 3 prepares for the eventual meeting of Omensetter and Furber. Watson is like Omensetter. Furber attacks with words-stones his kinsman. Scene is described as being like a stage. We are moving steadily toward the dramatic, though obviously the drama in this section is pretty subjective and peculiar. I like the Philly Kinsman poem and some of Furber's speeches—partly modeled on Ben Jonson. Studied the Alchemist, etc. for it. By god—this is a very traditional work. Like Pimber and Omensetter, Furber has trouble hearing everything.

Central theme of sermon repeats theme of mock-sermon in section one: transformation of good and evil.

Section 7. Omensetter vs Furber

Furber has been in hysterical fit most of the day. Omensetter is scared green. Furber begins to be reached by reality. Omensetter is suddenly not the dream figure he has had before him in the past. Omensetter defeats Furber, just as Furber has defeated Watson. He gets in. They exchange exactly similar words. The development is the same. Omensetter must seem to Furber very unreal. Furber tries to deal with Omensetter the way he did with Watson—hence the brutal hanging speech. Omensetter can't be reached. He has his own worries, and he gets his way. I've just reread the chapter. It was a tough one. Maybe it doesn't work, but it didn't seem so bad to me. I'd call the dangerous part the hanging speech, and I think it is justified in view of the condition of Furber, the events which have occurred, and the patterns previously established. P. 343 is risky.

Well, the book is seriously flawed. The middle is gross. It tries too much. There is too much narrative compromise. But large forms lack great emotional force because they take so long to complete. You can accumulate effect, but only easily remembered effect. The magnificent closes of FW or Uly. are only partly dependent upon the bodies of the books they finish. A work can have a bent back and get by, but it dare not have very many bad sentences in it. A writer must be able to write. Every dab of Braque's brush bespeaks the master. There his genius lies. One hears of badly written great books, but I don't believe in them. While there are architectural flaws in The Portrait of a Lady.

This has all been futile, I know. And you can see how rapidly my energy was consumed and my interest flagged. I love theory, but I hate my own work. I hate talking about it. I hate trying to justify it. And my theory tells me that no explanations suffice.

Hell—I've left out everything.

Who will help you sell this book? God knows. No one, likely. I can't claim to be popular. The few people who have given me any encouragement over the years are not people whose names form queues. The only author of any celebration I know well is Stan Elkin. I met Saul Bellow once, and though he gave a Longview award to the Tott piece once, I can't imagine his liking Omensetter's Luck. That is about the extent of it.

I like writers like John Barth, John Hawkes, Vladimir Nabokov; and poets like Lowell and Snodgrass. There's Beckett, of course, and Porter. But I'm not suggesting you pester any of these people. I happen to admire them. People I admire I leave alone.

Unfortunately this book was not written to have readers. It was written to *not* have readers, while still deserving them. This is the position I prefer, and I suspect encourages me to my best work. That is why your phone call was so salutary. From hopelessness—new hope.

Best,

Bill Gass

REYNOLDS PRICE

A Generous Man

News for the Mineshaft

IF WORKS OF art test their spectators at least as strenuously as spectators test them and if *A Generous Man* is a work of art (I believe it is, or would not have published it), then several in the audience who handily passed the test of *A Long and Happy Life* failed *A Generous Man.* The chief look on their faces was bafflement. At the time (five months after writing the end and still wired to it with threads of skin), I could offer them nothing more helpful than that the fault was theirs, not the book's or mine. And now at a distance—other work intervening, other hags in the saddle, half my cellular body replaced; when the book, reread, seems as separate and free as a book by a friend—I can offer little more: they were found lacking. *A Generous Man,* however imperfect (and I'm sure that I am the chief authority on its imperfections), whatever its place in the Sweepstakes-in-the-Sky, discovered holes in a number of its readers—in their appreciative agility (their reflexive ability to recognize a form and make the essential adjustments of expectation and attention which the form presupposes); in their senses of humor; their control of panic at the sight of the body engaged in its own delight and continuance; in short, in their lives. About most of these lacks, I would not attempt to write, outside the work itself (which speaks of little else); but perhaps I can be of some help with the first—the confusion of response resulting from failure to recognize form and producing in some readers (especially in the victims of modern literary education) a band of static whose only recognizable syllables are the station call-letters of College English—*symbol, myth, levels of meaning.*

The meaning of *A Generous Man* is itself, its physical shape which is both the product of its meaning and the container, limiter, protector; the shell of the crab (though the crab can slough its shell and grow). Anyone who has chosen to read it at all can discover its full content in how-it-looks—not in what it says, least of all in "what it says to you" (that bloodless scrap so often flung by exhausted artists to the gaining wolves). The famous little girl in Graham Wallas' *Art of Thought,* warned to think out her meaning first, says, "How can I know what I think till I see what I say?" And Wallas says she has the makings of a poet. The makings, granted—her crucial verb is *see;* but had she been a poet, she would certainly have substituted *you* for the first and third *I's.* Tolstoy said it impersonally, "This indeed is one of the significant facts about a true work of art—that its content in its entirety can be expressed only by itself." (I labor what may seem a thundering cliché because, however true, it is not honored—as any American novelist will swear who has skimmed his two-hundred-odd reviews or has had the hair-raising experience of looking into, say, *The Explicator* or any of the quarterly fiction studies. I can think of only one contemporary critic, since the death of Erich Auerbach, who has made it his steering principle—H. D. F. Kitto, in *Greek Tragedy* and *Form and Meaning in Drama*—and he has proceeded through Greek drama, producing startling illumination from a single assumption which, though he applies it only to drama, he holds valid for all other forms—"If the dramatist had something to say, and if he was a competent artist, the presumption is that he has said it, and that we, by looking at the form which he created, can find out what it is.")

The meaning therefore, for the audience or the artist himself, cannot be complete until the work is complete. This is not to say that the artist works automatically, unconsciously, without plan or continuous conscious control. It does say, though, that the plan for any work of the necessary length and complexity of a novel will (and must, for the sake of truthfulness and vivacity) undergo an elaborate and apparently uncontrollable bombardment of accident, accretion, whim—in addition to the more astonishing and satisfying discoveries of secret relations, the secret autonomous life of the story itself, its concealed fecundities (which will proceed in part from those accidents).

That process of continuous growth in the idea and shape of *A Generous Man* is, for me, most nearly recoverable now in the progressive titles which I find in the manuscript. The first page is dated 21 January 1964; the title is *A Mad Dog and a Boa Constrictor*. I kept no orderly notes for the story, as I had done—voluminously, a year in advance—for *A Long and Happy Life*; but my memory is that the story surfaced as I lay in bed, insomniac, one night in January '64, still beached like many others by the backwash of Kennedy's murder. What in fact had been beached was not so much I as the novel I had worked at for two years before, a story of waste and panic suddenly harmonious with recent events yet doomed by them, made irrelevant, inaudible, a clavichord note in a *Wozzeck* fortissimo. And what arrived that sleepless night—clicked up instantly formed in my head—was a story which seemed an antidote, a way back to work. The given was two tales, till then unrelated, which I had known for years—a runaway circus-snake and a mad dog whose rural owners set it free to rave (they could neither kill it nor watch it die slowly)—and my immediate grateful decision, seconds later, was that both tales were comic (the snake would be caught, the dog not actually mad) and that both could be yoked into a single story by the Mustian family, the central family of *A Long and Happy Life* (1962) and of my second short story, "A Chain of Love" (1955). The story, I thought, would be brief—eighty pages—and essentially a farce for my own good cheer. So within the next day or two I began, with very little more forethought than I've mentioned—the bones of a story, a set of characters ready-made and well-known for ten years. The title was as simple as the impulse seemed—*A Mad Dog and a Boa Constrictor*—and I rattled along through the early pages at, for me, a brisk clip (twenty-three pages in the first thirty days). My initial aim was being fulfilled—for the first time in more than ten years of writing, I was working with pleasure; without the reluctance, the neurotic obstacles which all craftsmen (Mozart and Handel excepted) strew between themselves and the desk (obstacles whose absence I have now come to fear; they being the surest danger signs that I'm nearing a center which shrinks from touch, the flesh puffing madly around the sore).

The first eighty pages exhibit that pleasure, in their larger shape (the quick tumbling of scenes; scene hitched to scene more tightly than appears, by outrageous surprise); in a quality of action (the literal movement of characters through space) balletic and clear-lined, whose faith is that, in the young characters at least, gesture and movement is revelation, that they cannot *lie* so long as they move (a quality of course which is at the mercy of each reader's sight, his willingness to yield to coercion from me and make his own sights from the actions offered); in the archeology of character (the creation of pasts for characters whose futures I had long since fixed); the guying of as many as possible of the sacred solemnities of Southern fiction, my own included (from the bow to *Tom Sawyer* in the opening sentence on through the humble but noble dog, the pathetic idiot, the sanctity of blood and name—"We use the names they give us, that's all. They called me Milo so that's how I act"—the hunters who think they are chasing bear or boar but end with nothing more edible than Beauty and Truth in their gassy bags, the young stud watering some parched lady's life); most intensely, in the rhythm and rate of language, the conversion of mid-South-farm-dialect into forms and meters which appear, I think, natural but are thoroughly made from the inside by pleasure (a sentence in the meter of the *William Tell* Overture—so far undetected, page 4*; scenes as on pages 11–15, which have both a

* All page references are to the first American and British editions of *A Generous Man;* Atheneum (1965), Chatto & Windus (1966).

mirror-accuracy to this family's life and a striking resemblance to, say, Rossini's scenes of comic confusion or the swirl of *ariette* in Verdi's *Falstaff*—three lines of passionate fun per man, which lay his life open to public view).

Yet there seems to me now, in those early pages, a high almost desperate pitch to the playfulness. Quite early, rifts begin to yawn in the farce and the buried strata are slowly revealed—though I did not know it, the theme was *loss*. My old impulse was asserting itself, humping up beneath the surface glaze—waste and destruction in their homeliest forms (the apparent loss of a dog to disease, remembered loss of a son-and-father to alcohol, the sudden separation by roaring adolescence of brother and sister, a drunk vet's drowning in loneliness, a woman's snake and chief means of support vanished, a middle-aged sheriff still panting to catch what he'd never had or earned—the love of his wife—and more). And the forms are progressive, dogs to men.

My working-title had changed by then (the end of part one). The manuscript does not show a date for the change, but it must have occurred between pages 48 and 67; for by page 67, I have twice used the phrase "clear day." The first time, without apparent intention of special weight for a common phrase—

> Eyes still shut, his mouth burst open on the surge of his joy, the sudden manhood that stood in his groin, that firmed the bones of his face and wrists as the truck bore him on through this clear day among his family, his first known girl, toward his life to come, his life he would make for himself as he wished. (p. 48)—

but at its recurrence, twenty pages on, in Rosacoke's dream of Milo's new manhood, with a sense, for me at least, of gravity, freight—

> She said, "You will die and ruin us, Milo." He said, not looking, "I am almost a man, I must fall to rise." He jumped and he rose and the last she saw—before she woke—was him rising not falling as he had foretold, above limbs and leaves into steady light, a single figure in clear day alone, no thought of when that day might end. (p. 67)

By then or within the next few pages (six months after the candid beginning), I had made the phrase my title—*Clear Day,* to which I added a protective description, *an escapade.* That remained my title, through to the end—October '65—and the book was announced thus by Atheneum, though by early that fall, I had begun to face the need for a change. A musical play had been announced for New York, called *On a Clear Day You Can See Forever.* The papers were calling it *Clear Day;* and I know exactly the spot where I heard, on my car radio, its title-song—"On a Clear Day"—and admitted to myself that I was cornered and must change.

Few readers, even editors, understand the importance of titles and names to most writers. It is difficult to discuss them at all without sounding precious or fraudulent; but surely what is involved is no stranger than the ancient and continuing magic of names—our names are organic to us, handles to our lives, vulnerable heels; chosen for us before we were born and our surest survivors, in an age of records. We all spent solitary hours as children, saying our names aloud until they metamorphosed from familiarity through abstract sound to final mystery, essence —so with a novelist who has spent two years or longer with a carefully named set of characters and with a satisfying title on his manuscript. The prospect of change is the threat of loss—name is essence and can be lost. A changed name will be a diminished name. (I remember my confusion and revulsion when, as a child, I learned the true names of several famous film stars. The apparent ease with which they had shed them seemed then—and now—a frightening display of gleeful self-hatred.)

Why had *Clear Day* insisted upon itself so early in the work and why at the end was I so reluctant to discard it? Habit—after eighteen months, I was used to the name. But also a weakness for its easy attractiveness of connotation. A clear day is a welcome experience. So is *calm sleep* or *steady love.* (So, supremely, is *a long and happy life,* though that bears a crippling sting in its tail.) And when I began to search for new titles, I at first turned up a series of approximations—*A Full Day, First Light, Morning Light, A Given Day, A Perfect Day, Fair Day.* None of them chimed. I was worried and since I was deep in revising the text, I tried to discover the meanings which *Clear Day* had collected, for me and for the story. This is not to say that I had not known its meaning since at least page 80—sixteen months before—but that the phrase, once chosen as title, had exerted its own control, tunneling always only just out of sight, surfacing at moments of intensity as sign and reminder, almost warning—to the characters, to me, to the future reader—that this story was steered, not hauled or pushed; and steered by a steady vision of Milo, the boy at the center, the pitch of his youth.

But more than his youth—I saw, looking back. The pitch of his life.

A consecutive list of the chief passages, beyond the two already given, which contain the phrase *clear day* (with its related words —*morning, afternoon, night, day* or the adjective only) would reveal—I saw, with some surprise—the spine of the story, the linked control—

> Rooster said "What's the time?"
> "Maybe eleven twenty-five."
> "And you think it's morning?"
> "For half an hour—sure."
> Rooster said "What's your age?"
> "I told you—fifteen."
> "And you think that's young?"
> "Well, I've met one or two older people through the years."
> Rooster said it to the road. "It is eleven twenty-five, a clear broad morning that will be noon soon. You are fifteen, a man and the Lord has hung gifts on you like a *hatrack* . . . Don't think it's morning when it's late afternoon." (pp. 85–86)

> [Milo] did not hear (he was whirling on down), but blinded and weak, he did feel her gaze, accept her hopes and turn them in his mind to a momentary dream—Lois at last, clear in perfect nakedness, waiting on a porch as he moved towards her, answered her smile, extended his open hands to hers and heard her say, "I have been afraid, waiting in the dark. I have kept my promise. Why have you failed? You said you would come to me long before night." He answered, "Night? It is still clear day" but looking up, saw it was really night, that the light was from her, her readiness, so he said, "I am sorry. I was tending to duties but now I am here and look, I am ready." (pp. 160–161)

[Rooster] thumbed towards Milo. "He's had his day . . ." (p. 211)

"But don't stop with taking," Mr. Favro said.
"I ain't," Milo said. "I been learning things—but I told you that. These past three nights, these two clear days. I been handing out stuff like the whole Red Cross, like loaves and fishes to people on the hills." (pp. 254–255)

So Rosa looked to Rooster—"Maybe this is the end?"
But Rooster looked to Milo, answered to him. "'Could be I guess. What could keep it from being? You've had *your* day. Maybe I've had mine—maybe never will." (p. 256)

But Milo paused above her on arms as straight as what stood ready beneath to serve, looked at her eyes—only them, nothing lower—and said unsmiling, "I have heard that the saddest thing on earth is to love somebody and they not love back."
"So have I," she said and by smiling fully, forced him to smile, then rocked the heel of her own tough hand in the pit of his neck (where nerves pierce the skull) and drew him forward, welcomed him down, and the rest was giving—pure gift for both, no thought of receipt though receipts poured in so long as they worked, as if fresh joy could flood your thighs, stream down through your legs, drown your heart, gorge throat and brain, offer (even threaten) a new clear life (so long as you moved) and yet roll on, roll past, leave you spared. (p. 266)

But Rato turned, faced Milo, grinned. "Morning," he said.
"Morning," Milo said. Then they both looked up to the lifting sky—Lois followed their eyes—and found they were right. It was morning (clear, cloudless, the oldest gift), would be morning oh six hours yet. (p. 275)

The phrase had become, since its first uncalculated appearance, both a controlling and a fertilizing device. It had become—without, I am almost sure, conscious knowledge by me—the emblem of the fullness of the impulse. Whether it was an initial fullness or a gradually gathering one, I cannot say. It was certainly one which I neither anticipated nor understood when I began the story. And an emblem of more than its fullness—its truthfulness. Truth to the final seriousness, even grimness, of a story I had thought was farce and to the shape of a quickly changing character—the boy Milo's—as he reaches (in three days) the height of his manhood, poises in clear broad day, descends (descends, not falls).

I had seen what I had not quite seen before, in the nearly two years since beginning the book (two years which include a ten-month gap between the last two lines of page 172)—that the story had made itself, and well (clearly, economically), in response to its own impulse and needs. What must go without saying is that it responded also to needs of mine; to observation of life around me in those two years; to personal bafflements, pleasures, and defeats; family deaths. I do not mean to play hierophant in barring the entrance to that one cave. It still contains matters of the greatest force and urgency for my daily life. I only confess my inability to talk sense—truthful usable sense, anyhow—about a process so gradual, complex and irrecoverable. Inability, and lack of curiosity. The *story* exists, is the thing that matters—existed, whole, as I searched it for a title. And the things which I saw it saying most strongly of Milo's life were in Rooster's voice. First, his early warning, "Don't think it's morning when it's late afternoon"; then his grim summation almost at the end, "You have had *your* day."

So he had—Milo—and the sense is heavy at the end (the final passage above is the end) that it was his last day, that—in Donne's use of the same metaphor—"his first minute, after noon, is night." The final light of the book is still morning, but morning for only "six hours yet." A limited, sentenced strip of day is what is left him as he turns from his vision, vague as it is, of a new clear life toward his home again, his ravenous duties at his old—and future—mill, which in nine years' time will have left him the charred and raucous figure of *A Long and Happy Life*.

But, ended as it is, it had *been* day at least (three days in fact, Saturday to Monday). A number of witnesses realize that—the sheriff, his wife, Rosacoke, Lois, Selma. And what a day—the single moment when Milo stood ready to offer freely, with rushing plenitude, the virtues he had earned or had laid upon him; virtues called from him by the shape of the story, the demands of every event and meeting. It had been, I saw, his manhood; not his "coming to manhood," as might appear.

So my search for a title was colored now by my retrospective findings; and the list of prospects lengthened—*The End of Day, First Dark, The Midst of Day, A Generous Man*. That the last was best, I would still maintain—as the fullest flag for the whole —though I have not seen one notice of the book which considered the title; and only a few which accepted its clear news. (How many readers accept or even notice the necessary help offered by such titles as *The Great Gatsby* and *Rabbit, Run*? An attempt to measure the degree of irony, if any, contained in that *Great* or the realization that the title of Updike's novel is an imperative, almost a plea, by the author to the hero, would carry a serious reader a good deal farther than he'd otherwise go toward the core of the books. So, conversely, might an attempt to rename a supreme but misleadingly named book like *Anna Karenina*. Maybe *Happy Families*? Or its early title, *Two Marriages*?)

I had called *Clear Day* an escapade, when I thought it was one. Perhaps I should have called *A Generous Man* a romance. If I had ended at what might appear a possible point, on page 244, the end of part two (with a further phrase to clarify that Milo has fainted not died), then I would have had a story that answered the classical tests for prose romance—a mode common from the first century to the present, deriving apparently from *The Odyssey* and New Comedy, in which stylized characters capable of allegorical expansion move through "strange adventures, separations, wanderings across seas and lands, rescues miraculously effected, dangers overcome and trials passed, until the final triumph of reunion with loved relatives. . . ."* But surely the minimal requirement for romance is a happy ending— Daphnis and Chloe married and bedded; Prospero restored to his dukedom a wiser, more merciful man; Ishmael alive in the wreck of the *Pequod,* planning his book; Catherine and Heathcliff joined in death on their rightful moors; the curse of the Pyncheons laid.

* Ernest Schanzer, introduction to Shakespeare's *Pericles*, New American Library, 1965, p. xxi.

Hawthorne's own definition of romance, in his preface to *The House of the Seven Gables,* is disappointingly exterior—

> When a writer calls his work a Romance, it need hardly be observed that he wishes to claim a certain latitude, both as to its fashion and material, which he would not have felt himself entitled to assume, had he professed to be writing a Novel. The latter form of composition is presumed to aim at a very minute fidelity, not merely to the possible, but to the probable and ordinary course of man's experience. The former—while, as a work of art, it must rigidly subject itself to laws, and while it sins unpardonably so far as it may swerve aside from the truth of the human heart—has fairly a right to present that truth under circumstances, to a great extent, of the writer's own choosing or creation.

But whatever a writer's reasons for choosing the form romance or, more probably, for producing one and then discovering he has done so, his basic strategy in prose romance will have been wish-fulfillment; or more exactly, the arousal and examination of a number of our oldest fears—that we are not the children of our parents, that lovers may be permanently parted, that nature is indifferent if not hostile—and then an at-least-partial allaying of those fears, a granting of our deepest needs—Here is your long-lost father/wife/daughter/beloved. All is well. The gods are not mocked.

All that could be said of *A Generous Man* at the end of part two (p. 244). The dead have worked through their blood-relations—and beasts and extraordinary events—to right their wrongs; old debts are paid by a golden boy who never incurred them; relations are clarified through recognitions; forgiveness, comprehension, gratitude abound. There is however a third part, thirty pages. Renunciations, further (and final) separations, a grim future seen, a grim present faced, its demands obeyed—and all that, not nailed on by a willfully sadistic author but inherent in the characters, their actions, the world.

So perhaps not *romance,* despite a passage in Northrop Frye's *Anatomy of Criticism* which tends my way (and the ways of Alain-Fournier, Kafka, Ralph Ellison, Joseph Heller, Thomas Pynchon)—

Certain elements of character are released in the romance which make it naturally a more revolutionary form than the novel. The novelist deals with personality, with characters wearing their *personae* or social masks. He needs the framework of a stable society, and many of our best novelists have been conventional to the verge of fussiness. The romancer deals with individuality, with characters *in vacuo* idealized by revery, and, however conservative he may be, something nihilistic and untamable is likely to keep breaking out of his pages.

Yet *A Generous Man* is not a novel—its resemblance to Japanese Noh drama or to *The Magic Flute* is closer than to most twentieth-century fiction—and permitting it to appear as a novel only confirmed some readers in their suspicions that I had intended to write the previous history of the Mustian family in the realistic mode of *A Long and Happy Life* and had, early in the job, lost all control. A python capable of conceptual thought; a ghost who assists at a flat-tire change, then attempts a murder, then repents and leads the way to a lost fortune; a teen-age palmist who foretells the plot of *A Long and Happy Life;* all accepted as apparently unexceptional by characters observed "realistically," recognizably the cast of an earlier sane novel—the man's lost hold.

Not this time. The form of the theme was new and different, and had taken hold. (The Milo of *A Generous Man* stands in roughly the same relation to Milo of *A Long and Happy Life* as Stephen Dedalus in *Ulysses* to Stephen in *Portrait of the Artist.*) The theme, I have said, was—for its own reasons and mine—*loss.* But loss in the midst of plenty or at the sudden end of plenty; loss-in-*time* too (three days' time)—*absence* before he had realized *presence.* The presence—of all Milo's resources and his use of them—had been, as their counterparts are in any person, miraculous; that is, inexplicable in terms of our present knowledge of heredity, environment or training. The form of his story is therefore miraculous. Laws are suspended, laws of the European and American realistic novel and those physical laws which, in fiction or in life, are our most elegant walls against the large world—that terrible perhaps even benevolent world which turns, huge, around and beneath our neater world which agrees to forbid it. The dead, incompletions, the past which is future. And *A Generous Man* proceeds under no law except its own—the demands of its meaning, demands of the large world to deal with ours. Demands which are met by the shape of the story; the resistance and yielding of character; finally, by language, the irreducible medium and servant and guide of the meaning.

Many readers and journalists compliment the language of an elaborate work of fiction as dictators compliment a free press— with bluster and suppression. The history of art and manners can be seen—and not entirely misleadingly—as an endless knock-up between the plain style and the elaborate. The good old days when men were men, could say what they meant in a telegram and wore linsey-woolsey against all weather—Aeschylus vs. Euripides, Athens vs. Alexandria, Giotto vs. Bernini, Heming- way vs. Faulkner. It should have been long-since obvious to ev- eryone that, in serious verse and fiction, the language (in its atomic structure of syllable, meter, order) proceeds from the pres- sure of the entire given impulse as it shoulders upward through one man (his unconscious, his conscious, his training, his *charac- ter*) and will therefore bear the marks, even the scars, of its unique journey. When Shakespeare writes,

> Poor naked wretches, wheresoe'er you are,
> That bide the pelting of this pitiless storm,
> How shall your houseless heads and unfed sides,
> Your loop'd and window'd raggedness, defend you
> From seasons such as these? . . .

and when Milton writes,

> Great pomp, and sacrifice, and praises loud
> To Dagon, as their God who hath deliver'd
> Thee, Samson, bound and blind into their hands,
> Them out of thine, who slew'st them many a slain.

what is at issue is not clarity vs. murk, sincerity vs. artifice, but fidelity to an impulse, a willingness by the poet to display lan- guage which bears whole strips of his private skin and entrails (because they are *his* entrails for good or bad, all he has to offer), and a refusal to contract with readers-on-horseback, racing by.

Or, another way, a line like

non sapei tu che qui è l'uom felice?,

simple as it sounds, may express an even more complicated reality than

But ah, but O thou terrible, why wouldst thou rude on me
Thy wring-world right foot rock? lay a lionlimb against me?
  scan
With darksome devouring eyes my bruisèd bones? . . .

but the clear-water was produced by Dante, the turbid by Hopkins. You may have strong reasons for thinking that Dante achieved a larger, worthier end; but you cannot therefore dismiss Hopkins as obscure, mannered, self-intoxicated, anymore than you can dismiss a turtle for failing to win the Kentucky Derby. *You* staged the race and entered him against his will and his nature. Your duty—if you mean to read at all and not just clock winners—is to discover the exact race which Hopkins has entered, the goal he approaches, and only then to judge his performance over his own course.

That is not to claim that all language produced by all artists is equally acceptable and could not admit change. The implicit threat to plain-style is oversimplification; to the elaborate, fancification—both, forms of lying. And, more particularly, any process which is both so sudden and slow and still so mysterious as inspiration is vulnerable to any number of accidents, from flu to madness, along the chain of transmission. Accidents which will be almost impossible to hide. The weaknesses of Shakespeare's character are as clearly on show in every hundred lines (for all his track-covering) as Rimbaud's in all the *Saison en Enfer* or mine in *A Generous Man.*

For the language of *A Generous Man,* so far as it differs from the "language really used by men" (what men? and when?) in complexity, density and compression, is neither a style nor a manner as either is generally understood nor a series of calculated "effects" nor the appliqué of decoration (raising the rural tone a notch). It is the literally reflexive response of all my available faculties to the moment at hand—a boy's first drunk, a girl's nightmare, the boy's sudden possession by an unfinished past—and to my vaguer sense of a total vision and structure, the story. The voice of the story is—with all faults of intonation and detail—the vision of the story.

This is not to say that I take no conscious care of language. It is the largest care I take (the other things, for better or worse, occurring beyond care); but—aside from obvious editings, omission of repetitions; the choice of a monosyllable here, a disyllable there, for sinew or speed—it is not a care directed toward elegance or memorability of diction. I never think, "This is a Price story and had better start sounding like one." What I think is roughly this (and it is really never a conscious thought)—my job is to make a language which is as faithful as my gift and craft permit to the complexity of knowledge and experience, the mystery and dignity of characters and objects, unearthed by this story; and finally, as clear and as quickly communicative as those prior fidelities will allow. (If you object that my argument rests on examples from verse and proves nothing for prose which is traditionally the plainer medium, I'd ask you to show me where on the hinges of the world is the engraved law which says that prose cannot be exactly as complex as its subject and the nature of its author require.)

A Generous Man—read through now for the first time since passing proof three years ago—stands for me, at a possible distance, as a story told, an object made. Another three years might well bring it down around my ears (so they might the world); but now, though I don't claim perfection for it all, I can say that I do not find a sentence I would cut or change. I think it is right, in the way it needs to be; and the question, I suppose, for a serious reader—who has somehow decided to spend several hours of his life going through it and has got to the end—is then, *so what?* What was it doing? Did it do it well, in terms of its aim? Then, did it seem worth doing at all, with such care, in a world already gagging on books (warehouses stuffed with Lord's Prayers on heads of pins)? You realize of course that it means to change your life? Has it made you begin? Would anything, anyone?

There are smaller questions which might follow those. How difficult is it for a reader not familiar with rural life in the American South to respond with serious attention to characters who speak and act in a dialect and manner which is simultaneously the manner—however coarsened—of a long and continuing tradition of comedy now most visible in Li'l Abner and the Beverly Hillbillies? Has "the South" been fouled beyond use, for now—and not merely by caricature but by its own follies—as a source of serious comedy? Aristophanes in Athens? (My faith is that existence is—or will prove to *have* been—comic and that a serious writer can use any matter which he knows and needs to know, in which he imagines a whole design; of course I wonder if it's my *belief*.) Was it, on balance, an error to use the Mustian family in a work whose conventions are so nearly incompatible with earlier work in which they appear? (I hope I have answered that. Not at all. Milo's early life—his quick manhood— was different in kind, not merely in degree, from the rest of his life. So is the youth of most men. Teach for a few years if you doubt that. *A Generous Man* may have been my "college novel.") Was it an error to call the snake *Death* and send the symbol-hounds howling down dark trails that ended blankly—not however before they had raced past, or over, the sense of the book? (Maybe it was. Maybe I should change the name. I meant it first as a joke-in-character. What would you call a twenty-foot python that you showed for a living at county fairs?—what better than *Death*? Then other jokes followed—"Death is dead," etc.—and I let the name become one more nail in the coffin I was building for the great Southern hunt—what are you boys hunting? Death, what else? I trusted the wit of the audience. I may not again.)

The final question, from reader to writer, might be, "There you stand with a smile on your face (or writhing at my feet). Explain and justify. Just what have you achieved that cheers (pains) you so?"

Today's answer might be, "The smile is of puzzlement not satisfaction, and will not wipe off." Mr. Ramsay thinks in *To the*

Lighthouse, "The very stone one kicks with one's boot will out-last Shakespeare." Quite possibly—though with the bomb in stock since Virginia Woolf's death, Shakespeare's chances are con-siderably improved. You could store him safely in an Arizona mineshaft; the stone's in trouble, though, like you and me. So the smile (if not the writhing) is apparently for that—that *A Gener-ous Man* will clearly outlast me and everyone alive as I write this line (so will my cufflinks). What else will it outlast and what will it say to whoever lasts with it or oars through drowned space to find it in the rubble? Would it be enough?—a jawbone sufficient to remake the old ass, and plan a new?

GEORGE P. ELLIOTT

Among the Dangs

Discovering the Dangs

IN THE GOOD old days, when magic was a useful art and the stars sang in the heavens, it was commonly believed that the circumstances under which a child was conceived might affect his whole character and development. A reasonable theory, but genetics, being even more reasonable, has pretty well done it in. However, until there is a genetics of artistic creation—which God forbid—I for one am going right on believing that the circumstances in which a story is conceived may very well condition its whole future growth and development. In me this condition often operates on the principle of opposition. "Among the Dangs" concerns some savages who in bleak surroundings are living a life dominated by religious practices, and it was conceived in as civilized, sumptuous, and secular a place as I have ever stayed in.

In Saratoga Springs, adjoining one of the race tracks, there is a large, park-like estate called Yaddo, which, according to the will of its makers, has been used since 1925 as a retreat where writers, painters, and composers might go for a few days or a few weeks to do their work without expense and free of any external care. Yaddo was built in the late 19th century by a tycoon named Spencer Trask. The opulent furnishings of the two mansions reflect the taste of his arts-loving wife, Katrina, whom he adored and who wrote. The smaller mansion contains Katrina's special bedroom, painted bone-white, with a wall-to-wall faded pink rug, windows on three sides looking across expanses of lawn and flowerbeds into a nearby elegant little forest of assorted conifers, the whole room some forty-five feet long and twenty-seven feet wide with a fireplace, some pretty little statues of nymphs, and its own sunporch. To Yaddo I went to stay for a couple of weeks in June of 1957.

I was assigned the maid's room just off the large pink bedroom. I felt right in the maid's room, which was only about twice as big as any bedroom in any place I'd ever been able to afford to rent. Moreover, I came straight from serving a one-year sentence in a New York City apartment, writing on a card table in a tiny, jam-packed storage room the window of which had a sunless view of a brick wall ten feet away. Psychologists have discovered that people behave very oddly when deprived of their dreams even when allowed to sleep all they want. For me, New York is a huge dream-deprivation depot; there, my dreaming powers are so occupied with resisting the alarms of the city that I seldom have dreams of my own. In Yaddo suddenly to have silence, spaciousness, no interruptions of any kind all day long, a stately view, the society of pleasant companions, good food, nothing to do but write—it was too much for me. After a day of it I came down with a fever. It wasn't enough of a fever to worry about; it didn't come from a cold or flu; it just kept up for a couple of days—though it abated for meals—burning the poisons out of my system, as my father would have said.

I was lying in a single bed on a quite firm mattress, flat on my back without a pillow, with one sheet stretched over me for it was a warm afternoon. I had the bodily discomforts that come with a temperature, but I was really quite content for I could feel that fever doing me all sorts of good. I was half asleep, perfectly willing to let any fever-images enter my mind that wanted to. The fever made my skin so sensitive that it seemed to me the sheet was binding me tight, with only my head free. Abruptly I imagined that I was lying bound in hides, with a poisoned spear point so close to each temple I dared not move my head, and with this chant stomping in my ears: The Dangs and the Urdangs, the Dangs and the Urdangs. After I had lain there stiff for a while, terrified and enchanted, I realized that I had just conceived a story. As soon as I realized this, I knew that the climax of the story would occur as the protagonist lay in the position I had half been in, half imagined myself in, and that it would have something to do with prophesying. I also thought at first that there would be two tribes, the Dangs and some sort of ancestors of theirs, the Urdangs—like *Hamlet* and the Ur-*Hamlet*. As it turned out, the Urdangs never emerged from the hills where, for all I know, they're still dwelling in caves. That night my fever broke. The next morning I began the story, and eight or nine days later it was finished, though I had to fiddle around with the ending off and on for a month or so longer.

For me to compose a longish story at the rate of a thousand words a day, particularly a story as complex as this one, is to go at two or three times my usual speed. However, I have occasionally done it, before and since then, though always *after* having thought through the details of what I was writing. What is extraordinary not only for me but for any writer is to sit down to write a sizable story the day after having got the idea for it, especially since I began with no plot in mind, no conception of any of the characters, and an utter lack of experience with any primitives whatever. Yet I wrote with excitement and less difficulty than usual: it flowed from my pen not only fast but easily.

The standard psychological explanation to apply to such an experience—an experience out of the ordinary but by no means unique—is that the story had been gestating in my unconscious mind and this accident merely started its parturition; that the writing of it was a sort of writing it down from internal dictation; that it was produced as a dream is produced, its order and components determined in the way Freud has best described. The classic instance of this process is Coleridge's composing "Kubla Khan." Coleridge wrote of his memory of writing in that opium dream: ". . . during which time he has the most vivid confidence, that he could not have composed less than from two to three hundred lines; if that indeed can be called composition in which all the images rose up before him as things, with a parallel production of the correspondent expressions, without any sensation or consciousness of effort." Then came that accursed emissary from common sense, "a person on business from Porlock," and after an hour of conversation with the person, Coleridge found to his mortification that "with the exception of some eight or ten scattered lines and images, all the rest had passed away like the images on the surface of a stream into which a stone has been cast." The creative impulse had ended with the dream; he was never able to re-enter the poem again, nor to recollect the rest of the lines composed while he was asleep. All we have, all he had, left of this loveliest of fantasy poems is 54 lines. Coleridge's experience certainly appears to support the usual explanation of these matters: the subject of the poem is a dream, the mood of it is marvelously dream-like, it was composed while he was dreaming, it faded from the waking author's consciousness just as a dream fades. Now there is probably enough truth in this explanation to make it dangerously easy for one to subside into it profitlessly—though I doubt that there can be any way of determining the gestation period of dreams and stories, and indeed I see no reason why some should not be delivered full-blown from their creator's head the hour they are conceived. The whole truth, I would judge from my experience, is far less comfortable, far more difficult and essentially mysterious.

To begin with, "Kubla Khan" was not a dream. According to Coleridge's own testimony, which I think it presumptuous not to take literally, "Kubla Khan" was a poem composed at the same time the author was dreaming. The dream provided images for the poem. Those images may have been no more than the manifest content of the dream, but as embodied in the words, they are of the very structure and essence of the poem. Why should a reader, while he is enjoying the poem, give a hoot about the analyzable meaning latent in Coleridge's mind behind these images? The images, the rhythms, the sound patterns of the words, these *are* the poem. It seems to me amazing that Coleridge could have composed any poem, much less so beautiful a one, which used the manifest content of a dream even as the dream was going along, amazing that his poetry-making powers worked so well so fast. But I am often amazed by what our minds can do. At the dinner table one evening I told a friend about an algebra problem which my daughter had brought home that afternoon and which I had wrestled with unsuccessfully for a couple of hours. In four or five minutes, while eating and keeping up his end of the general conversation, he solved the problem accurately. These separate actions of his mind were wholly conscious. The unconscious is yet more versatile and multifarious. I see no reason why a man of Coleridge's powers, supersaturated in poetry, should not be able simultaneously to dream and compose a poem about the dream; nor why one should not consider these actions, while intimately connected and to some degree similar, as being nevertheless radically different, quite as different as passing the salad, commenting on the weather, and solving an algebra problem.

Perhaps composing a dream and composing a poem ultimately derive from the same creative source. Freud's speculations on dream-formation did not penetrate beyond those elements in the psyche which he could treat as determining and determined. The power in us to shape, what Coleridge called the *esemplastic imagination,* that power as such Freud said little about. How could he? The prime wonder of dreams is that everyone has the power to create them. Confronted with this, all the how's and why's of dream-formation fade a bit. Freud, a master strategist, did not confront the mystery, and his speculations on how and why have had the limelight since the turn of the century.

Ultimately the power to make dreams and the power to make works of art may derive from the same root. But my own experience, available to me through memory, is that, wherever the ultimate power may come from, creating a story is as much unlike as it is like creating a dream.

In writing "Among the Dangs," I was faced with the literary problem of preventing a reader from worrying about the inconsistencies between the fantasy and the actual world. This is especially a problem at the points where the two conflict, as they always must. The writer must keep the reader from thinking about it. Suppose a real-seeming story opens with these words:

"As Gregor Samsa awoke one morning from uneasy dreams he found himself transformed in his bed into a gigantic insect." At no point in that story ought the writer to allow the reader to speculate on how it is possible for a man to turn into an insect. For when fantasy and reality collide, reality wins, hands down. As a writer I recognized and dealt with this problem as best I could. But the problem does not exist for a dreamer: the dreamer is his own spectator, the dream is its own reality. My work in composing "Among the Dangs" was made the easier because I was so little interested in all those aspects of the world which are recognizably arranged in a realistic story. The whole thrust of my story was to get away from the familiar world and deeper and deeper into a fantastic one. This left me quite free to use my odds and ends of knowledge about primitive customs and psychology in any way that pleased my fancy; in the story these bits and pieces are analogous to the manifest content of a dream. It also left me free to fabricate any details that suited my purpose. The idea for the vatic drug came from a recent article in *Life* magazine about trance-producing mushrooms; but the custom of disposing of corpses by floating them down the river, I just made up. The idea for making the protagonist an anthropologist came from my hearing about an anthropology professor, a dignified doctor of his science, who had entered a tribe of savages and taught them one major technical advantage (something like the wheel); his purpose was to observe the effect of this novelty upon their behavior-patterns over the years; one thing they did was, in gratitude, to make him a god—Professor John Johnson, Ph. D., LL.D., God. But the equally important idea of making prophesy the chief activity of the Dangs does not correspond to the practice of any actual primitives I have ever heard of. The word Dangs does not derive from the tribe of that name in India; I first heard of the actual one seven or eight years later. It derives from Urdang, which was then no more to me than the name of an editor of an anthology in which one of my stories had appeared. In other words, what I included, omitted, distorted, or fabricated depended scarcely at all upon the actuality either of primitive customs or of my daily experience and almost entirely upon what the internal order of the story called for, as in dream-making; but unlike dream-making it depended also upon various literary considerations, which can be suggested by the question: "What will this mean to a reader?"

For example, I had no notion that the protagonist was going to be a Negro until I got well into the first paragraph. It was obviously a convenience to me for him to be dark-skinned for the simple reason that, since all the primitives left in the world are in fact dark of skin, it would be a huge and distracting element if the story were to make them beige or peach-colored. However, there is the difficulty that the moment an educated Negro is introduced into a contemporary American setting, The Problem rears its ugly head. The Problem may matter to a dreamer or it may not. But to a story-teller it must matter just because it matters to so many of his hoped-for readers. I had to work consciously at my craft to control the reader's response to The Problem. There is another reason for the protagonist to be a Negro. The story is partly a social satire, and satire is an undreamy quality depending for its existence on an audience of others; it was appropriate enough that a character torn between two cultures, between America and the Dangs, in but not of either of them, should be a contemporary intellectual American Negro. Indeed, this and not the narrative convenience is the chief justification for his color.

The crux of the similarity and difference between making a dream and making a literary fantasy is to be found, I believe, in the question of revising. In a sense a dream may be said to undergo revision: when a dream or portion of a dream is repeated with variations. It is as though the unconscious dream-making mind wanted to disguise some latent content yet more effectually or else to taunt the soon-to-be conscious sleeper into an open understanding and recognition of this content. Quite apart from the esthetic considerations involved in revising a poem, the poet may revise his fantasy with a similar intention —to disguise yet more or yet less revealingly the fantasy's hidden meaning. But the poet aims to shape a fantasy which will preserve this power and be able to exert it over many, whereas the dream's power is over no one but the dreamer and it fades with waking. Poems aspire to perfection of form and meaning; dreams aspire to keep the dreamer from waking up, by releasing some of his enlabyrinthed spirits. To revise a poem means to intensify it, deepen the significance of what it says, prune it, mold it, improve it—none of which have anything to do with dreaming or re-dreaming.

What I was given as the germ of this story was an image from a dream. My fevered imagination had taken my actual physical situation and made of it an image which, even at the time, my dim consciousness knew to be fantastic; but this image, as I also knew at the time, was somehow surcharged with significance. The movement of the story is from here to there—from the recognizable order of our civilization to an imaginary world ordered barbarously. That strange world I aimed to render with the vividness of hallucination and yet also with suggestions of meaning referring not back into my own private mind but out into what a number of readers are concerned about. This fictional movement, of which I was aware and which affected the execution of the story in many ways, corresponds very closely to the movement of my imagination in writing the story—from here to there. I knew where I was: sitting with a pen in my hand, conscious and excessively rational, at a table in a room in Saratoga Springs. I knew where I was going: to a re-creation and comprehension of that image which had been the seed of the story, its mummied sperm. My whole purpose was to get from here to there—from that straight cane-bottomed chair in a maid's room in Yaddo, into a swathing of deerhide flat on my back in peril of my life among the Dangs, whoever they were. I was bent on discovering what complexities of meaning were latent in that image, discovering them, however, not just for my own benefit, as in a dream, but in such a way as to make it possible for a reader to make a similar discovery. I could discover for myself what it meant only as I revealed it to you.

My aim in this story, like Coleridge's in "Kubla Khan," like any science-fiction writer's, was to make my fantasy the reader's fantasy. Doing this is as different from dreaming as it is different from telling a dream to a friend in conversation, and as like them too. What this shaping and transferring power is I cannot really know. The hair on the back of my neck stands up when I even imagine it.

When the fantasy image reaches out in a story to the conscious minds of others, ceasing to refer back only into its creator's unconscious mind, when it becomes public, then its nature essentially changes. In talking about it, one must use psychoanalytic insights only with tact and discretion. For a new mystery has entered—language, the language which is common to stenographers gossiping during a coffee break, and to Coleridge's sleep-created but not dream-created poem, and to an essay on logic assembled by Bertrand Russell, that conscious man.

Though the dreaming mind ordinarily uses language, it has no essential need of words: sounds are enough to make a dream with. A dream's words, when it uses words, serve their function quite as well nonsense as sense. "Zumbly doo" can serve a dream as well as "the Dangs and the Urdangs," and both can serve it as well, and in the same way, as "How are you, my dear?" or "Please come in." For a news reporter a given word is like a little boat which always carries the same cargo; the cargo is what matters. For a dream a given word may carry the usual cargo or any other cargo the dream unconscionably wants, though the dream usually disguises its special cargo as the customary thing. The word "toothless" always means about the same thing to reporters, "without teeth," and usually, for convenience, it means that to a dreamer. But it can mean all sorts of things to a dreamer; as a dream greeting, "toothless" could melt him with joy, as a curse it could scare him half to death. To the society which gave him his language, the dreamer's unconscious is wholly irresponsible in its choice, use, and fabrication of words. However, to a creative writer, to one making with words, and especially to the writer of a fantasy, all this is different. Language is given to the poet by society, by those before and about him, and it means to him what it means to them. Yet his writer's fantasy enters into those very words; it is nowhere if not in those words and in the way he arranges them. He must return the words to society from whom he got them, return them recognizable and changed at once.

The words of a reporter are as little his as "hello" and "good-bye" are yours or mine; the community, far more than the individual, is responsible for the way they are used. The words and word-components of a dream come from the community, or at least from the outer world, but only the dreamer is responsible for the way they are used. The words of a creating writer are both at once. This is true even of *Finnegans Wake*. By the time

Joyce came to write that huge simile to a dream, he was as solipsistic as a sane man gets—every dreamer of course is a total solipsist. Joyce altered the word-boats and changed their cargoes to suit his special purposes. Yet he did not so do it that he was his only audience. I find it possible to enjoy a few passages of the book quite as I enjoy any other poem or story, and some say they have worked hard enough to enjoy all of it. The words of *Finnegans Wake* retain most of their communal function most of the time. The words of "Kubla Khan" retain all of it. Joyce the waking solipsist used words in a more dream-like way than did Coleridge the poet, who kept the rest of us in mind even in his sleep. Except for a couple of words which Coleridge invented but which are obviously proper names, every word in "Kubla Khan" means what it means in the dictionary, that guide to social custom. He makes the language his own by shearing it of all but its syntax, its sound, and its image-making power.

In "Among the Dangs" I aimed to use words in a sociable way, but I also aimed to make them the story's by playing a few rhetorical tricks—by juxtaposition, by ambiguity, by figure of speech. The turning point of the story occurs when the protagonist understands the words "Stone is Stone." Those words as words are about as simple as words get. "Stone" appears to mean here what it means in the dictionary. Yet in the context, that little boat "Stone is Stone" just about founders; its tiny social cargo just barely disguises its huge private cargo—not private to me but private to the story and therefore accessible to you when you read the story. This is the crucial sentence in which it occurs: "I understood Stone is Stone, and that understanding became my consciousness." Now that sentence communicates a meaning only as it is prepared for within and as the climax to the story; and even then one cannot easily say what the meaning is. Structurally, narratively, the function of the statement seems as clear as its dictionary meaning does. The tricky problem is: What real-life experience, what possible revelation can that simple tautology refer to?

This problem is made all the more acute because the situation of the narrator is so fraught with conventional symbolisms. He is in a cave, lying with his head emerging from a channel at the bottom of a large boulder, on which are two breast-like protuberances. Well, I guess: REBIRTH. "Stone is Stone" is a magic formula involved in his being re-born—that fits into this archetypal interpretation all right, though it hardly explains why it should be this formula rather than some other. Moreover (as the students in a class taught by a friend of mine pointed out) the narrator, who has been prophesying the story of Christ, has endured up to this point experiences which have a great deal in common with the essential events in Christ's story. He has appeared to them from on high; he has performed what must seem to them a miracle with fishes; he has just been prodded in the side with spears till he bled; he is lying as it were in bonds of death with spears sharp as thorns pointed at the sides of his head; he must endure this torment in order to save his people who are not his people. At this moment he identifies himself with Christ, and "Stone is Stone" is a sign of that identification—though, once again, why it should be this formula rather than some other is hardly clear. But aside from the psychoanalytic and the Christian interpretations, how can the tautology be justified in the story?

In itself, "Stone is Stone" means no more to me than it does to you. The statement refers back into the story, not back into its author. I happen to know where the formula came from. I'd come across it, in slightly different form, earlier that year in Suzuki's book on Zen Buddhism. "One of the masters remarked: 'When I began to study Zen, mountains were mountains; when I thought I understood Zen, mountains were not mountains; but when I came to full knowledge of Zen, mountains were again mountains.' " The idea charmed me. But "Among the Dangs" is not a story about Zen. That I got the notion from Suzuki's book is as little relevant to this story as the fact that I got the notion for the Dangs' custom of standing on the left leg with the right foot against the left knee from a photograph in a picture magazine in a waiting room in a dentist's office.

What the narrator says at that crucial moment can be said to have this public meaning: "I understand that this boulder over me is a big rock and is also what both geologists and Dangs think it is; this sensible fact is at once the thing and its meanings, and I accept this state of affairs; what is, is." Very well. But even in paraphrase this sounds dangerously near to Margaret Fuller's famous "I accept the universe," to which Carlyle answered for all people of good sense, "Gad, madam, you'd better!" Now, as a matter of fact, I didn't intend "Stone is Stone" to mean much in a dictionary way when I wrote it; but I did intend it to seem to mean a lot, at least it seemed to mean a lot when I was writing it. It is wise-sounding and obscure, like "I am Who am." "Stone is Stone" has the aura of portentousness without having, outside the story at least, enough content to justify the portentousness. For this revelation which the narrator experiences is not so profound as he thinks it is; it is temporary; it becomes his consciousness for a while but that's all of him it becomes. Ninety-nine per cent of the purpose of those words in this story is not denotative but structural, in a way analogous to, but only analogous to, the dream-use of words. They mean the little they would mean in ordinary speech, but mostly they are vehicles and instruments to accomplish a purpose peculiar to this story.

Within the story "Stone is Stone" is asked to mean: a thing is itself and is not another thing; also a thing is what science says it is and is simultaneously what religion says it is. The narrator's salvation is to reach the point of accepting this difficult meaning as true. Yet all he can salvage of this experience next day in the light of common sense, in ordinary language, is the mere tautology. This tautology lacks the power to preserve the experience, either for him or for the reader, with anything like the profundity it promises.

I do not mean that the narrator's experience was phony. Earlier, to be sure, he recited the story of Christ not because he believed it was true but because he believed it was useful. Now, in danger of his life, he has to some extent identified himself with Christ, and his experience is as genuine as it can be. At this point he does not utter Christ's message. He utters a tautology which lacks the power to hold his experience.

I, flat on my back in Yaddo, in imaginary danger of my life, uttered words even emptier than his: "The Dangs and the Urdangs." But I, sitting at a desk, set about finding words public enough to generate an experience analogous to mine and strong enough to hold it once it was created. Only as I wrote did I discover the nature of this experience. I had to identify myself with a character who was identifying himself with Christ before I found the meaning my experience had generated. This meaning is not Christ's message, nor is it "Stone is Stone." As nearly as I can paraphrase it, this meaning is: Without words adequate to contain it, insight may not endure but seems to be, perhaps is, illusory.

At least that's what I find the story means when I reread it, I who am by now able to re-enter this story only as another reader.

TRUMAN CAPOTE

Other Voices, Other Rooms

Voice from a Cloud

Other Voices, Other Rooms (my own title: it is not a quotation) was published in January 1948. It took two years to write and was not my first novel, but the second. The first, a manuscript never submitted and now lost, was called *Summer Crossing*—a spare, objective story with a New York setting. Not bad, as I remember: technically accomplished, an interesting enough tale, but without intensity or pain, without the qualities of a private vision, the anxieties that then had control of my emotions and imagination. *Other Voices, Other Rooms* was an attempt to exorcise demons: an unconscious, altogether intuitive attempt, for I was not aware, except for a few incidents and descriptions, of its being in any serious degree autobiographical. Rereading it now, I find such self-deception unpardonable.

Surely there were reasons for this adamant ignorance, no doubt protective ones: a fire curtain between the writer and the true source of his material. As I have lost contact with the troubled youth who wrote this book, since only a faded shadow of him is any longer contained inside myself, it is difficult to reconstruct his state of mind. However, I shall try.

At the time of the appearance of *Other Voices, Other Rooms*, critics, ranging from the warmest to the most hostile, remarked that obviously I was much influenced by such Southern literary artists as Faulkner and Welty and McCullers, three writers whose work I knew well and admired. Nevertheless, the gentlemen were mistaken though understandably. The American writers who had been most valuable to me were, in no particular order, James, Twain, Poe, Cather, Hawthorne, Sarah Orne Jewett; and, overseas, Flaubert, Jane Austen, Dickens, Proust, Chekhov, Katherine Mansfield, E. M. Forster, Turgenev, De Maupassant, and Emily Brontë. A collection more or less irrelevant to *Other Voices, Other Rooms;* for clearly no one of these writers, with the conceivable exception of Poe (who was by then a blurred childhood enthusiasm, like Dickens and Twain), was a necessary antecedent to this particular work. Rather, they *all* were, in the sense that each of them had contributed to my literary intelligence, such as it was. But the real progenitor was my difficult, subterranean self. The result was both a revelation and an escape: the book set me free, and, as in its prophetic final sentence, I stood there and looked back at the boy I had left behind.

I was born in New Orleans, an only child; my parents were divorced when I was four years old. It was a complicated divorce with much bitterness on either side, which is the main reason why I spent most of my childhood wandering among the homes of relatives in Louisiana, Mississippi, and rural Alabama (off and on, I attended schools in New York City and Connecticut). The reading I did on my own was of greater importance than my official education, which was a waste and ended when I was seventeen, the age at which I applied for and received a job at *The New Yorker* magazine. Not a very grand job, for all it really involved was sorting cartoons and clipping newspapers. Still, I was fortunate to have it, especially since I was determined never to set a studious foot inside a college classroom. I felt that either one was or wasn't a writer, and no combination of professors could influence the outcome. I still think I was correct, at least in my own case; however, I now realize that most young writers have more to gain than not by attending college, if only because their teachers and classroom comrades provide a captive audience for their work; nothing is lonelier than to be an aspiring artist without some semblance of a sounding board.

I stayed two years at *The New Yorker,* and during this period published a number of short stories in small literary magazines. (Several of them were submitted to my employers, and none accepted, though once one was returned with the following comment: "Very good. But romantic in a way this magazine is not.") Also, I wrote *Summer Crossing.* Actually, it was in order to complete the book that I took courage, quit my job, left New York, and settled with relatives, a cotton-growing family who lived in a remote part of Alabama: cotton fields, cattle pastures, pinewoods, dirt roads, creeks and slow little rivers, jaybirds, owls, buzzards circling in empty skies, distant train whistles—and, five miles away, a small country town: the Noon City of the present volume.

It was early winter when I arrived there, and the atmosphere of the roomy farmhouse, entirely heated by stoves and fireplaces, was well suited to a fledgling novelist wanting quiet isolation. The household rose at four-thirty, breakfasted by electric light, and was off about its business as the sun ascended—leaving me alone and, increasingly, in a panic. For, more and more, *Summer Closing* seemed to me thin, clever, unfelt. Another language, a secret spiritual geography, was burgeoning inside me, taking hold of my night-dream hours as well as my wakeful day-dreams.

One frosty December afternoon I was far from home, walking in a forest along the bank of a mysterious, deep, very clear creek, a route that led eventually to a place called Hater's Mill. The mill, which straddled the creek, had been abandoned long ago; it was a place where farmers had brought their corn to be ground into cornmeal. As a child, I'd often gone there with cousins to fish and swim; it was while exploring under the mill that I'd been bitten in the knee by a cottonmouth moccasin—precisely as happens to Joel Knox. And now as I came upon the forlorn mill with its sagging silver-gray timbers, the remembered shock of the snakebite returned; and other memories too—of Idabel, or rather the girl who was the counterpart of Idabel, and how we used to wade and swim in the pure waters, where fat speckled fish lolled in sunlit pools; Idabel was always trying to reach out and grab one.

Excitement—a variety of creative coma—overcame me. Walking home, I lost my way and moved in circles round the woods, for my mind was reeling with the whole book. Usually when a story comes to me, it arrives, or seems to, *in toto:* a long, sustained streak of lightning that darkens the tangible, so-called real world, and leaves illuminated only this suddenly seen pseudo-imaginary landscape, a terrain alive with figures, voices, rooms, atmospheres, weather. And all of it, at birth, is like an angry, wrathful tiger cub; one must soothe and tame it. Which, of course, is an artist's principal task: to tame and shape the raw creative vision.

It was dark when I got home, and cold, but I didn't feel the cold because of the fire inside me. My Aunt Lucille said she had been worried about me, and was disappointed because I didn't want any supper. She wanted to know if I was sick; I said no. She said, "Well, you *look* sick. You're white as a ghost." I said good night, locked myself in my room, tossed the manuscript of *Summer Crossing* into a bottom bureau drawer, collected several sharp pencils and a fresh pad of yellow lined paper, got into bed fully clothed, and with pathetic optimism, wrote: *"Other Voices, Other Rooms*—a novel by Truman Capote." Then: "Now a traveler must make his way to Noon City by the best means he can . . ."

It is unusual, but occasionally it happens to almost every writer that the writing of some particular story seems outerwilled and effortless; it is as though one were a secretary transcribing the words of a voice from a cloud. The difficulty is maintaining contact with this spectral dictator. Eventually it developed that communication ran highest at night, as fevers are known to do after dusk. So I took to working all night and sleeping all day, a routine that distressed the household and caused constant disapproving comment: "But you've got everything turned upside down. You're ruining your health." That is why, in the spring of the year, I thanked my exasperated relatives for their generosity, their burdened patience, and bought a ticket on a Greyhound bus to New Orleans.

There I rented a bedroom in the crowded apartment of a Creole family who lived in the French Quarter on Royal Street. It was a small hot bedroom almost entirely occupied by a brass bed, and it was noisy as a steel mill. Streetcars racketed under the window, and the carousings of sightseers touring the Quarter, the boisterous whiskey brawlings of soldiers and sailors, made for continuous pandemonium. Still, sticking to my night schedule, I progressed; by late autumn the book was half finished.

I need not have been as lonely as I was. New Orleans was my hometown and I had many friends there but because I did not desire that familial world and preferred to remain sealed off in the self-created universe of Zoo and Jesus Fever and the Cloud Hotel, I called none of my acquaintances. My only company was the Creole family, who were kindly working-class people (the father was a dockhand and his wife a seamstress), or encounters with drugstore clerks and café folk. Curiously, for New Orleans is not that sizable a town, I never saw a soul I knew. Except, by accident, my father. Which was ironic, considering that though I was unaware of it at the time, the central theme of *Other Voices, Other Rooms* was my search for the existence of this essentially imaginary person.

I seldom ate more than once a day, usually when I finished work. At that dawn hour I would walk through the humid, balconied streets, past St. Louis Cathedral and on to the French Market, a square crammed in the murky early morning with the trucks of vegetable farmers, Gulf Coast fishermen, meat vendors, and flower growers. It smelled of earth, of herbs and exotic, gingery scents, and it rang, clanged, clogged the ears with the sounds of vivacious trading. I loved it.

The market's chief gathering place was a café that served only bitter-black chicory coffee and the crustiest, most delicious fresh-fried doughnuts. I had discovered the place when I was fifteen, and had become addicted. The proprietor of the café gave all its habitués a nickname; he called me the Jockey, a reference to my height and build. Every morning as I plowed into the coffee and doughnuts, he would warn me with a sinister chuckle, "Better watch it, Jockey. You'll never make your weight."

It was in the café that five years earlier I'd met the prototype of Cousin Randolph. Actually, Cousin Randolph was suggested by two people. Once, when I was a very young child, I had spent a few summer weeks in an old house in Pass Christian, Mississippi. I don't remember much about it, except that there was an elderly man who lived there, an asthmatic invalid who smoked medicinal cigarettes and made remarkable scrap-quilts. He had been the captain of a fishing trawler, but illness had forced him to retire to a darkened room. His sister had taught him to sew; in consequence, he had found in himself a beautiful gift for designing cloth pictures. I used often to visit his room, where he would spread his tapestry-like quilts on the floor for me to admire: rose bouquets, ships in full sail, a bowl of apples.

The other Randolph, the character's spiritual ancestor, was the man I met in the café, a plump blond fellow who was said to be dying of leukemia. The proprietor called him the Sketcher, for he always sat alone in a corner drawing pictures of the clientele, the truckers and cattlemen, in a large loose-leaf notebook. One night it was obvious that I was his subject; after sketching for a while, he moseyed over to the counter where I was sitting and said, "You're a *Wunderkind*, aren't you? I can tell by your hands." I didn't know what it meant—*Wunderkind*; I thought that either he was joking or making a dubious overture. But then he defined the word, and I was pleased: it coincided with my own private opinion. We became friends; afterwards I saw him not only at the café, but we also took lazy strolls along the levee. We did not have much conversation, for he was a monologuist obsessed with death, betrayed passions, and unfulfilled talent.

All this transpired during one summer. That autumn I went to school in the East, and when I returned in June and asked the proprietor about the Sketcher, he said, "Oh, he died. Saw it in the *Picayune*. Did you know he was rich? Uh huh. Said so in the paper. Turned out his family owned half the land around Lake Pontchartrain. Imagine that. Well, you never know."

The book was completed in a setting far removed from the one in which it was begun. I wandered and worked in North Carolina, Saratoga Springs, New York City, and, ultimately, in a rented cottage on Nantucket. It was there, at a desk by a window with a view of sky and sand and arriving surf, that I wrote the last pages, finishing them with disbelief that the moment had come, a wonder simultaneously regretful and exhilarated.

I am not a keen rereader of my own books: what's done is done. Moreover, I am always afraid of finding that my harsher detractors are correct and that the work is not as good as I choose to think it. But recently I read *Other Voices, Other Rooms* straight through, the first time I had done so since it was published.

And? And, as I have already indicated, I was startled by its symbolic subterfuges. Also, while there are passages that seem to me accomplishments, others arouse uneasiness. On the whole, though, it was as if I were reading the fresh-minted manuscript of a total stranger. I was impressed by him. For what he had done has the enigmatic shine of a strangely colored prism held to the light—that, and a certain anguished, pleading intensity like the message of a shipwrecked sailor stuffed into a bottle and thrown out to sea.

ROSS MACDONALD

The Galton Case

A Preface to *The Galton Case*

For Donald Davie

DETECTIVE STORY WRITERS are often asked why we devote our talents to working in a mere popular convention. One answer is that there may be more to our use of the convention than meets the eye. I tried to show in an earlier piece* how the literary detective has provided writers since Poe with a disguise, a kind of welder's mask enabling us to handle dangerously hot material.

One night in his fifth year when we were alone in my house, my grandson Jimmie staged a performance which demonstrated the uses of disguise. His main idea seemed to be to express and discharge his guilts and fears, particularly his overriding fear that his absent parents might punish his (imperceptible) moral imperfections by never coming back to him. Perhaps he had overheard and been alarmed by the name of the movie they were attending, *Divorce American Style*.

Jimmie's stage was the raised hearth in the kitchen, his only prop a towel. He climbed up on the hearth and hid himself

* "The Writer as Detective Hero," *Essays Classic and Contemporary*, ed., R. W. Lid (Lippincott, 1967), pp. 307-315.

behind the back of an armchair. "Grandpa, what do you see?"

"Nothing."

He put the towel in view. "What do you see now?"

"Your towel."

He withdrew the towel. There was a silence. "What am I doing with my towel?"

I guessed that he was doing something "wrong," and that he wanted me to suspend judgment. "You're chewing it," I said boldly.

"No. But I have it in my mouth."

My easy acceptance of his wickedness encouraged him to enact it before my eyes. His head popped up. He was completely hooded with the towel, like a miniature inductee into the Ku Klux Klan.

"I'm a monster," he announced.

Then he threw off the towel, laughing. I sat and watched him for a time while the hooded monster and the laughing boy took alternate possession of the stage. Finally, soothed and purged by his simple but powerful art, Jimmie lay down on the cushioned hearth and went to sleep.

His little show speaks for itself, and needs no Aristotle. But let me point out some connections between his monodrama and my detective fiction. Both draw directly on life and feed back into it. Both are something the artist does for his own sake. But they need an audience to fulfill even their private function, let alone their public ones. Disguise is the imaginative device which permits the work to be both private and public, to half-divulge the writer's crucial secrets while deepening the whole community's sense of its own mysterious life.

I was forty-two when I wrote *The Galton Case*. It had taken me a dozen years and as many books to learn to tell highly personal stories in terms of the convention I had chosen. In the winter of 1957–1958 I was as ready as I would ever be to cope in fiction with some of the more complicated facts of my experience.

Central among these was the fact that I was born in California, in 1915, and was thus an American citizen; but I was raised in Canada by Canadian relatives. After attending university in Canada, I taught high school there for two years. In 1941, in one of the decisive moves of my life, I came back to the United States with my wife and young daughter, and started work on a doctorate in English at the University of Michigan.

It was a legitimate move, but the crossing of the border failed to dispel my dual citizen's sense of illegitimacy, and probably deepened it. This feeling was somewhat relieved by a couple of years in the American Navy. After the war I closed a physical circle, if not an emotional one, by settling in California, in Santa Barbara. At the same time I took up my lifelong tenancy in the bare muffled room of the professional writer where I am sitting now, with my back to the window, writing longhand in a Spiral notebook.

After ten years this writing routine was broken by circumstances which my later books more than adequately suggest. My wife and I lived in the San Francisco area for a year, and then came back to Santa Barbara. We rented a house on a cliff overlooking the sea and lived in it for a winter and a summer.

The Pacific had always lapped like blue eternity at the far edge of my life. The tides of that winter brought in old memories, some of which had drifted for forty years. In 1919, I remembered, my sea-captain father took me on a brief voyage and showed me a shining oceanic world from which I had felt exiled ever since, even during my sea duty in the Navy.

Exile and half-recovery and partial return had been the themes of at least two earlier books, *Blue City* and *The Three Roads* (which got its title from *Oedipus Tyrannus*). I wrote them in 1946, the year I left the Navy and came back to California after my long absence. These novels borrowed some strength from my return to my native state but they missed the uniquely personal heart of the matter—matter which I will call Oedipal, in memory of that Theban who was exiled more than once.

In the red Spiral notebook where I set down my first notes for *The Galton Case,* Oedipus made an appropriately early appearance. His ancient name was surrounded by a profusion of ideas and images which I can see in retrospect were sketching out the groundwork for the novel. A crude early description of its protagonist turns up in two lines of verse about a tragicomic track meet:

A burst of speed! Half angel and half ape,
The youthful winner strangles on the tape.

Two lines from another abortive poem—

Birds in the morning, scattered atomies:
The voice is one, the voice is not my own.—

were to supply an important detail to the closing page of the completed novel. The morning birds appear there as reminders of a world which encloses and outlasts the merely human.

A third and final example of these multitudinous early notes is one for an unwritten story—" 'The Fortieth Year' (downgrade reversed by an act of will)"—which recalls my then recent age and condition and suggests another character in the novel, the poet Chad Bolling. This middle-aged San Francisco poet is at the same time an object of parody and my spokesman for the possibilities of California life. Bolling's involvement in the Galton case takes him back to a sea cliff which he had visited as a young man, and he recovers some of a young man's high spirits:

He flapped his arms some more. "I can fly! I breast the windy currents of the sky. I soar like Icarus toward the sun. The wax melts. I fall from a great height into the sea. Mother Thalassa."
"Mother who?"
"Thalassa, the sea, the Homeric sea. We could build another Athens. I used to think we could do it in San Francisco, build a new city of man on the great hills. A city measured with forgiveness. Oh, well."

Not long after this outburst, Bolling sits down to write his best poem in years, as he says. While I am not a true poet, I am content to have Bolling represent me here. He shows the kite-flying exuberance of a man beginning a lucky piece of work, and speaks unashamedly for the epic impulse which almost all writers of fiction try to serve in some degree.

It was a complex business, getting ready to write even this moderately ambitious novel. Dozens of ideas were going through my mind in search of an organizing principle. The central idea which was to magnetize the others and set them in narrative order was a variation on the Oedipus story. It appears in the red notebook briefly and abruptly, without preparation: "Oedipus angry vs. parents for sending him away into a foreign country."

This simplification of the traditional Oedipus stories, Sophoclean or Freudian, provides Oedipus with a conscious reason for turning against his father and suggests that the latter's death was probably not unintended. It rereads the myth through the lens of my own experience, and in this it is characteristic of my plots. Many of them are founded on ideas which question or invert or criticize received ideas and which could, if brevity were my forte, be expressed in aphorisms.

Neither plots nor characters can be borrowed, even from Freud or Sophocles. Like the moving chart of an encephalograph, the plot of a novel follows the curve of the mind's intention. The central character, and many of the other characters, are in varying degrees versions of the author. Flaubert said that he was Madame Bovary, William Styron that he became Nat Turner. The character holding the pen has to wrestle and conspire with the one taking shape on paper, extracting a vision of the self from internal darkness—a self dying into fiction as it comes to birth.

My mind had been haunted for years by an imaginary boy whom I recognized as the darker side of my own remembered boyhood. By his sixteenth year he had lived in fifty houses and committed the sin of poverty in each of them. I couldn't think of him without anger and guilt.

This boy became the central figure of *The Galton Case*. His nature and the nature of his story are suggested by some early titles set down in the red notebook: "A Matter of Identity," "The Castle and the Poorhouse," "The Impostor." He is, to put it briefly and rather inexactly, a false claimant, a poorhouse graduate trying to lie his way into the castle.

"The Castle and the Poorhouse," old-fashioned and melodramatic as the phrase is, accurately reflects the vision of the world which my adult imagination inherited from my childhood. It was a world profoundly divided, between the rich and the poor, the upright and the downcast, the sheep and the goats. We goats knew the moral pain inflicted not so much by poverty as by the doctrine, still current, that poverty is always deserved.

In the first winters of the Depression in Ontario, skilled factory workers were willing to put in a full week on piecework for as little as five dollars. The year I left high school, 1932, I was glad to work on a farm for my board alone. Healthy as that year of farm life was, it was a year of waiting without much hope. I shared with many others the dilemma of finding myself to be at the same time two radically different kinds of people, a pauper and a member of the middle class. The dilemma was deepened by my fear that I'd never make it to college, and by my feeling of exile, which my mother had cultivated by teaching me from early childhood that California was my birthplace and natural home.

Such personal dilemmas tend to solidify along traditional philosophic lines. In a puritanical society the poor and fatherless, suffering the quiet punishments of despair, may see themselves as permanently and justifiably damned for crimes they can't remember having committed.

The Platonic split between more worthy and less worthy substances, idea and matter, spirit and flesh, widens under pressure. The crude pseudo-Darwinian dualism of my own phrase, "half angel and half ape," suggests an image of man not only divided but at war.

The Galton Case was an attempt to mend such gross divisions on the imaginative level. It tried to bring the Monster and the Laughing Boy into unity or congruence at least, and build a bridge, or a tunnel, between the poorhouse and the castle.

The castle is represented by the Galton family's Southern California estate, described as if it was literally a medieval demesne: "The majestic iron gates gave a portcullis effect. A serf who was cutting the lawn with a power-mower paused to tug at his forelock as we went by." The old widow who presides over this estate had quarreled with her son Anthony some twenty years ago, and Anthony had walked out and disappeared. Now Mrs. Galton has begun to dream of a reconciliation with her son. Through her attorney she hires the detective Lew Archer to look for him.

My earliest note on Anthony Galton will give an idea of his place in the story. A very young man and a poet, Anthony deliberately declassed himself in an effort, the note says, "to put together 'the castle and the poorhouse.' He changed his name [to John Brown] and became a workingman. . . . Married under his pseudonym, to the common law wife of a man in jail," he was murdered when the other man got out.

About one-third of the way through the novel, the detective Archer is shown an incomplete set of human bones which prove to be Anthony Galton's. At the same time and the same place— not many miles up the coast from the Northern California town where I was born—Archer finds or is found by a boy who represents himself as Anthony's son and calls himself John Brown. The rest of the novel is concerned with this boy and his identity.

Perhaps I have encouraged the reader to identify this boy with me. If so, I must qualify that notion. The connections between a writer and his fiction, which are turning out to be my present subject, are everything but simple. My nature is probably better represented by the whole book than by any one of its characters. At the same time John Brown, Jr.'s life is a version of my early life: the former could not have existed without the latter.

The extent of this symbiosis can be seen in the two false starts I made on the novel, more clearly than in the finished product, where personal concerns were continually reshaped by overriding artistic needs. The most striking fact about these early versions is that they begin the story approximately where the completed novel ends it. Both Version One and Version Two, as I'll call them, are narrated by a boy who recalls aspects of my Canadian boyhood. The other characters including the father and mother are imaginary, as they are in the published novel.

In Version One the narrator's name is Tom. He lives on the poorer side of London, Ontario (where I attended university and in a sense graduated from the "poorhouse" of my childhood.) Tom has finished high school but has no prospects. At the moment he is playing semi-pro pool.

He is challenged to a game by an American named Dawson who wears an expensive suit with a red pin-stripe in it. Tom wins easily and sees, when Dawson pays, that his wallet is "thick with money—American money, which always seems a little bit like stage money to me." From the standpoint of a poor Canadian boy, the United States and its riches seem unreal.

Tom has a taste for unreality. He has done some acting in high school, he tells Dawson.

> *"Did you enjoy acting?"*
> *Did I? It was the only time I ever felt alive, when I could forget myself and the hole I lived in, and turn into an imaginary character.*
> *"I liked it, yeah."*

Tom is not speaking for me here. I don't like acting. But it is probably not a coincidence that the American, Dawson, is a Ph.D. trained, as I was trained at the University of Toronto, "in the evaluation of intelligence."

Dawson is testing the boy's memory and acting ability and talking vaguely about hiring him, as Version One died in mid-sentence on its thirteenth page. This version suffered from lack of adequate planning, and from the associated difficulty of telling the boy's complicated story in his own simple person. Neither structure nor style was complex enough to let me discover my largely undiscovered purposes.

But immediately I made a second stab at having the boy narrate his own story. His name is Willie now, and he lives in Toronto, almost as if he was following in my footsteps. He has an appointment with an American, now named Mr. Sablacan, who is waiting for him at the Royal York Hotel.

Willie never gets there. All of Version Two takes place in his home, in the early morning. This rather roughly written six-page scene breaks the ground for my book and introduces some of its underlying themes: the hostility between father and son, for instance, here brought to an extreme pitch:

> *The old man was sitting at the kitchen table when I went down. He looked like a ghost with a two-day beard. The whole room stank of wine, and he was holding a partly empty bottle propped up between his crotch.*
> *. . . I kept one eye on him while I made breakfast. . . . He wouldn't throw the bottle as long as it had wine in it. After that, you never knew.*

The shades of Huck Finn and his father are pretty well dispelled, I think, when the boy's mother comes down. She approaches her drunken husband "with that silly adoring look on her face, as if he was God Almighty giving her a break just by letting her live. 'You've been working and thinking all night,' she said. 'Your poor head needs a rest. I'll fix you a nice cup of tea. . . .' "

Later, she stops an argument between the father and the boy by silencing the father.

> *He sat in his chair and looked down into his bottle. You'd think from the expression on his face that it was a telescope which let him see all the way down to hell. All of a sudden his face went slack. He went to sleep in his chair. The old lady took the bottle away from him as if he was a baby. . . .*
> *. . . I sat and ate my breakfast in silence. With the old man propped up opposite me, eyes closed and mouth open, it was a little like eating with a dead man at the table.*

My story had begun to feed on its Oedipal roots, both mythical and psychological. Relieved by the mother of his crotch-held bottle, the father has undergone symbolic death. The short scene ends with the boy's determination to get away not only from his father but from his mother:

> *She'd go on feeding me until I choked. She'd be pouring me cups of tea until I drowned in the stuff. She'd give me loving encouragement until I suffocated.*

Version Two was a good deal more than a false start. Swarming with spontaneous symbolism, it laid out one whole side, the sinister side, of the binocular vision of my book. In fact it laid it out so completely that it left me, like Willie, nowhere to go but away. I couldn't begin the novel with the infernal vision on which part of its weight would finally rest; the novel must converge on that gradually. But by writing my last scene first, in effect, and facing its Medusa images—poverty and family failure and hostility—my imagination freed itself to plan the novel without succumbing to the more obvious evasions.

Even so, as I was trying to finish the first draft, I got morally tired and lost my grip on my subject, ending the book with a dying fall in Nevada. My friend John Mersereau read this draft

—entitled, appropriately, "The Enormous Detour"—and reminded me that a book like mine could not succeed as a novel unless it succeeded in its own terms as a detective novel. For my ending I went back to Version Two, which contains the dramatic essense of the final confrontations. Willie's scene with his parents served me well, leading me into the heart of my subject not just once but again.

A second break-through at the beginning, more technical and less obviously important, came with my decision to use the detective Archer as the narrator. This may seem a small matter, but it was not. The decision on narrative point-of-view is a key one for any novelist. It determines shape and tone, and even the class of detail that can be used. With this decision I made up my mind that the convention of the detective novel, in which I had been working for fifteen years, would be able to contain the materials of my most ambitious and personal work so far. I doubt that my book could have been written in any other form.

Miss Brigid Brophy has alleged against the detective story that it cannot be taken seriously because it fails to risk the author's ego and is therefore mere fantasy. It is true as I have noted that writers since Poe have used detectives like Dupin as a sort of rational strong point from which they can observe and report on a violent no-man's-land. Unfortunately this violent world is not always fantastic, although it may reflect psychological elements. Miss Brophy's argument disregards the fact that the detective and his story can become means of knowing oneself and saying the unsayable. You can never hit a distant target by aiming at it directly.

In any case I have to plead not guilty to unearned security of the ego. As I write a book, as I wrote *The Galton Case*, my ego is dispersed through several characters, including usually some of the undesirable ones, and I am involved with them to the limit of my imaginative strength. In modern fiction the narrator is not always the protagonist or hero, nor is the protagonist always single. Certainly my narrator Archer is not the main object of my interest, nor the character with whose fate I am most concerned. He is a deliberately narrowed version of the writing self, so narrow that when he turns sideways he almost disappears. Yet his semi-transparent presence places the story at one remove from the author and lets it, as we say (through sweat and tears), write itself.

I remember the rush of invention that occurred when the emotional and imaginative urges, the things *The Galton Case* was to be about, were released by Willie's scene with his parents, and channeled by my decision to write the book from Archer's point of view. The details came unbidden in a benign avalanche which in two or three days filled the rest of the red notebook. The people and the places weren't all final, but they were definite enough to let me begin the wild masonry of laying detail on detail to make a structure. (Naturally many of the details came in already organized gestalts: people in relationship, events in narrative order.)

Detective novels differ from some other kinds of novel, in having to have a rather hard structure built in logical coherence. But the structure will fail to satisfy the mind, writer's or reader's, unless the logic of imagination, tempered by feelings and rooted in the unconscious, is tied to it, often subverting it. The plans for a detective novel in the making are less like blueprints than like travel notes set down as you once revisited a city. The city had changed since you saw it last. It keeps changing around you. Some of the people you knew there have changed their names. Some of them wear disguises.

Take for example Dr. Dawson who lost a game of pool to Tom in Version One and became, in Version Two, a Mr. Sablacan waiting for Willie at the Royal York. In my final notes and in the novel itself he has become Gordon Sable, identifiable with his earlier personae by his name and by the fact that, like Dr. Dawson, he wears a suit with a wicked red pin-stripe in it. His occupation has changed, and his function in the novel has expanded. Gordon Sable is the attorney who hires Lew Archer on Mrs. Galton's behalf to look for her lost son Anthony.

Archer and Gordon Sable know each other. The nature of their relationship is hinted at by a small incident on the first page of the novel. A line of it will illustrate some of the implications of style, which could be described as structure on a small scale. Archer sits down on a Harvard chair in Gordon Sable's office, and then gets up. "It was like being expelled."

In a world of rich and poor, educated and disadvantaged,

Archer's dry little joke places him on the side of the underdog. It suggests that he is the kind of man who would sympathize with the boy impostor waiting in the wings. And of course it speaks for the author—my own application for a graduate fellowship at Harvard was turned down thirty years ago—so that like nearly everything in fiction the joke has a private side which partly accounts for its having been made. The University of Michigan gave me a graduate fellowship in 1941, by the way, and my debt to Ann Arbor is duly if strangely acknowledged in the course of John Brown, Jr.'s story.

Detective stories are told backward, as well as forward, and full revelation of the characters and their lives' meanings is deferred until the end, or near the end. But even deeper structural considerations require the main dynamic elements of a story to be laid in early. For this and other reasons, such as the further weight and dimension imparted by repetition, it is sometimes a good idea to let a character and his story divide. One part or aspect of him can perform an early function in the story which foreshadows the function of his later persona, without revealing too much of it.

John Brown, Jr., as I've already said, doesn't enter the story until it is one-third told. I decided, though hardly on the fully conscious level, to provide John with a stand-in or alter ego to pull his weight in the early part of the narrative. When I invented this other boy, and named him Tom Lemberg, I had totally forgotten that Tom was the name of the boy in Version One who beat Dr. Dawson at pool. But here he is in the novel: an earlier stage in the development of my boy impostor. A specimen of fiction, like a biological specimen, seems to recapitulate the lower stages of its evolution. I suspect Tom had to be brought in to validate my novel, proving that I had touched in order all the bases between life and fiction. At any rate the book comes alive when Archer and Tom Lemberg, two widely distinct versions of the author, confront each other in Chapter Five.

This confrontation with Tom of course prefigures Archer's confrontation with the boy impostor John. Tom serves an even more important purpose at the beginning of the book, when he is held responsible for the murder of Peter Culligan. The structure of the story sufficiently identifies Culligan with the wino father, so that Culligan's death parallels and anticipates the final catastrophe. Like the repeated exile of Oedipus, the crucial events of my novel seem to happen at least twice. And like a young Oedipus, Tom is a "son" who appears to kill a "father," thus setting the whole story in circular motion.

I have told a little too much of that story for comfort, and a little too much of my own story. One final connection between the private story and the public one should suffice. When Archer opens the dead Culligan's suitcase, "Its contents emitted a whiff of tobacco, sea water, sweat, and the subtler indescribable odor of masculine loneliness." These were the smells, as I remembered and imagined them, of the pipe-smoking sea-captain who left my mother and me when I was about the age that grandson Jimmie was when he became a monster in my poor castle, and then a laughing boy, and fell asleep.

JOHN FOWLES

The French Lieutenant's Woman

Notes on an Unfinished Novel

THE NOVEL I am writing at the moment (provisionally entitled *The French Lieutenant's Woman*) is set about a hundred years back. I don't think of it as a historical novel, a genre in which I have very little interest. It started four or five months ago as a visual image. A woman stands at the end of a deserted quay and stares out to sea. That was all. This image rose in my mind one morning when I was still in bed half asleep. It corresponded to no actual incident in my life (or in art) that I can recall, though I have for many years collected obscure books and forgotten prints, all sorts of flotsam and jetsam from the last two or three centuries, relics of past lives—and I suppose this leaves me with a sort of dense hinterland from which such images percolate down to the coast of consciousness.

These mythopoeic "stills" (they seem almost always static) float into my mind very often. I ignore them, since that is the best way of finding whether they really are the door into a new world.

So I ignored this image; but it recurred. Imperceptibly it stopped coming to me. I began deliberately to recall it and to try to analyze and hypothesize why it held some sort of imminent power. It was obviously mysterious. It was vaguely romantic. It also seemed, perhaps because of the latter quality, not to belong to today. The woman obstinately refused to stare out of the window of an airport lounge; it had to be this ancient quay—as I happen to live near one, so near that I can see it from the bottom of my garden, it soon became a specific ancient quay. The woman had no face, no particular degree of sexuality. But she was Victorian; and since I always saw her in the same static long shot, with her back turned, she represented a reproach on the Victorian Age. An outcast. I didn't know her crime, but I wished to protect her. That is, I began to fall in love with her. Or with her stance. I didn't know which.

This—not literally—pregnant female image came at a time (the autumn of 1966) when I was already halfway through another novel and had, still have, three or four others planned to follow it. It was an interference, but of such power that it soon came to make the previously planned work seem the intrusive element in my life. This accidentality of inspiration has to be allowed for in writing; both in the work one is on (unplanned development of character, unintended incidents, and so on) and in one's works as a whole. Follow the accident, fear the fixed plan—that is the rule.

*

Narcissism, or pygmalionism, is the essential vice a writer must have. Characters (and even situations) are like children or lovers, they need constant caressing, concern, listening to, watching, admiring. All these occupations become tiring for the active partner—the writer—and only something akin to love can provide the energy. I've heard people say "I want to write a book." But wanting to write a book, however ardently, is not enough. Even to say "I want to be possessed by my own creations" is not enough; all natural or born writers are possessed, and in the old magical sense, by their own imaginations long before they even begin to think of writing.

*

This fluke genesis must break all the rules of creative writing; must sound at best childlike, at worst childish. I suppose the orthodox method is to work out what one wants to say and what one has experience of, and then to correlate the two. I have tried that method and started out with an analytically arrived-at theme and a set of characters all neatly standing for something; but the manuscripts have all petered out miserably. *The Magus* (written before *The Collector,* which also originated in a single image) sprang from a very trivial visit to a villa on a Greek island; nothing in the least unusual happened. But in my unconscious I kept arriving at the place again and again; something wanted to happen there, something that had not happened to me at the time. Why it should have been at *that* villa, *that* one visit, among so many thousands of other possible launching-pads, I do not know. Only a month ago someone showed me some recent photographs of the villa, which is now deserted; and it was just a deserted villa. Its mysterious significance to me fifteen years ago remains mysterious.

*

Once the seed germinates, reason and knowledge, culture and all the rest, have to start to grow it. You cannot create a world by hot instinct; but only by cold experience. That is one good reason why so many novelists produce nothing until, or do all their best work after, the age of forty.

*

I find it very difficult to write if I don't know I shall have several days absolutely clear. All visits, all intrusions, all daily duties become irksome. This is during the first draft. I wrote the first draft of *The Collector* in under a month; sometimes ten thousand words a day. Of course a lot of it was poorly written and had to be endlessly amended and revised. First-draft and revision writing are so different they hardly seem to belong to the same activity. I never do any "research" until the first draft is finished; all that matters to begin with is the flow, the story, the narrating. Research material then is like swimming in a strait-jacket.

During the revision period I try to keep some sort of discipline. I make myself revise whether I feel like it or not; in some ways, the more disinclined and dyspeptic one feels, the better—one is harsher with oneself. All the best cutting is done when one is sick of the writing.

But all this advice from senior writers to establish a discipline always, to get down a thousand words a day whatever one's mood, I find an absurdly puritanical and impractical approach. Writing is like eating or making love; a natural process, not an artificial one. Write, if you must, because you feel like writing; never because you feel you ought to write.

*

I write memoranda to myself about the book I'm on. On this one: *You are not trying to write something one of the Victorian novelists forgot to write; but perhaps something one of them failed to write. And: Remember the etymology of the word. A novel is something new. It must have relevance to the writer's now—so don't ever pretend you live in 1867; or make sure the reader knows it's a pretence.*

*

In the matter of clothes, social manners, historical background, and the rest, writing about 1867 is merely a question of research. But I soon get into trouble over dialogue, because the genuine dialogue of 1867 (insofar as it can be heard in books of the time) is far too close to our own to sound convincingly old. It very often fails to agree with our psychological picture of the Victorians—it is not stiff enough, not euphemistic enough, and so on; and here at once I have to start cheating and pick out the more formal and archaic (even for 1867) elements of spoken speech. It is this kind of "cheating," which is intrinsic to the novel, that takes the time.

Even in modern-novel dialogue the most real is not the most conformable to actual current speech. One has only to read a transcribed tape of actual conversation to realize that it is, in the literary context, not very real. Novel dialogue is a form of shorthand, an *impression* of what people actually say; and besides that it has to perform other functions—to keep the narrative moving (which real conversation rarely does), to reveal character (real conversation often hides it), and so on.

This is the greatest technical problem I have; it is hard enough with modern characters, and doubly so with historical ones.

*

Memorandum: *If you want to be true to life, start lying about the reality of it.*

164

And: *One cannot describe reality; only give metaphors that indicate it. All human modes of description (photographic, mathematical and the rest, as well as literary) are metaphorical. Even the most precise scientific description of an object or movement is a tissue of metaphors.*

*

Alain Robbe-Grillet's polemical essay *Pour un nouveau roman* (1963) is indispensable reading for the profession, even where it produces no more than total disagreement. His key question: *Why bother to write in a form whose great masters cannot be surpassed?* The fallacy of one of his conclusions—we must discover a new form to write in if the novel is to survive—is obvious. It reduces the purpose of the novel to the discovery of new forms: whereas its other purposes—to entertain, to satirize, to describe new sensibilities, to record life, to improve life, and so on—are clearly just as viable and important. But his obsessive pleading for new form places a kind of stress on every passage one writes today. To what extent am I being a coward by writing inside the old tradition? To what extent am I being panicked into avant-gardism? Writing about 1867 doesn't lessen the stress; it increases it, since so much of the subject matter must of its historical nature be "traditional."

There are apparent parallels in other arts: Stravinsky's eighteenth century rehandlings, Picasso's and Francis Bacon's use of Velasquez. But in this context words are not nearly so tractable as musical notes or brush-strokes. One can parody a rococo musical ornament, a baroque face. Very early on I tried, in a test chapter, to put modern dialogue into Victorian mouths. But the effect was absurd, since the real historical nature of the characters is hopelessly distorted; the only people to get away with this (Julius Caesar speaking with a Brooklyn accent, and so on) are the professional funny men. One is led inevitably, by such a technique, into a comic novel.

*

My two previous novels were both based on more or less disguised existentialist premises. I want this one to be no exception; and so I am trying to show an existentialist awareness before it was chronologically possible. Kierkegaard was, of course, totally unknown to the British and American Victorians; but it has always seemed to me that the Victorian Age, especially from 1850 on, was highly existentialist in many of its personal dilemmas. One can almost invert the reality and say that Camus and Sartre have been trying to lead us, in their fashion, to a Victorian seriousness of purpose and moral sensitivity.

Nor is this the only similarity between the 1960's and 1860's. The great nightmare of the respectable Victorian mind was the only too real one created by the geologist Lyell and the biologist Darwin. Until then man had lived like a child in a small room. They gave him—and never was a present less welcome—infinite space and time, and a hideously mechanistic explanation of human reality into the bargain. Just as we "live with the bomb" the Victorians lived with the theory of evolution. They were hurled into space. They felt themselves infinitely isolated. By the 1860's the great iron structures of their philosophies, religions, and social stratifications were already beginning to look dangerously corroded to the more perspicacious.

Just such a man, an existentialist before his time, walks down the quay and sees that mysterious back, feminine, silent, also existentialist, turned to the horizon.

*

Magnificent though the Victorian novelists were, they almost all (an exception, of course, is the later Hardy) failed miserably in one aspect; nowhere in "respectable" Victorian literature (and most of the pornography was based on the brothel—or eighteenth-century accounts) does one see a man and a woman described together in bed. We do not know how they made love, what they said to each other in their most intimate moments, what they felt then.

Writing as I have been today—about two Victorians making love—with no guides except my imagination and vague deductions from the spirit of the age and so on—is really science fiction. A journey is a journey, backwards or forwards.

*

The most difficult task for a writer is to get the right "voice" for his material; by voice I mean the overall impression one has of the creator behind what he creates. Now I've always liked the ironic voice that the line of great nineteenth-century novelists, from Austen through to Conrad, all used so naturally. We tend

today to remember the failures of that tone—the satirical over-
kill in Dickens, the facetiousness of Thackeray, the strained
sarcasm of Mark Twain, the priggishness in George Eliot—rather
than its virtues. The reason is clear enough: irony needs the
assumption of superiority in the ironist. Such an assumption
must be anathema to a democratic, egalitarian century like our
own. We suspect people who pretend to be omniscient; and that
is why so many of us twentieth-century novelists feel driven into
first-person narration.

I have heard writers claim that this first-person technique is a
last bastion of the novel against the cinema, a form where the
camera dictates an inevitable third-person point of view of what
happens, however much we may identify with one character. But
the matter of whether a contemporary novelist uses "he" or "I" is
largely irrelevant. The great majority of modern third-person
narration is "I" narration very thinly disguised. The real "I" of
the Victorian writers—the writer himself—is as rigorously re-
pressed there (out of fear of seeming pretentious, etc.) as it is, for
obvious semantic and grammatical reasons, when the narration is
in literal first-person form.

But in this new book, I shall try to resurrect this technique. It
seems in any case natural to look back at the England of a
hundred years ago with a somewhat ironical eye—and "I"—although it is my strong belief that history is horizontal in terms of
the ratio between understanding and *available* knowledge and
(far more important) horizontal in terms of the happiness the
individual gets from being alive. In short, there is a danger in
being ironic about the apparent follies and miseries of any past
age. So I have written myself another memorandum: *You are not
the "I" who breaks into the illusion, but the "I" who is a part of
it.*

In other words, the "I" who will make first-person commen-
taries here and there in my story, and who will finally even enter
it, will not be my real "I" in 1967; but much more just another
character, though in a different category from the purely fictional
ones.

*

An illustration. Here is the beginning of a minor novel (*Lovel
the Widower,* 1861) by Thackeray:

Who shall be the hero of this tale? Not I who write it. I am but the Chorus of the Play. I make remarks on the conduct of the characters: I narrate their simple story.

Today I think we should assume (not knowing who the writer was) that the "I" here is the writer's "I." For three or four pages more we might still just believe this; but then suddenly Thackeray introduces his eponymous hero as "my friend Lovel" and we see we've been misled. "I" is simply another character. But then a few pages on the "I" cuts in again in the description of a character.

She never could speak. Her voice was as hoarse as a fishwoman's. Can that immense stout old box-keeper at the ——— theatre . . . be the once brilliant Emily Montanville? I am told there are *no* lady box-keepers in the English theatres. This, I submit, is a proof of my consummate care and artifice in rescuing from a prurient curiosity the individual personages from whom the characters of the present story are taken. Montanville is *not* a box-opener. She *may,* under another name, keep a trinket-shop in the Burlington Arcade, for what you know: but this secret no torture shall induce me to divulge. Life has its rises and downfalls, and you have had yours, you hobbling old creature. Montanville, indeed! Go thy ways! Here is a shilling for thee. (Thank you, sir.) Take away that confounded footstool, and never let us see thee more!

We can just still suppose that the "I" is another character here; but the strong suspicion is that it is Thackeray himself. There is the characteristic teasing of the reader, the shock new angle of the present tense, the compensatory self-mocking in the already revealed "secret no torture shall induce me to divulge." But clearly he doesn't mean us to be sure; it is not the whole Thackeray.

Lovel rates poorly by Thackeray's own standards elsewhere; it is nevertheless a brilliant technical exercise in the use of "voice." I cannot believe that it is a dead technique. Nothing can get us off the charge of omniscience—and certainly not the *nouveau roman* theory. Even that theory's most brilliant practical demonstrations—say Robbe-Grillet's own *La Jalousie*—fail to answer the accusation. Robbe-Grillet may have removed the writer Robbe-Grillet totally from the text; but he has never denied he wrote it. If the writer really believes in the statement "I know nothing about my characters except what can be tape-recorded and photographed (and then 'mixed' and 'cut')," the logical step is to take up tape-recording and photography—not writing. But if he still writes, and writes well, as Robbe-Grillet does, then he is self-betrayed: he belongs to Cosa Nostra, and is transparently far more deeply implicated than he will admit.

*

September 2nd, 1967. Now I am about two thirds of the way through. Always a bad stage, when one begins to doubt major things like basic motivations, dramatic design, the whole bloody enterprise; in the beginning one tends to get dazzled by each page, by one's fertility, those nice Muses always at one's shoulder . . . but then the inherent faults in the plot and characters begin to emerge. One starts to doubt the wisdom of the way the latter make things go; at the stage in an *affaire,* when one begins to thank God that marriage never raised its ugly head. But here one is condemned to a marriage of sorts—I have the woman on the quay (whose name is Sarah) for better or for worse, so to speak; and all seems worse.

*

I have to break off for a fortnight to go down to Majorca, where they're filming *The Magus.* I have written the script, but like most scripts it's really a team effort. The two producers have had their say, and the director; and a number of non-human factors, such as the budget, the nature of the locations, and the casting of the main roles, have had theirs. Most of the time I feel like a skeleton at the feast; this isn't what I had imagined, either in the book or in the script.

Yet it is interesting to watch, on a big film production, how buttressed each key man is by the other key men; to see how often one will turn to the other and say "Will it work?" I compare this with the loneliness of the long-distance writer; and I come back with a sort of relief, a re-affirmation in my faith in the novel. For all its faults, it is a statement by one person. In my novels I am the producer, director, and all the actors; I photograph it. This may seem a megalomania beside which the more celebrated cases from Hollywood pale to nothingness. There *is* a vanity about it, a wish to play the godgame, which all the random and author-removing devices of avant-garde technique cannot hide. But there must be a virtue, in an age that is out to exterminate both the individual and the enduring, in the individual's attempt to endure by his own efforts alone. The truth is, the novel is a free form. Unlike the play or the filmscript, it has no limits other than those of the language. It is like a poem; it can be what it wants. This is its downfall and its glory; and explains why both forms have been so often used to establish freedom in other fields, social and political.

*

A charge all of us who sell film rights have to answer is that we wrote our books with this end in view. What has to be distinguished here is the legitimate and the illegitimate influence of the cinema on the novel. I saw my first film when I was six; I suppose I've seen on average—and discounting television—a film a week ever since: let's say some two and a half thousand films up to now. How can so frequently repeated an experience not have indelibly stamped itself on the *mode* of imagination? At one time I analyzed my dreams in detail; again and again I recalled purely cinematic effects . . . panning shots, close shots, tracking, jump cuts, and the rest. In short, this mode of imagining is far too deep in me to eradicate—not only in me, in all my generation.

This doesn't mean we have surrendered to the cinema. I don't share the general pessimism about the so-called decline of the novel and its present status as a minority cult. Except for a brief period in the nineteenth century, when a literate majority and a lack of other means of entertainment coincided, it has always been a minority cult.

One has in fact only to do a filmscript to realize how inalienably in possession of a still vast domain the novel is; how countless the forms of human experience only to be described in and by it. There is too an essential difference in the quality of image evoked by the two media. The cinematic visual image is virtually the same for all who see it; it stamps out personal imagination, the response from individual *visual* memory. A sentence or paragraph in a novel will evoke a different image in each reader. This necessary co-operation between writer and reader, the one to suggest, the other to make concrete, is a privilege of *verbal* form; and the cinema can never usurp it.

Nor is that all. Here (the opening four paragraphs of a novel) is a flagrant bit of writing for the cinema. The man has obviously spent too much time on filmscripts, and can now think only of his movie sale.

The temperature is in the 90's and the boulevard is absolutely empty.
Lower down, the inky water of a canal reaches in a straight line. Midway between two locks is a barge full of timber. On the bank, two rows of barrels.
Beyond the canal, between houses separated by workyards, a huge cloudless tropical sky. Under the throbbing sun white façades, slate roofs and granite quays hurt the eyes. An obscure distant murmur rises in the hot air. All seems drugged by the Sunday peace and the sadness of summer days.
Two men appear.

It first appeared on March 25, 1881. The writer's name is Flaubert. All I have done is to transpose his past historic into the present.

*

I woke in the small hours, and the book tormented me. All its failings rose up in the darkness. I saw the novel I dropped in order to write *The French Lieutenant's Woman* was much better. This one was not my sort of book; but an aberration, a folly, a delusion. Sentences from vitriolic reviews floated through my mind . . . "a clumsy pastiche of Hardy," "pretentious imitation of an inimitable genre," "pointless exploration of an already over-explored age . . . ," and so on and so on.

Now it is day, I am back on it again, and it denies what I felt in the night. But the horror of such realizations is that someone, some reader or reviewer, *will* realize them. The nightmare of the writer is that all his worst private fears and self-criticisms will be made public.

*

The shadow of Thomas Hardy, the heart of whose "country" I can see in the distance from my workroom window, I cannot avoid. Since he and Peacock are my two favourite male novelists of the nineteenth century I don't mind the shadow. It seems best to use it; and by a curious coincidence, which I didn't realize when I placed my own story in that year, 1867 was the crucial year in Hardy's own mysterious personal life. It is somehow encouraging that while my fictitious characters weave their own story in their 1867, only thirty miles away in the real 1867 the pale young architect was entering his own fatal life-incident.

*

My female characters tend to dominate the male. I see man as a kind of artifice, and woman as a kind of reality. The one is cold idea, the other is warm fact. Daedalus faces Venus, and Venus must win. If the technical problems hadn't been so great, I should have liked to make Conchis in *The Magus* a woman. The character of Mrs. de Seitas at the end of the book was simply an aspect of his character; as was Lily. Now Sarah exerts this power. She doesn't realize how. Nor do I yet.

*

I was stuck this morning to find a good answer from Sarah at the climax of a scene. Characters sometimes reject all the possibilities one offers. They say in effect: *I would never say or do a thing like that.* But they don't say what they would say; and one has to proceed negatively, by a very tedious coaxing kind of trial and error. After an hour over this one wretched sentence, I realized that she had in fact been telling me what to do: silence from her was better than any line she might have said.

*

By the time I left Oxford I found myself much more at home in French than in English literature. There seems to me to be a vital distinction between the French and Anglo-Saxon cultures in this field. Since 1650 French writers have assumed an international audience; and the Anglo-Saxons a national one. This may be no more than a general tendency; the literatures of the two cultures offer hundreds of exceptions, even among the best-known books. Nevertheless I have always found this French assumption that the proper audience of a book is one without frontiers more attractive than the extreme opposite view, which is still widely held in both Britain and America, that the proper job of a writer is to write of and for his own country and countrymen.

I am aware of this when I write, and especially when I revise.

English references that will mean nothing to a foreigner I usually cut out, or avoid in the first place. In the present book I have the ubiquity in the West of the Victorian ethos: that helps greatly.

*

Various things have long made me feel an exile in England. Some years ago I came across a sentence in an obscure French novel: *Ideas are the only motherland.* Ever since I have kept it as the most succinct summary I know of what I believe. Perhaps "believe" is the wrong verb—if you are without national feeling, if you find many of your fellowcountrymen and most of their beliefs and their institutions foolish and antiquated, you can hardly *believe* in anything, but only accept the loneliness that results.

So I live completely away from other English writers and the literary life of London. What I have to think of as my "public" self is willy-nilly absorbed into or rejected by (mostly the latter, in my case) the national literary "world." Even to me it seems, that public self, very remote and often distastefully alien and spurious; just one more thing that I feel my real self in exile from.

My real self is here and now, writing. Whenever I think of this (the writing, not the written) experience, images to do with exploring, singlehanded voyages, lone mountain ascents always spring unwanted to my mind. They sound romantic, but they're not meant to. It's the damned solitude, the fear of failure (by which I do *not* mean bad reviews), the tedium of the novel form, the often nauseating feeling that one is prey to an unhealthy obsession. . . .

When I go out and meet other people, become mixed in their lives and social routines, my own solitude, routinelessness, and freedom (which is a subtle imprisonment) from economic "worries" often make me feel like a visitor from outer space. I like earthmen, but I'm not quite sure what they're at. I mean we regulate things better at home. But there it is—I've been posted here. And there's no transport back.

Something like this lies behind all I write.

*

This total difference between the written and the writing world is what non-writers never realize about us. They see us as we were; we live with what we are. It is not subjects that matter to writers; but the experience of handling them. In those romantic terms, a difficult pitch scaled, a storm survived, the untrodden moon beneath one's feet. Such pleasures are unholy; and the world in general does right to regard us with malice and suspicion.

*

I loathe the day a manuscript is sent to the publisher, because on that day the people one has loved die; they become what they are—petrified, fossil organisms for others to study and collect. I get asked what I meant by this and by that. But what I wrote is what I meant. If it wasn't clear in the book, it shouldn't be clear now.

I find Americans especially, the kind people who write and ask questions, have a strangely pragmatic view of what books are. Perhaps because of the miserable heresy that creative writing can be taught ("creative" is here a euphemism for "imitative") they seem to believe that a writer always knows exactly what he's doing. Obscure books, for them, are a kind of crossword puzzle. Somewhere, they feel, in some number of a paper they missed, all the answers have been given to all the clues.

They believe, in short, that a book is like a machine; that if you have the knack, you can take it to bits.

*

Ordinary readers can hardly be blamed for thinking like this. Both academic criticism and weekly reviewing have in the last forty years grown dangerously scientific, or pseudoscientific, in their general tenor. Analysis and categorization are indispensable scientific tools *in the scientific field;* but the novel, like the poem, is only partly a scientific field. No one wants a return to the kind of bellelettrist and onanistic accounts of new books that were fashionable in the early years of the century; but we could do with something better than what we have got.

I am an interested party? I confess it. Ever since I began writing *The French Lieutenant's Woman* I've been reading obituaries of the novel; a particularly gloomy one came from Gore Vidal in the December 1967 issue of *Encounter.* And I have been watching novel-reviewing in England become this last year increasingly impatient and dismissive. Any moment now I expect

one of our fashionable newspapers to decide to drop their *New
Novels* column for good and give the released space over to television or pop music. Of course I am interested—but, like Mr.
Vidal, I can hardly be personally resentful. If the novel is dead,
the corpse still remains oddly fertile. We are told no one reads
novels any more; so the authors of *Julian* and *The Collector*
must be grateful to the two million ghosts or more who have
bought copies of their respective books. But I don't want to be
sarcastic. More is at issue here than self-interest.

One has the choice of two views: either that the novel, along
with printed-word culture in general, is moribund or that there
is something sadly shallow and blinded in our age. I know which
view I hold; and the people who astound me are the ones who
are sure that the first view is true. If you want omniscience, you
have it there; and it ought to worry you, you the reader who is
neither critic nor writer, that this omniscient contempt for print is
found so widely among people who make a living out of literary
dissection. Surgery is what we want, not dissection. It is not only
the extirpation of the mind that kills the body; the heart will do
the trick just as well.

*

October 27th, 1967. I finished the first draft, which was begun on
January 25th. It is about 140,000 words long, and exactly as I
imagined it: perfect, flawless, a lovely novel. But that, alas, is
indeed only how I imagine it. When I re-read it I see 140,000
things need to be changed; then it will, perhaps, be less imperfect. But I haven't the energy; the dreaded research now, the
interminable sentence-picking. I want to get on with another
book. I had a strange image last night . . .

VANCE BOURJAILY

Confessions of a Spent Youth

A Certain Kind of Work

THERE ARE VARIOUS images offered for what it is like to write a novel. It is like childbirth, like an affair, like fighting an angel, like plotting the destruction of the world.

While I should be glad to have you think of me as engaged in a mysterious act of pain, sex, struggle and sedition, I see no real signs of it looking around my studio. It's a mess all right, but without blood, sperm, bombs or broken furniture.

Images have their uses in my trade, but for explanation I prefer simple-mindedness: writing is a certain kind of work.

I am talking only about the writing itself, the process, not its result in publication and sales and manner of acceptance (nor the result of that, which is how we live and behave, having become writers).

There'd be some pretty sour stuff if I got into any of those areas, no fun to read and no fun to write.

But for the process, I have respect and affection; sometimes, these days, a little fear, a little weariness; often, still, a good deal of zest; now and then a moment of genuine awe.

It is these feelings which make me want to present writing a book quite plainly as a certain kind of work, more of which went into my fourth novel, *Confessions of a Spent Youth*, than into any of the others.

It took longer, its technical problems were more perplexing, its examination of emotion more exacting; and there was, though I don't know that anyone but me has ever seen it, experiment involved.

If an experiment succeeds, something new has been done. Megalo as the next man, I'm going to claim it has.

2.

Writing is, of course, brain work, but there is something that feels to me like physiological involvement, too, quite distinct from the mild effort of sitting at a machine, courting eyestrain, and watching the awkward play of the two index fingers trying to cover a ten-finger keyboard.

The way it feels is this: there is, first, always a kind of contracting and relaxing movement going on in the front part of my head just behind the forehead as I write. It even seems to tire up there, with too much contraction, which can cut short a day's work.

If it sounds preposterous for me to maintain that I can feel the movement of thought in my skull, wait till you hear the rest of it: I think it goes together with signals for movement to other organs, glands and muscles, and that there is likely to be a feeling of predominance by one of these others connected with each book one writes.

Let me illustrate the kind of signal I mean: bring to mind a song, say, "I'm in the Mood for Love." Stop, and remember how it goes. The point is, where did you remember it? With what part of your body? I suggest that it was in your throat, that there was actual sensation there, because you were remembering vocally, singing to yourself. Now think of a big orchestral passage, strings in a big extended harmony with tympani pounding and brass going counter—isn't the feeling of recollection now in behind your ears? Aural recollection feels, too.

These two kinds of recall are a constant part of the writing process. Sentences are formed, either concurrently with the writing or gathered unconsciously from a night's dreams and a morning's waking. Then they are recalled or collected vocally at the machine; we speak them to ourselves soundlessly as we write them, a kind of interior dictation. And almost instantly, reading back from the page, we listen to them again, hearing them now, to see if the sound matches an aural recall of what we meant them to be.

There is yet another part to this physiology of writing which I'm proposing which has to do with where the sentences—and the scenes, characters and ideas—come from. It is in this area that I feel the dominance of one or another part of the body over each of my books.

My first novel, *The End of My Life*, for example, seems to me to have been written chiefly by ear, aural recollection reaching out as well as in. I heard that book at the age of twenty-five, twenty years ago, the ear picking up and putting together rhythms and resonances that other men (Hemingway and Fitzgerald, mostly) had left around in the air of the century. There is a particular spirit in which each book is written, too, and it seems to me to have been a spirit that I started with each time, and that it somehow determined which part of the body I'd be working from.

Again, taking up the first book, the spirit was one of perfect, naive faith in me and my talent, probably about the same kind of faith a pretty, silly girl has in what her looks can do for her. In that spirit I really could sit there, a dumb, happy kid, listen to my book and take it down, without ever wondering where the transmission came from.

Then I wrote a second book, which was not published. I lost the sonofabitch, somewhere between a good enough first draft and revisions which got worse and worse. It seems to me, looking back, a negative demonstration of what I am trying to describe as physiological focus and dominant spirit; by the time I was done I was simply dispirited, and I was writing only with my fingers.

The third novel I wrote—the second published—was called *The Hound of Earth*. The spirit in which it was written was desperation. It has enough vitality to stay in print, most likely, because of the energy that fear put into me, fear of failure, not just of a book but of a life. I think the physiological focus was glandular, an adrenal response to my situation, dark, painful, almost involuntary spurts so that the work went very fast, almost frighteningly fast.

The Violated, my third and longest novel, seems to me to have been a work of the muscles—shoulders, back, arms and legs. This may be partly because of its length, and the great stretches of hours I spent at it. Sitting at a machine requires endurance if you go on past the eighth, ninth, tenth hours, and on *The Violated* I frequently did. But apart from the hours, I have the feeling of the whole system of muscles working away at it, building and lifting and arranging—that sounds as if I'm moving towards metaphor, I know, but in my own mind I'm not. I feel that I made the big pieces of that big book and heaved them into place, and was enabled to work that way because the dominant spirit now was a feeling that I knew what I was doing and had the strength for the job. I got up and down a lot, did knee bends and push-ups, and sometimes typed standing. I would have liked an electric typewriter with each key the size of a saucer and padded, mounted vertically on the wall. I could set the pressure required to make each of those keys connect, and could punch them, lean into them, kick them, or, letting off, whirl at them in a kind of dance. I remember myself there in a bare room, alone with my growing pile of manuscript, grinning and exhilarated much of the time.

Naive energy, nervous energy, physical energy. There was yet another kind, I learned while I wrote *Confessions.* Cerebral energy and a spirit of discovery. It was the first book I wrote by means of thought, and it felt as if my whole, not particularly outstanding brain, was involved, rather than just the anterior lobes and the signaling apparatus.

And let me bring this up to date before I go on with my preface: I think I carried the spirit and the focus of *Confessions* into a book about hunting, *The Unnatural Enemy,* which means to be Thoreauvian. The latest novel, *The Man Who Knew Kennedy,* is inevitably an emotional book. It begins with the assassination, and there is a lot of open feeling in it. When one feels, one speaks; the fifth novel seems to me as much a spoken book as the first was a heard book.

In the novel I am presently working on, no particular physiological focus has established itself yet, and I suspect that the work will go slowly until it does. It may be one of those I seem to have used before, or a combination, or something new.

3.

These next paragraphs are going to have to be somewhat defensive. I've got to establish that there is some sort of interest in having me say any more about *Confessions of a Spent Youth* than it says for itself. An author taking his own work seriously in public, if no one else takes it so, is either pathetic or pompous but certainly ridiculous.

The thought of being ridiculous is a pretty strong inhibiting factor among us preface writers.

I've got to explain that, except for the latest, none of my books has been immediately successful. This gets over into that sour area I wanted to avoid, but I'll get out again as quick as I can. Eventual success in American writing careers is a big bore. About all you can do with it is tell yourself—I favor a W. C. Fields, interior voice for this—"Well, boy. Books a little ahead of their time, are they?" And start looking for a teaching job.

Enough of that. What I started to say is that a particular difficulty of eventual success is that it's never clear when it begins or what it really amounts to. In a big country, the difference between isolated voices and a chorus, spread out over a little time, is imperceptible.

I could quote four or five strongly affirmative recent critical remarks; there's no way of my knowing, unless I made a much more deliberate and systematic study than the matter is worth, whether these should be taken as a statistical sample or a bunch of nuts. Naturally, I prefer to take them as the former and to reassure myself that the book has people going for it.

Think of me as addressing these nuts, or this sample, seriously in writing this preface. Listen in or not, as you will, and if you will, thank you. And if you won't—to quote from one of Henry James' prefaces, the model for us all—up yours, buddy. I've been at this novel-writing just about long enough not to care.

4.

The material of fiction is experience. I can count four kinds.

They are obvious enough, but I need to note them in order to be able to describe what I wish to call my experiment.

The four kinds of experience are: recollected, fantasized, invented, learned.

Learned experience is what we hear about from others, or get from research, and try to fit to our characters. It happened historically.

Invented experience is what we imagine for our characters with no reference to similar events in our own lives. It could happen.

Fantasized experience does start with an actual event but, for our characters, we give it a different outcome. It might well have happened, given a change or two of factors.

Recollected experience sounds simplest: it happened personally. For my first 310,000 words of fiction—three published novels and one not published—I managed to avoid it.

It is part of the style of a writer, I told myself, once I had realized this, that he favors one or two of these kinds of experience, and very few of us use them all with equal facility.

I couldn't tell myself that for long. If I was avoiding recollection in writing, I was nevertheless using—perhaps wasting—it freely enough in anecdotal conversation ("I'll never forget the time that . . ."). Whatever the reasons of inhibition, or being unable to trust life to be interesting, or wanting to protect people's privacy, I thought I had better get myself over that.

But I didn't begin by thinking that, because I didn't think of the first piece of what was to become *Confessions of a Spent Youth* as fiction; I thought of it as an article.

In 1952, John W. Aldridge and I were getting together material for the first issue of a new-writing periodical called *discovery*. We had a dozen stories we liked, and enough poetry, but only one piece of nonfiction. We felt we should have two, to indicate the balance of content we favored.

I said I would write the second myself, a sort of mock confession piece, in which I'd offer as accurate a recollection as I could of a series of experiences with marijuana. That it was mild, and less destructive physically than alcohol, was not a matter of general knowledge then. My real experience could be compared with the horror stories and exaggerations about the drug which circulated, both in and out of print, a good deal more gaudily then than now.

It may be hard to realize, fifteen years later, when almost anyone who is curious about marijuana has tried it without fear except of arrest, that it had nearly the same monstrous character in the public mind of 1952 as heroin or cocaine.

To be truthful, I had not in 1952 read Thomas DeQuincey's *Confessions of an English Opium Eater* except in excerpts, but it seemed to me that the ironic point I wanted to make could be started in a title, "Confessions of an American Marijuana Smoker." And I needed a pseudonym, because that would be a further irony—to present the material as if there were someone writing who needed to conceal his identity, when actually all I wanted to conceal was that I was using our new magazine to publish a piece of my own stuff.

U. S. D. 'Quincey, O.K.

It took seven years before I found out against whom the irony of my piece, its title and the pseudonym were directed. Among the literary and journalistic misrepresentations of marijuana and its effects which I was kidding was one in particular that I knew quite thoroughly, though something kept it from coming immediately to mind. It was the marijuana scene from my own first novel, *The End of My Life.*

However well the scene fits the novel's purposes, it was not drawn from my own experience. It came from books, hearsay and imagination. Experience, if I had let myself use it, rather contradicted the scene.

Like citizens of any culture, we have our myths—believe and tend not to reexamine them. Today they are revealed and repeated in the set pieces of realistic fiction and the movies: How a Gangster Dies, What Happens at a Party, How Flirts Operate, The Dialogue Tone of a Bad Marriage, Businessmen are Corrupt. . . .

More often than I like to remember, when I began writing fiction, I would forget to compare what I knew from life with the cultural assumptions based on these myths.

Confessions, when I finally decided to write it, and that it would be a novel, makes quite a few of the comparisons overtly, and many more implicitly.

For example: Chapter One, of Section Four, takes as its topic whores and whoring. Now the mythic whore is either Fat and Goodhearted, or Diseased and Vindictive, or A Captive with a Child's Mind. But the ones I remembered and put in my chapter were a New England smallbusiness woman, a sad South African of a certain gentility, a merry Japanese girl and several others.

And the experience of whoring was not a single experience, but quite various—I tried to make some distinctions, as in an episode which begins, "Whoring alone is like drinking alone. The companionable whorer commits a social act, the solitary whorer a compulsive one."

And again, a more complicated example: too often, in a writer's autobiographical novel, the youth is a young writer with special sensibilities. But my youth wasn't a writer yet—like many others, out spending, he thought he might be. It doesn't seem to me that anybody is a writer until he is really writing, most of the time and for publication (as: we all take music lessons, but when is it correct to start calling oneself a musician?). So I decided it would be most accurate to omit my boy's fitful composition of seven-line sonnets and half-act plays, since many of his friends were doing the same sort of thing. When it becomes necessary in the book for the author to describe what his young protagonist has turned into, it seems to me accurate to say: "I am . . . an established man . . . even somewhat prominent, in an inconspicuous field which [the boy] and I both value."

5.

But in the early fifties, I was a long way away from seeing any of what I've been discussing, and just past the middle of the decade I seem to have decided to write a second autobiographical piece. U. S. D. Quincy—I dropped the *e*, now, Americanizing—was on hand. Eventually he became Quince, in my mind, a half-rhyme for Vance; the pseudonym was now a character.

In the new piece I was taking out after the myth—admittedly not one of the most common ones—that there is something instinctual about religious feeling, and once again I subverted myself a title from literature: "Varieties of Irreligious Experience."

It was published in *Esquire,* and there were now two Quince Quincy pieces extant.

6.

All the stories I have ever written and liked have either been conceived as, or become, parts of novels. This, by the way, is poor strategy for the American writer; it gets you left out of, shucks, anthologies.

I wrote "The Poozle Dreamers" third.

Here is something odd about that. I had my teaching job, by then, at the University of Iowa. It was 1958. And even though I'd published three books, and was 36, I found myself quite capable of feeling competitive with one or two of my students. There were a couple (Tom Williams and Jim Buechler) who were such good writers, and such good short story writers in particular, that I had to acknowledge myself unskilled in that form.

The sense of competition with another writer centers on a particular piece of work, not on the immeasurable quality called talent, and is interior. I wrote "The Poozle Dreamers" to show myself (not Tom and Jim) that I could handle the short story form perhaps as well as Tom had in one story and Jim in another. And for a third time found myself wanting to use Quincy.

Liked what I did, and may even have thought, "There, by God. There's one for the anthologies." But if I thought that, I knew at the same time that I had a book going because I had started programmatically now, not just on occasion, on the comparison of novelists' set-pieces with life experience. I'd picked the most evident of the cliché scenes—sexual initiation—and was trying to expose it through comparison with an actual initiation. In the tenth paragraph I said openly that this was what I meant to do.

So I had three chapters for an autobiographical novel (they would eventually be two, eight and ten). I didn't know yet where and how they'd fit. What I did know was that the book would be one of correction, would be a fictional critique of fiction (as *Don Quixote* is), taking as its most frequent example—since it would cover the same ground; the war; the middle east—my own first novel. I did not mean to repudiate *The End of My Life*, but rather to see the same kind of experience, which it dealt with romantically, with tough, early-middle-aged clarity. This was one element of experiment.

What I needed now was an idea for structure.

7.

Structure in a novel comes from how you decide to handle time.

It also comes, more obviously but less crucially, from how you decide to organize episodes internally and relate them to one another. It was already evident that *Confessions* would be the kind of book in which each chapter runs on its own power, with its own start and stop. What I decided to do—probably not all at once—was to organize the book topically. This is the way of the essay, but it is also often the way of conversation. I would say all I knew in one chapter, already cited, about whores, and in another about adolescent drunks, and in another about origins, and so on.

These things would overlap, of course, but this was to be a novel, not a collection of autobiographical essays illustrated by narrative passages; that was merely its form. The structural decision was that each topic taken up could start wherever it began in Quince's life, but that within each section, each chapter should end by advancing the life past the point of the close of the preceding chapter. Each section must follow the same rule, beginning wherever its first concern began, but advancing past the closing point of the section preceding.

These decisions on form and structure—and material—would, I hoped, give the novel a strong, basic veracity, which is intended to be the essential characteristic of the work. The material was to be unaltered recall, nothing else.

A novel of veracity is not a work either of realism or naturalism in my mind, but something new. I do not mean that it has no antecedents. Robert Graves' *Goodbye to All That* is one, and Henry Miller's work certainly another. Isherwood's *Berlin Stories* were in my mind at times, and so was the fiction of recall developed by *The New Yorker* (which used some parts of *Confessions*).

But I believed, and believe, that I was adding weight, order, and a more total candor to these models, through posing experience against literary assumption, and through finding a form with which to make the confrontation constant and specific, if not always overt. It is on this my claim of innovation rests; make of it what you will.

8.

Three separated chapters of a novel is more outline than I generally work with. Once I knew where the three might fit, and what further topics I wanted to cover, the rest of the book became a matter of remembering, analysing, exposing, assigning, evaluating, trying to understand. And writing. A lot of this was done in South America, for which I left with my family in 1959, returning home in 1960.

I will not try to tell the whole story of that dumb year. In summary, my wife and I in our late thirties started off with two young children to take the sort of adventurous trip suited to a vigorous couple, without kids, in their middle twenties. We didn't have the resiliency, we didn't have the money, and that old phrase, "hostages to fortune," so well described the children I had gaily brought along that it haunted me everywhere we went.

I could not have felt more distracted or more pressed than I did the morning in Santiago, Chile, when I finished the chapter called "The Fractional Man." We were living in a white-collar slum apartment, at street level on a shabby-elegant street called Avenida Brazil. There was heat in part of it, but in the little front room in which I had my typewriter, I had to put my hands in my pockets from time to time to warm them up.

I was reluctant to change my working place because of the opportunity that might come to shoot: I kept my nine-year-old daughter's BB gun, which we had bought in Uruguay, on the table with my writing things, and sat facing the street, under the window, with the window open eight inches.

The idea was to catch a moment when none of the decayed Chilean gentlewomen who shared the neighborhood was looking, and shoot a street pigeon out the window for supper.

Evidence I could see of our folly: a lovely Jaguar car, British racing green, sitting in front, out of gas with one tire flat. It was worth thousands of black market dollars, but could not legally be sold.

I thought of shooting a BB at it. I also thought that maybe I should shave, and find a clean shirt, and go out to see the Chileans I knew, one by one, looking for a connection to make the illegal car sale, which many had told me could perhaps be done.

Instead, I did my certain kind of work: I wrote. I started by rereading yesterday's paragraphs of "The Fractional Man." I had Quince sitting with his great aunt in an exotic place, now, ready to say goodbye. I knew, because I was using recalled material only, what he had done in response to the situation.

I analysed why, and tried to analyse why the old aunt had behaved as she behaved as well. I wrote a few lines of narrative and analysis (you can follow this in the final seven paragraphs of that chapter, if it seems worth while). Then I began to expose. I did this, since there was no particular literary model to contradict this time by describing the ending in two ways: the way in which Quince has ended the story before, telling it as an anecdote. And in terms of how that anecdotal ending has contained certain lies. And then I read back, feeling the lines vocally, listened to them, thought about the lies to be sure I was telling the truth about them, noted that this would give me a reference all the way back to the opening of the book, and wrote another half dozen words.

A pigeon came into BB range just then, chesty and grazing dung, but he was perfectly safe as long as I stayed in midsentence. The thought for how to end it was completing itself in my mind; my hands weren't moving yet. The words for the thought neither spoke nor sounded; they were projected and seen with some kind of inverted eye, in rear of head center, as on a screen. The focus on the screen clarified, and I could transfer the line vocally now, and then to my fingers. The pigeon, as I looked up, was nearly gone from my line of sight, but I cared no more for shooting him than I did for selling the car now—not with that sentence right and the next one forming.

And soon it was all inseparable, hands going fast, and I was excited—losing my consciousness of pressure, along with car and pigeon, in precisely the same way as in the perfectly common experience of losing oneself while reading.

And that is what the work of writing is really like.

I have no idea how long the paragraph took me to do, but I remember having no question in my mind about what I'd done being good, being right.

That piece, which I wrote to write us out of a most dismal corner, because it was all I knew how to do (but, stubbornly, as part of my book, too) was the first of those that sold to *The New Yorker*.

9.

For me the opening and closing chapters of a novel are likely to be the final things written in the first draft. It was this way with *Confessions.* The first chapter, an announcement, had to wait until I knew what I had to announce.

The last gathers up the narrative threads and makes, since our form is mock essay, the crucial statements of conclusion. About experience (for this is a novel of education) ". . . I was always a tourist in the worlds of your world, and never found the one in which I could belong until I learned to make my own."

There is, and I cannot be displeased with my impertinence, a comment on the preceding page on the synthetic, plot-induced affirmations of novelists as great as Joyce and Lawrence, in which it is a sign of Quince's health that, contradicting Molly Bloom, he is not yelling "yes"; he affirms by yelling "no."

And there is, too, the final questioning of veracity, the last line of the book: "Readers and doctors, my truths are real, unless, since dreams are, as you've told me, a form of memory, memory is no more finally than a form of dream."

Finally, just to complete the log, I had to rewrite the whole book from first to last; it was especially difficult to redo the earliest chapters, on religion and marijuana. But I had time, and was free of pressure by then, back once more at Iowa.

The University job, resumed, had seen me through the book, and has by now seen me through two more. I would feel mean if I overlooked the opportunity to say that I'm grateful, and I guess that's my answer to the people who ask funny questions about whether the academic life doesn't stifle writing. I shall be glad, if it comes, to be done with wage-earning, but nothing stifles writing if that is what you want to do, and the University stifles least of all.

10.

I'm not sure what to say about the prose in *Confessions of A Spent Youth.* One can never know what one's voice sounds like, nor how one's prose reads.

I know that I had a sort of ideal of prose for myself that I used to describe to my students (though I did not prescribe it for them) as being invisible. I felt that, in *The Violated,* I'd been trying to write prose like a pane of good glass, which would come as little as possible between the reader and the things seen. I'd thought it would be okay, in writing invisible prose, to start or close a sequence now and then with something ornamental. Even as I was earnestly telling my students how fine invisible prose could be, I was rewriting *Confessions* in prose which is really quite mannered.

I think I was trying to keep, by means of this, the distance, in the reader's mind, between the man who is telling the story and the youth who is living it.

The prose itself, then, might be a comment on the young man's prose of *The End of My Life*.

I should add, I guess, that the comparison of the two books cannot be made in terms of perfect parallels. Only occasionally, since I was using life and not inventing, is there a scene in *Confessions* which directly comments on a similar one in *The End of My Life*. Parallels between characters are easier to see: Skinner, of TEOML, is mostly Eddie, of *Confessions*—only rarely Quince. Freak is Richie Banks of *Confessions,* but is also a boy I knew and liked in college. Benny, of TEOML, is George Love, Christ Jennings, Stork and a man I used to play bridge with later in the army. Rod is O'Gorman, Hal and even, just a touch, Ben Hines. Cindy, I'm afraid, is Jeannie Childress.

The correspondences of characters in *Confessions* to real-life originals is one-to-one. In a novel of veracity, it has to be so. The correspondence in TEOML varies greatly, but almost all the characters in the earlier book, as you can see above, are composites.

I have no way of judging which are more credible fictional characters.

II.

For a man who has written six books and no prefaces, it is difficult to write a preface to one and not deal with them all.

Okay, what the hell:

It seems to me I have spent half a career trying to document and dramatize and, if I can, make art out of, an observation which is made directly in my second published novel. I wrote this in 1954, and it seems to me, in my search for pride, that now nearly everyone is saying it. I'll condense the passage quite a bit:

The United States of America has had a strange, foreshortened history. There were conventional enough amounts of time between discovery and colonization and assertion of independence, but then the cells of progress began to multiply too rapidly. Too many inventions, too much communication, too many resources, too much wealth, too much responsibility. And in consequence, the United States, within 175 years of its establishment, had already completed much of the cycle which, for great nations of the past, had spread out over six and seven centuries. In what ought to have been late childhood, it had run all the ages of national experience so rapidly that hardly any of the cultural achievement could hope to stick, no national characteristics could form without being destroyed a decade later. Having reached zenith as a prodigy, it must now, instead of enjoying the comforts and splendors of decline, finish its course as a place of curious unhappiness, history's first neurotic nation.

That condensation is about a fifth of the full argument, but it should be enough to show what is meant when a character says, "Crazy. That's where the road maps lead, Al. Crazy, population a hundred and eighty million."

In my first book I had written of something I called "prewar neurosis," an affliction of educated youth overprepared for the Second World War. In the third I wrote of interwoven, specimen lives, and of the terrible gap between adolescent promise and adult achievement in our country. In the fourth I tried to take a true, unaltered look at the specimen of American life I knew best. In the fifth I wrote of our unhappy relationship to nature and enjoyment. In the sixth, of the death of hope.

And in the seventh? I don't know exactly. And may be wrong, for that matter, as to what the others say.

All I know is that now has come the time of the sinister clowns in high office, of small and evil wars, the squandering of our resources for petty pride, the open abandonment of fine ideas. . . . I must get back to work.

It is late, fellow Romans, and we are not yet happy or wise.

NORMAN MAILER

The Deer Park

The Last Draft of *The Deer Park*

IN HIS REVIEW of *The Deer Park*, Malcolm Cowley said it must have been a more difficult book to write than *The Naked and The Dead*. He was right. Most of the time, I worked on *The Deer Park* in a low mood; my liver, which had gone bad in the Philippines, exacted a hard price for forcing the effort against the tide of a long depression, and matters were not improved when nobody at Rinehart & Co. liked the first draft of the novel. The second draft, which to me was the finished book, also gave little enthusiasm to the editors, and open woe to Stanley Rinehart, the publisher. I was impatient to leave for Mexico, now that I was done, but before I could go, Rinehart asked for a week in which to decide whether he wanted to do the book. Since he had already given me a contract which allowed him no option not to accept the novel (a common arrangement for writers whose sales are more or less large) any decision to reject the manuscript would cost him a sizable advance. (I learned later he had been hoping his lawyers would find the book obscene, but they did not, at least not then in May 1954.) So he had really no choice but to agree to put the book out in February, and gloomily he consented. To cheer him a bit, I agreed to his request that he delay paying me my advance until publication, although the first half was due on delivery of the manuscript. I thought the favor might improve our relations.

Now, if a few of you are wondering why I did not take my book back and go to another publishing house, the answer is that I was tired, I was badly tired. Only a few weeks before, a doctor had given me tests for the liver, and it had shown itself to be sick and depleted. I was hoping that a few months in Mexico would give me a chance to fill up again.

But the next months were not cheerful. *The Deer Park* had been done as well as I could do it, yet I thought it was probably a minor work, and I did not know if I had any real interest in starting another book. I made efforts of course; I collected notes, began to piece together a few ideas for a novel given to bullfighting, and another about a concentration camp; I wrote "David Reisman Reconsidered" during this time, and "The Homosexual Villain"; read most of the work of the other writers of my generation (I think I was looking for a level against which to measure my third novel) went over the galleys when they came, changed a line or two, sent them back. Keeping half busy I mended a bit, but it was a time of dull drifting. When we came back to New York in October, *The Deer Park* was already in page proof. By November, the first advertisement was given to *Publishers' Weekly*. Then, with less than ninety days to publication, Stanley Rinehart told me I would have to take out a small piece of the book—six not very explicit lines about the sex of an old producer and a call girl. The moment one was ready to consider losing those six lines they moved into the moral center of the novel. It would be no tonic for my liver to cut them out. But I also knew Rinehart was serious, and since I was still tired, it seemed a little unreal to try to keep the passage. Like a miser I had been storing energy to start a new book; I wanted nothing to distract me now. I gave in on a word or two, agreed to rewrite a line, and went home from that particular conference not very impressed with myself. The next morning I called up the editor in chief, Ted Amussen, to tell him I had decided the original words had to be put back.

"Well, fine," he said, "fine. I don't know why you agreed to anything in the first place."

A day later, Stanley Rinehart halted publication, stopped all ads (he was too late to catch the first run of *Publishers' Weekly* which was already on its way to England with a full page for *The Deer Park*) and broke his contract to do the book. I was started on a trip to find a new publisher, and before I was done, the book had gone to Random House, Knopf, Simon and Schuster, Harper's, Scribner's, and unofficially to Harcourt, Brace. Some day it would be fine to give the details, but for now little more than a few lines of dialogue and an editorial report:

Bennett Cerf: This novel will set publishing back twenty years.
Alfred Knopf to an editor: Is this your idea of the kind of book which should bear a Borzoi imprint?

The lawyer for one publishing house complimented me on the six lines, word for word, which had excited Rinehart to break his contract. This lawyer said, "It's admirable the way you get around the problem here." Then he brought out more than a hundred objections to other parts of the book. One was the line, "She was lovely. Her back was adorable in its contours." I was told that this ought to go because "The principals are not married, and so your description puts a favorable interpretation upon a meretricious relationship."

Hiram Hayden had lunch with me some time after Random House saw the book. He told me he was responsible for their decision not to do it, and if I did not agree with his taste, I had to admire his honesty—it is rare for an editor to tell a writer the truth. Hayden went on to say that the book never came alive for him even though he had been ready to welcome it. "I can tell you that I picked the book up with anticipation. Of course I had heard from Bill, and Bill had told me that he didn't like it, but I never pay attention to what one writer says about the work of another. . . ." Bill was William Styron, and Hayden was his editor. I had asked Styron to call Hayden the night I found out Rinehart had broken his contract. One reason for asking the favor of Styron was that he sent me a long letter about the novel after I had shown it to him in manuscript. He had written, "I don't like *The Deer Park,* but I admire sheer hell out of it." So I thought to impose on him.

Other parts of the account are not less dreary. The only generosity I found was from the late Jack Goodman. He sent me a photostat of his editorial report to Simon and Schuster and, because it was sympathetic, his report became the objective estimate of the situation for me. I assumed that the book when it came out would meet the kind of trouble Goodman expected, and so when I went back later to work on the page proofs I was not free of a fear or two. But that can be talked about in its place. Here is the core of his report.

> Mailer refuses to make any changes . . . [He] *will* consider suggestions, but reserves the right to make final decisions, so we must make our decision on what the book now is.
>
> That's not easy. It is full of vitality and power, as readable a novel as I've ever encountered. Mailer emerges as a sort of post-Kinsey F. Scott Fitzgerald. His dialogue is uninhibited and the sexuality of the book is completely interwoven with its purpose, which is to describe a segment of society whose morality is nonexistent. Locale is evidently Palm Springs. Chief characters are Charles Eitel, movie director who first defies the House Un-American Committee, then becomes a friendly witness, his mistress, a great movie star who is his ex-wife, her lover who is the narrator, the head of a great movie company, his son-in-law, a strange, tortured panderer who is Eitel's conscience and, assorted demimondaines, homosexuals, actors.
>
> My layman's opinion is that the novel will be banned in certain quarters and that it may very well be up for an obscenity charge, but this should of course be checked by our lawyers. It it were possible to recognize this at the start, to have a united front here and treat the whole issue positively and head-on, I would be for our publishing. But I am afraid such unanimity may be impossible of attainment and if so, we should reject, in spite of the fact that I am certain it will be one of the best-selling novels of the next couple of years. It is the work of a serious artist. . . .

The eighth house was G. P. Putnam's. I didn't want to give it to them, I was planning to go next to Viking, but Walter Minton kept saying, "Give us three days. We'll give you a decision in three days." So we sent it over to Putnam, and in three days they took it without conditions, and without a request for a single change. I had a victory, I had made my point, but in fact I was not very happy. I had grown so wild on my diet of polite letters from publishing houses who didn't want me, that I had been ready to collect rejections from twenty houses, publish *The Deer Park* at my own expense, and try to make a kind of publishing history. Instead I was thrown in with Walter Minton, who has since attracted some fame as the publisher of *Lolita*. He is the only publisher I ever met who would make a good general. Months after I came to Putnam, Minton told me, "I was ready to take *The Deer Park* without reading it. I knew your name would sell enough copies to pay your advance, and I figured one of these days you're going to write another book like *The Naked and The Dead*," which is the sort of sure hold of strategy you can have when you're not afraid of censorship.

Now I've tried to water this account with a minimum of tears, but taking *The Deer Park* into the nervous system of eight publishing houses was not so good for my own nervous system, nor was it good for getting to work on my new novel. In the ten weeks it took the book to travel the circuit from Rinehart to Putnam, I squandered the careful energy I had been hoarding for months; there was a hard comedy at how much of myself I would burn up in a few hours of hot telephone calls; I had never had any sense for practical affairs, but in those days, carrying *The Deer Park* from house to house, I stayed as close to it as a stage-struck mother pushing her child forward at every producer's office. I was amateur agent for it, messenger boy, editorial consultant, Machiavelli of the luncheon table, fool of the five o'clock drinks, I was learning the publishing business in a hurry, and I made a hundred mistakes and paid for each one by wasting a new bout of energy.

In a way there was sense to it. For the first time in years I was having the kind of experience which was likely to return some day as good work, and so I forced many little events past any practical return, even insulting a few publishers en route as if to discover the limits of each situation. I was trying to find a few new proportions to things, and I did learn a bit. But I'll never know what that novel about the concentration camp would have been like if I had gotten quietly to work when I came back to New York and *The Deer Park* had been published on time. It is possible I was not serious about the book, it is also possible I lost something good, but one way or the other, that novel disappeared in the excitement, as lost as "the little object" in *Barbary Shore,* and it has not stirred since.

The real confession is that I was making a few of my mental connections those days on marijuana. Like more than one or two of my generation, I had smoked it from time to time over the years, but it never had meant anything. In Mexico, however, down in my depression with a bad liver, pot gave me a sense of something new about the time I was convinced I had seen it all, and I liked it enough to take it now and again in New York.

Then *The Deer Park* began to go like a beggar from house to house and en route Stanley Rinehart made it clear he was going to try not to pay the advance. Until then I had had sympathy for him. I thought it had taken a kind of displaced courage to be able to drop the book the way he did. An expensive moral stand, and wasteful for me; but a moral stand. When it turned out that he did not like to bear the expense of being that moral, the experience turned ugly for me. It took many months and the service of my lawyer to get the money, but long before that, the situation had become real enough to drive a spike into my cast-iron mind. I realized in some bottom of myself that for years I had been the sort of comic figure I would have cooked to a turn in one of my books, a radical who had the nineteenth-century naïveté to believe that the people with whom he did business were 1) gentlemen, 2) fond of him, and 3) respectful of his ideas even if in disagreement with them. Now, I was in the act of learning that I was not adored so very much; that my ideas were seen as nasty; and that my fine America which I had been at pains to criticize for so many years was in fact a real country which did real things and ugly things to the characters of more people than just the characters of my books. If the years since the war had not been brave or noble in the history of the country, which I certainly thought and do think, why then did it come as surprise that people in publishing were not as good as they used to be, and that the day of Maxwell Perkins was a day which was gone, really gone, gone as Greta Garbo and Scott Fitzgerald? Not easy, one could argue, for an advertising man to admit that advertis-

ing is a dishonest occupation, and no easier was it for the working novelist to see that now were left only the cliques, fashions,
vogues, snobs, snots, and fools, not to mention a dozen bureauc-
racies of criticism; that there was no room for the old literary
idea of oneself as a major writer, a figure in the landscape. One
had become a set of relations and equations, most flourishing
when most incorporated, for then one's literary stock was ready
for merger. The day was gone when people held on to your
novels no matter what others might say. Instead one's good
young readers waited now for the verdict of professional young
men, academics who wolfed down a modern literature with an
anxiety to find your classification, your identity, your similarity,
your common theme, your corporate literary earnings, each reference to yourself as individual as a carloading of homogenized
words. The articles which would be written about you and a
dozen others would be done by minds which were expert on the
aggregate and so had senses too lumpy for the particular. There
was a limit to how much appraisal could be made of a work
before the critic exposed his lack of the critical faculty, and so it
was naturally wiser for the mind of the expert to masticate the
themes of ten writers rather than approach the difficulties of any
one.

I had begun to read my good American novels at the end of an
era—I could remember people who would talk wistfully about
the excitement with which they had gone to bookstores because it
was publication day for the second novel of Thomas Wolfe, and
in college, at a Faculty tea, I had listened for an hour to a
professor's wife who was so blessed as to have known John Dos
Passos. My adolescent crush on the profession of the writer had
been more lasting than I could have guessed. I had even been so
simple as to think that the kind of people who went into publishing were still most concerned with the few writers who made the
profession not empty of honor, and I had been taking myself
seriously, I had been thinking I was one of those writers.

Instead I caught it in the face and deserved it for not looking
at the evidence. I was out of fashion and that was the score; that
was all the score; the publishing habits of the past were going to
be of no help for my *Deer Park*. And so as the language of
sentiment would have it, something broke in me, but I do not

know if it was so much a loving heart, as a cyst of the weak, the unreal, and the needy, and I was finally open to my anger. I turned within my psyche I can almost believe, for I felt something shift to murder in me. I finally had the simple sense to understand that if I wanted my work to travel further than others, the life of my talent depended on fighting a little more, and looking for help a little less. But I deny the sequence in putting it this way, for it took me years to come to this fine point. All I felt then was that I was an outlaw, a psychic outlaw, and I liked it, I liked it a good night better than trying to be a gentleman, and with a set of emotions accelerating one on the other, I mined down deep into the murderous message of marijuana, the smoke of the assassins, and for the first time in my life I knew what it was to make your kicks.

I could write about that here, but it would be a mistake. Let the experience stay where it is, and on a given year it may be found again in a novel. For now it is enough to say that marijuana opens the senses and weakens the mind. In the end, you pay for what you get. If you get something big, the cost will equal it. There is a moral economy to one's vice, but you learn that last of all. I still had the thought it was possible to find something which cost nothing. Thus, *The Deer Park* resting at Putnam, and new good friends found in Harlem, I was off on that happy ride where you discover a new duchy of jazz every night and the drought of the past is given a rain of new sound. What has been dull and dead in your years is now tart to the taste, and there is sweet in the illusion of how fast you can change. To keep up with it all, I began to log a journal, a wild set of thoughts and outlines for huge projects—I wrote one hundred thousand words in eight weeks, more than once twenty pages a day in a style which came willy-nilly from the cramp of the past, a lockstep jargon of sociology and psychology that sours my teeth when I look at those pages today. Yet this journal has the start of more ideas than I will have again; ideas which came so fast and so rich that sometimes I think my brain was dulled by the heat of their passage. (With all proportions kept, one can say that cocaine may have worked a similar good and ill upon Freud.)

The journal wore down by February, about the time *The Deer*

Park had once been scheduled to appear. By then I had decided
to change a few things in the novel, nothing in the way of lawyer's deletions, just a few touches for style. They were not happy
about this at Putnam. Minton argued that some interest in the
book would be lost if the text were not identical to Rinehart's
page proofs, and Ted Purdy, my editor, told me more than once
that they liked the book "just the way it is." Besides, there was
thought of bringing it out in June as a summer book.

Well, I wanted to take a look. After all, I had been learning
new lessons. I began to go over the page proofs, and the book
read as if it had been written by someone else. I was changed
from the writer who had labored on that novel, enough to be
able to see it without anger or vanity or the itch to justify myself.
Now, after three years of living with the book, I could at last
admit the style was wrong, that it had been wrong from the time
I started, that I had been strangling the life of my novel in a
poetic prose which was too self-consciously attractive and formal,
false to the life of my characters, especially false to the life of my
narrator who was the voice of my novel and so gave the story its
air. He had been a lieutenant in the Air Force, he had been cool
enough and hard enough to work his way up from an orphan
asylum, and to allow him to write in a style which at its best
sounded like Nick Carraway in *The Great Gatsby* must of course
blur his character and leave the book unreal. Nick was legitimate, out of fair family, the Midwest and Princeton—he would
write as he did, his style was himself. But the style of Sergius
O'Shaugnessy, no matter how good it became (and the Rinehart
Deer Park had its moments) was a style which came out of nothing so much as my determination to prove I could muster a fine
style.

If I wanted to improve my novel, yet keep the style, I would
have to make my narrator fit the prose, change his past, make
him an onlooker, a rich pretty boy brought up let us say by two
old-maid aunts, able to have an affair with a movie star only by
luck and/or the needs of the plot, which would give me a book
less distracting, well written but minor. If, however, I wanted to
keep that first narrator, my orphan, flier, adventurer, *germ*—for
three years he had been the frozen germ of some new theme—
well, to keep him I would need to change the style from the

inside of each sentence. I could keep the structure of my book, I thought—it had been put together for such a narrator—but the style could not escape. Probably I did not see it all so clearly as I now suggest. I believe I started with the conscious thought that I would tinker just a little, try to patch a compromise, but the navigator of my unconscious must already have made the choice, because it came as no real surprise that after a few days of changing a few words I moved more and more quickly toward the eye of the problem, and in two or three weeks I was tied to the work of doing a new *Deer Park*. The book was edited in a way no editor could ever have time or love to find; it was searched sentence by sentence, word for word, the style of the work lost its polish, became rough, and I can say real, because there was an abrupt and muscular body back of the voice now. It had been there all the time, trapped in the porcelain of a false style, but now as I chipped away, the work for a time became exhilarating in its clarity—I never enjoyed work so much—I felt as if finally I was learning how to write, learning the joints of language and the touch of a word, felt as if I came close to the meanings of sound and could say which of two close words was more female or more forward. I even had a glimpse of what Flaubert might have felt, for as I went on tuning the book, often five or six words would pile above one another in the margin at some small crisis of choice. (Since the Rinehart page proof was the usable copy, I had little space to write between the lines.) As I worked in this fine mood, I kept sending pages to the typist, yet so soon as I had exhausted the old galley pages, I could not keep away from the new typewritten copy—it would be close to say the book had come alive, and was invading my brain.

Soon the early pleasure of the work turned restless; the consequences of what I was doing were beginning to seep into my stamina. It was as if I were the captive of an illness whose first symptoms had been excitement, prodigies of quick work, and a confidence that one could go on forever, but that I was by now close to a second stage where what had been quick would be more like fever, a first wind of fatigue upon me, a knowledge that at the end of the drunken night a junkie cold was waiting. I was going to move at a pace deadly to myself, loading and overloading whatever little centers of the mind are forced to make the hard decisions. In ripping up the silk of the original syntax, I was tearing into any number of careful habits as well as whatever subtle fleshing of the nerves and the chemicals had gone to support them.

For six years I had been writing novels in the first person; it was the only way I could begin a book, even though the third person was more to my taste. Worse, I seemed unable to create a narrator in the first person who was not overdelicate, oversensitive, and painfully tender, which was an odd portrait to give, because I was not delicate, not physically; when it was a matter of strength I had as much as the next man. In those days I would spend time reminding myself that I had been a bit of an athlete (house football at Harvard, years of skiing) that I had not quit in combat, and once when a gang broke up a party in my loft, I had taken two cracks on the head with a hammer and had still been able to fight. Yet the first person seemed to paralyze me, as if I had a horror of creating a voice which could be in any way bigger than myself. So I had become mired in a false style for every narrator I tried. If now I had been in a fight, had found out that no matter how weak I could be in certain ways, I was also steady enough to hang on to six important lines, that may have given me new respect for myself, I don't know, but for the first time I was able to use the first person in a way where I could suggest some of the stubbornness and belligerence I also might have, I was able to color the empty reality of that first person with some real feeling of how I had always felt, which was to be outside, for Brooklyn where I grew up is not the center of anything. I was able, then, to create an adventurer whom I believed in, and as he came alive for me, the other parts of the book which had been stagnant for a year and more also came to life, and new things began to happen to Eitel my director and to Elena his mistress and their characters changed. It was a phenomenon. I learned how real a novel is. Before, the story of Eitel had been told by O'Shaugnessy of the weak voice; now by a confident young man: when the new narrator would remark that Eitel was his best friend and so he tried not to find Elena too attractive, the man and woman he was talking about were larger than they had once been. I was no longer telling of two nice people who fail at love because the world is too large and too cruel for them; the new O'Shaugnessy had moved me by degrees to the more painful story of two people who are strong as well as weak, corrupt as much as pure, and fail to grow despite their bravery in a poor world, because they are finally not brave enough, and so do more damage to one another than to the unjust world outside them. Which for me was exciting, for here and there *The Deer Park* now had the rare tenderness of tragedy. The most powerful leverage in fiction comes from point of view, and giving O'Shaugnessy courage gave passion to the others.

But the punishment was commencing for me. I was now creating a man who was braver and stronger than me, and the more my new style succeeded, the more was I writing an implicit portrait of myself as well. There is a shame about advertising yourself that way, a shame which became so strong that it was a psychological violation to go on. Yet I could not afford the time to digest the self-criticisms backing up in me, I was forced to drive myself, and so more and more I worked by tricks, taking marijuana the night before and then drugging myself into sleep with an overload of Seconal. In the morning I would be lithe with new perception, could read new words into the words I had already, and so could go on in the pace of my work, the most scrupulous part of my brain too sluggish to interfere. My powers of logic became weaker each day, but the book had its own logic, and so I did not need close reason. What I wanted and what the drugs gave me was the quick flesh of associations, and there I was often oversensitive, could discover new experience in the lines of my text like a hermit savoring the revelation of Scripture; I saw so much in some sentences that more than once I dropped into the pit of the amateur: since I was receiving such emotion from my words, I assumed everyone else would be stimulated as well, and on many a line I twisted the phrase in such a way that it could read well only when read slowly, about as slowly as it would take for an actor to read it aloud. Once you write that way, the quick reader (who is nearly all your audience) will stumble and fall against the vocal shifts of your prose. Then you had best have the cartel of a Hemingway, because in such a case it is critical whether the reader thinks it is your fault, or is so in awe of your reputation that he returns on the words, throttles his pace, and tries to discover why he is so stupid as not to swing on the off-bop of your style.

An example: in the Rinehart *Deer Park* I had this:

"They make Sugar sound so good in the newspapers," she declared one night to some people in a bar, "that I'll really try him. I really will, Sugar." And she gave me a sisterly kiss.

I happened to change that very little, I put in "said" instead of "declared" and later added "older sister," so that it now read:

And she gave me a sisterly kiss. Older sister.

Just two words, but I felt as if I had revealed some divine law of nature, had laid down an invaluable clue—the kiss of an older sister was a worldly universe away from the kiss of a younger sister—and I thought to give myself the Nobel Prize for having brought such illumination and *division* to the cliché of the sisterly kiss.

Well, as an addition it wasn't bad fun, and for two words it did a bit to give a sense of what was working back and forth between Sergius and Lulu, it was another small example of Sergius' hard eye for the world, and his cool sense of his place in it, and all this was to the good, or would have been for a reader who went slowly, and stopped, and thought. But if anyone was in a hurry, the little sentence "Older sister" was like a finger in the eye, it jabbed the unconscious, and gave an uncomfortable nip of rhythm to the mind.

I had five hundred changes of this kind. I started with the first paragraph of the book, on the third sentence which pokes the reader with its backed-up rhythm, "Some time ago," and I did that with intent, to slow my readers from the start, like a fighter who throws his right two seconds after the bell and so gives the other man no chance to decide on the pace.

There was a real question, however, whether I could slow the reader down, and so as I worked on further, at some point beginning to write paragraphs and pages to add to the new Putnam galleys, the attrition of the drugs and the possibility of failure began to depress me, and Benzedrine entered the balance, and I was on the way to wearing badly. Because, determined or no that they would read me slowly, praying my readers would read me slowly, there was no likelihood they would do anything of the sort if the reviews were bad. As I started to worry this it grew worse, because I knew in advance that three or four of my major reviews had to be bad—*Time* magazine for one, because Max Gissen was the book review editor, and I had insulted him in public once by suggesting that the kind of man who worked for a mind so exquisitely and subtly totalitarian as Henry Luce was not likely to have any ideas of his own. The New York Daily *Times* would be bad because Orville Prescott was well known for his distaste of books too forthrightly sexual; and *Saturday Review* would be bad. That is, they would probably be bad; the mentality of their reviewers would not be above the level of their dean of reviewers, Mr. Maxwell Geismar, and Geismar didn't seem to know that my second novel was titled *Barbary Shore* rather than *Barbary Coast*. I could spin this out, but what is more to the point is that I had begun to think of the reviews before finishing the book, and this doubtful occupation came out of the kind of inner knowledge I had of myself in those days. I knew what was good for my energy and what was poor, and so I knew that for the vitality of my work in the future, and yes even the quantity of my work, I needed a success and I needed it badly if I was to shed the fatigue I had been carrying since *Barbary Shore*. Some writers receive not enough attention for years, and so learn early to accommodate the habits of their work to little recognition. I think I could have done that when I was twenty-five. With *The Naked and The Dead* a new life had begun, however; as I have written earlier in this book, I had gone through the psychic labor of changing a good many modest habits in order to let me live a little more happily as a man with a name which could arouse quick reactions in strangers. If that started as an overlarge work, because I started as a decent but scared boy, well I had come to live with the new life, I had learned to like success—in fact I had probably come to depend on it, or at least my new habits did.

When *Barbary Shore* was ambushed in the alley, the damage to my nervous system was slow but thorough. My status dropped immediately—America is a quick country—but my ego did not permit me to understand that, and I went through tiring years of subtle social defeats because I did not know that I was no longer as large to others as I had been. I was always overmatching myself. To put it crudely, I would think I was dropping people when they were dropping me. And of course my unconscious knew better. There was all the waste of ferocious if unheard discussion between the armies of ego and id; I would get up in the morning with less snap in me than I had taken to sleep. Six or seven years of breathing that literary air taught me a writer stayed alive in the circuits of such hatred only if he were unappreciated enough to be adored by a clique, or was so overbought by the public that he excited some defenseless nerve in the snob. I knew if *The Deer Park* was a powerful best seller (the magical figure had become one hundred thousand copies for me) that I would then have won. I would be the first serious writer of my generation to have a best seller twice, and so it would not matter what was said about the book. Half of publishing might call it cheap, dirty, sensational, second-rate, and so forth and so forth, but it would be weak rage and could not hurt, for the literary world suffers a spot of the national taint—a serious writer is certain to be considered major if he is also a best seller; in fact, most readers are never convinced of his value until his books do well. Steinbeck is better known than Dos Passos, John O'Hara is taken seriously by people who dismiss Farrell, and indeed it took three decades and a Nobel Prize before Faulkner was placed on a level with Hemingway. For that reason, it would have done no good if someone had told me at the time that the financial success of a writer with major talent was probably due more to what was meretricious in his work than what was central. The argument would have meant nothing to me—all I knew was that seven publishing houses had been willing to dismiss my future, and so if the book did poorly, a good many people were going to congratulate themselves on their foresight and be concerned with me even less. I could see that if I wanted to keep on writing the kind of book I liked to write, I needed the energy of new success, I needed blood. Through every bit of me, I knew *The Deer Park* had damn well better make it or I was close to some serious illness, a real apathy of the will.

Every now and again I would have the nightmare of wondering what would happen if all the reviews were bad, as bad as *Barbary Shore.* I would try to tell myself that could not happen, but I was not certain, and I knew that if the book received a unanimously bad press and still showed signs of selling well, it was likely to be brought up for prosecution as obscene. As a delayed convulsion from the McCarthy years, the fear of censorship was strong in publishing, in England it was critically bad, and so I also knew that the book could lose such a suit—there might be no one of reputation to say it was serious. If it were banned, it could sink from sight. With the reserves I was throwing into the work, I no longer knew if I was ready to take another beating—for the first time in my life I had worn down to the edge, I could see through to the other side of my fear, I knew a time could come when I would be no longer my own man, that I might lose what I had liked to think was the incorruptible center of my strength (which of course I had had money and freedom to cultivate). Already the signs were there—I was beginning to avoid new lines in the Putnam *Deer Park* which were legally doubtful, and once in a while, like a gambler hedging a bet, I toned down individual sentences from the Rinehart *Deer Park,* nothing much, always a matter of the new O'Shaugnessy character, a change from "at last I was able to penetrate into the mysterious and magical belly of a movie star," to what was more in character for him: "I was led to discover the mysterious brain of a movie star." Which "brain" in context was fun for it was accurate, and "discover" was a word of more life than the legality of "penetrate," but I could not be sure if I were chasing my new aesthetic or afraid of the cops. The problem was that *The Deer Park* had become more sexual in the new version, the characters had more force, the air had more heat, and I had gone through the kind of galloping self-analysis which makes one very sensitive to the sexual nuance of every gesture, word, and object—the book now seemed overcharged to me, even a terror of a novel, a cold chisel into all the dull mortar of our guilty society. In my mind it became a more dangerous book than it really was, and my drug-hipped paranoia saw long consequences in every easy line of dialogue. I kept the panic in its place, but by an effort of course, and once in a while I would weaken enough to take out a line because I could not see myself able to defend it happily in a court of law. But it was a mistake to nibble at the edges of censoring myself, for it gave no life to my old pride that I was the boldest writer to have come out of my flabby time, and I think it helped to kill the small chance of finding my way into what could have been a novel as important as *The Sun Also Rises.*

But let me spell it out a bit: originally *The Deer Park* had been about a movie director and a girl with whom he had a bad affair, and it was told by a sensitive but faceless young man. In changing the young man, I saved the book from being minor, but put a disproportion upon it because my narrator became too interesting, and not enough happened to him in the second half of the book, and so it was to be expected that readers would be disappointed by this part of the novel.

Before I was finished, I saw a way to write another book altogether. In what I had so far done, Sergius O'Shaugnessy was given an opportunity by a movie studio to sell the rights to his life and get a contract as an actor. After more than one complication, he finally refused the offer, lost the love of his movie star Lulu, and went off wandering by himself, off to become a writer. This episode had never been an important part of the book, but I could see that the new Sergius was capable of accepting the offer, and if he went to Hollywood and became a movie star himself, the possibilities were good, for in O'Shaugnessy I had a character who was ambitious, yet in his own way, moral, and with such a character one could travel deep into the paradoxes of the time.

Well, I was not in shape to consider that book. With each week of work, bombed and sapped and charged and stoned with lush, with pot, with benny, saggy, Miltown, coffee, and two packs a day, I was working live, and overalert, and tiring into what felt like death, afraid all the way because I had achieved the worst of vicious circles in myself, I had gotten too tired, I was more tired than I had ever been in combat, and so as the weeks went on, and publication was delayed from June to August and then to October, there was only a worn-out part of me to keep protesting into the pillows of one drug and the pinch of the other that I ought to have the guts to stop the machine, to call back the galleys, to cease—to rest, to give myself another two years and write a book which would go a little further to the end of my particular night.

But I had passed the point where I could stop. My anxiety had become too great. I did not know anything any more, I did not have that clear sense of the way things work which is what you need for the natural proportions of a long novel, and it is likely I would not have been writing a new book so much as arguing with the law. Of course another man might have had the stamina to write the new book and manage to be indifferent to everything else, but it was too much to ask of me. By then I was like a lover in a bad, but uncontrollable affair; my woman was publication, and it would have cost too much to give her up before we were done. My imagination had been committed—to stop would leave half the psyche in limbo.

Knowing, however, what I had failed to do, shame added momentum to the punishment of the drugs. By the last week or two, I had worn down so badly that with a dozen pieces still to be fixed, I was reduced to working hardly more than an hour a day. Like an old man, I would come up out of a Seconal stupor with four or five times the normal dose in my veins, and drop into a chair to sit for hours. It was July, the heat was grim in New York, the last of the book had to be in by August 1. Putnam had been more than accommodating, but the vehicle of publication was on its way, and the book could not be postponed beyond the middle of October or it would miss all chance for a large fall sale. I would sit in a chair and watch a baseball game on television, or get up and go out in the heat to a drugstore for sandwich and malted—it was my outing for the day: the walk would feel like a patrol in a tropical sun, and it was two blocks, no more. When I came back, I would lie down, my head would lose the outer wrappings of sedation, and with a crumb of Benzedrine, the first snake or two of thought would wind through my brain. I would go for some coffee—it was a trip to the kitchen, but when I came back I would have a scratch-board and pencil in hand. Watching some afternoon horror on television, the boredom of the performers coming through their tense hilarities with a bleakness to match my own, I would pick up the board, wait for the first sentence—like all working addicts I had come to an old man's fine sense of inner timing—and then slowly, but picking up speed, the actions of the drugs hovering into collaboration like two ships passing in view of one another, I would work for an hour, not well but not badly either. (Pages 195 to 200 of the Putnam edition were written this way.) Then my mind would wear out, and new work was done for the day. I would sit around, watch more television and try to rest my dulled mind, but by evening a riot of bad nerves was on me again, and at two in the morning I'd be having the manly debate of whether to try sleep with two double capsules, or settle again for my need of three.

Somehow I got the book done for the last deadline. Not perfectly—doing just the kind of editing and small rewriting I was doing, I could have used another two or three days, but I got it almost the way I wanted, and then I took my car up to the Cape and lay around in Provincetown with my wife, trying to mend, and indeed doing a fair job because I came off sleeping pills and the marijuana and came part of the way back into that world which has the proportions of the ego. I picked up on *The Magic Mountain*, took it slowly, and lowered *The Deer Park* down to modest size in my brain. Which events proved was just as well.

A few weeks later we came back to the city, and I took some mescaline. Maybe one dies a little with the poison of mescaline in the blood. At the end of a long and private trip which no quick remark should try to describe, the book of *The Deer Park* floated into mind, and I sat up, reached through a pleasure garden of velveted light to find the tree of a pencil and the bed of a notebook and brought them to union together. Then, out of some flesh in myself I had not yet known, with the words coming one by one, in separate steeps and falls, hip in their turnings, all cool with their flights, like the touch of being coming into other being, so the last six lines of my bloody book came to me, and I was done. And it was the only good writing I ever did directly from a drug, even if I paid for it with a hangover beyond measure.

That way the novel received its last sentence, and if I had waited one more day it would have been too late, for in the next twenty-four hours, the printers began their cutting and binding. The book was out of my hands.

Six weeks later, when *The Deer Park* came out, I was no longer feeling eighty years old, but a vigorous hysterical sixty-three, and I laughed like an old pirate at the indignation I had breezed into being with the equation of sex and time. The important reviews broke about seven good and eleven bad, and the out-of-town reports were almost three-to-one bad to good, but I was not unhappy because the good reviews were lively and the bad reviews were full of factual error, indeed so much so that it would be monotonous to give more than a good couple.

Hollis Alpert in the *Saturday Review* called the book "garish and gauche." In reference to Sergius O'Shaugnessy, Alpert wrote: "He has been offered $50,000 by Teppis to sell the rights to his rather dull life story. . . ." As a matter of detail, the sum was $20,000, and it must have been mentioned a half dozen times in the pages of the book. Paul Pickrel in *Harper's* was blistering about how terrible was my style and then quoted the following sentence as an example of how I was often incomprehensible:

> (he) could talk opening about his personal life while remaining a dream of espionage in his business operations.

I happened to see Pickrel's review in *Harper's* galleys, and so was able to point out to them that Pickrel had misquoted the sentence. The fourth word was not "opening" but "openly." *Harper's* corrected his incorrect version, but of course left his remark about my style.

More interesting is the way reviews divided in the New York magazines and newspapers. *Time,* for example, was bad, *Newsweek* was good; *Harper's* was terrible but the *Atlantic* was adequate; the New York Daily *Times* was very bad, the Sunday *Times* was good; the Daily *Herald Tribune* gave a mark of zero, the Sunday *Herald Tribune* was better than good; *Commentary* was careful but complimentary, the *Reporter* was frantic; the *Saturday Review* was a scold and Brendan Gill writing for the *New Yorker* put together a series of slaps and superlatives which went partially like this:

> . . . a big, vigorous, rowdy, ill-shaped, and repellent book, so strong and so weak, so adroit and so fumbling, that only a writer of the greatest and most reckless talent could have flung it between covers.

It's one of the three or four lines I've thought perceptive in all the reviews of my books. That Malcolm Cowley used one of the same words in saying *The Deer Park* was "serious and reckless" is also, I think, interesting, for reckless the book was—and two critics, anyway, had the instinct to feel it.

One note appeared in many reviews. The strongest statement of it was by John Hutchens in The New York Daily *Herald Tribune:*

. . . the original version reputedly was more or less rewritten and certain materials eliminated that were deemed too erotic for public consumption. And, with that, a book that might at least have made a certain reputation as a large shocker wound up as a cipher. . . .

I was bothered to the point of writing a letter to the twenty-odd newspapers which reflected this idea. What bothered me was that I could never really prove I had not "eliminated" the book. Over the years all too many readers would have some hazy impression that I had disemboweled large pieces of the best meat, perspiring in a coward's sweat, a publisher's directive in my ear. (For that matter, I still get an occasional letter which asks if it is possible to see the unbowdlerized *Deer Park*.) Part of the cost of touching the Rinehart galleys was to start those rumors, and in fact I was not altogether free of the accusation, as I have tried to show. Even the six lines which so displeased Rinehart had been altered a bit; I had shown them once to a friend whose opinion I respected, and he remarked that while it was impossible to accept the sort of order Rinehart had laid down, still a phrase like the "fount of power" had a Victorian heaviness about it. Well, that was true, it was out of character for O'Shaugnessy's new style and so I altered it to the "thumb of power" and then other changes became desirable, and the curious are invited to compare the two versions of this particular passage in this collection, but the mistake I made was to take a small aesthetic gain on those six lines and lose a larger clarity about a principle.

What more is there to say? The book moved fairly well, it climbed to seven and then to six on *The New York Times* best-seller list, stayed there for a week or two, and then slipped down. By Christmas, the tone of the *Park* and the Christmas spirit being not all that congenial, it was just about off the lists forever. It did well, however; it would have reached as high as three or two or even to number one if it had come out in June and then been measured against the low sales of summer, for it sold over fifty thousand copies after returns which surprised a good many in publishing, as well as disappointing a few, including myself. I discovered that I had been poised for an enormous sale or a failure—a middling success was cruel to take. Week after week I kept waiting for the book to erupt into some dramatic change of pace which would send it up in sales instead of down, but that never happened. I was left with a draw, not busted, not made, and since I was empty at the time, worn-out with work, waiting for the quick transfusions of a generous success, the steady sales of the book left me deeply depressed. Having reshaped my words with an intensity of feeling I had not known before, I could not understand why others were not overcome with my sense of life, of sex, and of sadness. Like a starved revolutionary in a garret, I had compounded out of need and fever and vision and fear nothing less than a madman's confidence in the identity of my being and the wants of all others, and it was a new dull load to lift and to bear, this knowledge that I had no magic so great as to hasten the time of the apocalypse, but that instead I would be open like all others to the attritions of half-success and small failure. Something God-like in my confidence began to leave, and I was reduced in dimension if now less a boy. I knew I had failed to bid on the biggest hand I ever held.

Now a few years have gone by, more years than I thought, and I have begun to work up another hand, a new book which will be the proper book of an outlaw, and so not publishable in any easy or legal way. Two excerpts from this novel come later in this collection, and therefore I'll say here only that O'Shaugnessy will be one of the three heroes, and that if I'm to go all the way this time, the odds are that my beat senses will have to do the work without the fires and the wastes of the minor drugs.

But that is for later, and the proper end to this account is the advertisement I took in *The Village Voice*. It was bought in November 1955, a month after publication, it was put together by me and paid for by me, and it was my way I now suppose of saying good-by to the pleasure of a quick triumph, of making my apologies for the bad flaws in the bravest effort I had yet pulled out of myself, and certainly for declaring to the world (in a small way, mean pity) that I no longer gave a sick dog's drop for the wisdom, the reliability, and the authority of the public's literary mind, those creeps and old ladies of vested reviewing.

Besides, I had the tender notion—believe it if you will—that the ad might after all do its work and excite some people to buy the book.

But here it is:

In the cactus wastes of Southern California, a distance of two hundred miles from the capital of cinema, is the town of Desert D'Or. There I went from the Air Force to look for a good time.

Whether or not it is enough of an explanation, I can only say that I arrived at the resort with fourteen thousand dollars, a particular sum I picked up in a poker game while waiting with other fliers in Tokyo for our plane home. The irony is that I was never a gambler. I did not even like the game, and perhaps for such a reason I accepted the luck of my cards. Let me leave it at that. I came out of the Air Force with no place to go, no family to visit, and I wandered down to Desert D'Or.

Built since the Second World War, it is the only place I know which is altogether new. Desert D'Or, one is told, was called originally Desert Door by the prospectors who assembled their shanties at the edge of its oasis, and from there went into the mountains overhanging the desert to look for gold. There is nothing left, however, of such men; when the site of Desert D'Or was chosen, not enough of the abandoned shacks remained to create even one of those many California museums the size of a two-car garage.

No, everything is of the present, and in the months I stayed at the resort, I came to know its developed and cultivated real estate in a way given us to know few places. I can still see the straight paved roads and the curved roads, each laid out by the cross hair of the surveyor's transit. The hotels with their pastel colors are visible again in the subtle camouflage which dominated all style in Desert D'Or. It was a place built out of no other need than commercial profit and therefore no sign of commerce was allowed to appear. Desert D'Or was without a main street, and its shops, where nothing but a variety of luxuries could be bought, looked like anything but stores. In those buildings which sold clothing, no clothing was displayed, and one waited in a modern living room while salesmen opened panels in the wall to

In the cactus wild of Southern California, a distance of two hundred miles from the capital of cinema as I choose to call it, is the town of Desert D'Or. There I went from the Air Force to look for a good time. Some time ago.

Almost everybody I knew in Desert D'Or had had an unusual career, and it was the same for me. I grew up in a home for orphans. Still intact at the age of twenty-three, wearing my flying wings and a first lieutenant's uniform, I arrived at the resort with fourteen thousand dollars, a sum I picked up via a poker game in a Tokyo hotel room while waiting with other fliers for our plane home. The curiosity is that I was never a gambler, I did not even like the game, but I had nothing to lose that night, and maybe for such a reason I accepted the luck of my cards. Let me leave it at that. I came out of the Air Force with no place to go, no family to visit, and I wandered down to Desert D'Or.

Built since the Second World War, it is the only place I know which is all new. A long time ago, Desert D'Or was called Desert Door by the prospectors who put up their shanties at the edge of its oasis and went into the mountains above the desert to look for gold. But there is nothing left of those men; when the site of Desert D'Or was chosen, none of the old shacks remained.

No, everything is in the present tense, and during the months I stayed at the resort, I came to know it in a way we can know few places. It was a town built out of no other obvious motive than commercial profit and so no sign of commerce was allowed to appear. Desert D'Or was without a main street, and its stores looked like anything but stores. In those places which sold clothing, no clothing was laid out, and you waited in a modern living room while salesmen opened panels in the wall to exhibit summer suits, or held between their hands the blooms and sprays of a tropical scarf. There was a jewelry store built like a cabin cruiser; from the street one peeped through a porthole to see a thirty-thousand-dollar necklace hung on the silver antlers of a piece of drift-

exhibit summer slacks, or displayèd between their hands the lush blooms of a tropical scarf. There was a jewelry store built like a cabin cruiser; on the street one peered through no more than a porthole to see a necklace hung upon the silver antlers of a piece of driftwood transported across the desert from Pacific waters. None of the hotels I remember so well—not the Yacht Club, nor the Debonair, not the Yucca Plaza, the Sandpiper, the Creedmor, nor the Desert D'Or Arms—could even be seen from outside. Concealed behind cement-brick fences or wooden palings painted in the prevalent palette of Desert D'Or, one rarely saw a building which was not green, yellow, rose, orange, or pink, and the approach on a twisting sandy road was obscured by a shrubbery of bright flowers. As an instance, one passed through the gate to the Yacht Club, the most important hotel in the resort, and followed its private road, expecting a mansion at the end, but came to no more than a carport, a swimming pool in the shape of a free-form coffee table with curved-wall cabanas and canasta tables, and a set of lawn-tennis courts, unique through all that region of Southern California. From there, along yellow sidewalks which crossed and crossed again a meandering artificial creek by way of trellised footbridges, illumined at night with paper lanterns suspended from the tropical trees, one passed the guest bungalows dispersed through the grounds, their anonymous pastel-colored doors serving to emphasize the intimacy of the arrangement.

We soon developed another dispute. I had discovered that to make love to Lulu was to make myself an accessory to the telephone. It was always ringing, and no moment was rare enough to hinder her from answering. Her delight was to ignore the first few rings. "Don't be so nervous, Sugar," she would say, but before the phone

PUTNAM EDITION (Pages 1-3) continued

wood. None of the hotels—not the Yacht Club, nor the Debonair, not the Yucca Plaza, the Sandpiper, the Creedmor, nor the Desert D'Or Arms—could even be seen from outside. Put behind cement-brick fences or wooden palings, one hardly came across a building which was not green, yellow, rose, orange, or pink, and the approach was hidden by a shrubbery of bright flowers. You passed through the gate to the Yacht Club, the biggest and therefore the most exclusive hotel in the resort, and followed its private road which twisted through the grounds for several hundred yards, expecting a mansion at the end, but came instead to no more than a carport, a swimming pool in the shape of a freeform coffee table with curved-wall cabanas and canasta tables, and a set of lawn-tennis courts, the only lawn in all that part of Southern California. At night, along yellow sidewalks which crossed a winding artificial creek, lit up with Japanese lanterns strung to the tropical trees, you could wander by the guest bungalows scattered along the route, their flush pastel-colored doors another part of the maze of the arrangement.

PUTNAM EDITION (Pages 134-139)

We soon found something new to fight about. I discovered that to make love to Lulu was to make myself a scratch-pad to the telephone. It was always ringing, and no moment was long enough to keep her from answering. Her delight was to pass the first few rings. "Don't be so nervous, Sugar," she would say, "let the switchboard

had pealed five times, she would have picked it up. Invariably, it was business. She would be talking to Herman Teppis, or Munshin who was back in the capital, or a writer, or her director for the next picture, or once even her hairdresser—Lulu was interested in a coiffure she had seen. The conversation could not go on for long before she was fondling me again; to make love and talk business possessed a special attraction for her.

"Of course I'm being a good girl, Mr. Teppis," she would say, giving me a lewd wink. "How can you think these things of me?" As the ultimate in virtuosity, she succeeded one time in weeping through a phone call with Teppis while entertaining a passage with me.

I would try to get her to visit my place but she had developed a sudden aversion. "It depresses me, Sugar, it's in such bland taste. Do you know you're a bland boy?" For a while everything would be bland. Her own place was now spoiled by that word. To my amazement at her prodigality, she insisted one day upon having her room suite redecorated. Between morning and evening its beige walls were transformed to a delicate blue, which Lulu claimed was her most flattering color. So, too, were the sheets. Now she lay with her gold head on pale-blue linen, ordering from that telephone, as essential as any limb or organ, pink roses and red roses; the florist at the Yacht Club must arrange them himself. She would buy a dress and give it to her maid before she had even worn it, she would complain she had not a thing to wear. Her convertible she traded in one afternoon for another car almost its duplicate, and yet the exchange must have cost her a thousand dollars. When she remembered she must drive the new car slowly until it had accumulated the necessary mileage, she hired a chauffeur to trundle it through the desert and spare her the bother. Her first phone bill was five hundred dollars for the month.

Yet when it came to making money she was not without talent. While I knew her, negotiations were in progress for a three-picture contract. She would phone

PUTNAM EDITION (Pages 134-139) continued

suffer," but before the phone had screamed five times, she would pick it up. Almost always, it was business. She would be talking to Herman Teppis, or Munshin who was back in the capital, or a writer, or her director for the next picture, or an old boy friend, or once her hairdresser—Lulu was interested in a hair-do she had seen. The conversation could not go on for two minutes before she was teasing me again; to make love and talk business was a double-feature to her.

"Of course I'm being a good girl, Mr. Teppis," she would say, giving me the wink. "How can you think these things of me?" As the end in virtuosity, she succeeded one time in weeping through a phone call with Teppis while rendering a passage with me.

I would try to get her to visit my place but she had grown an aversion. "It depresses me, Sugar, it's in such bland taste." For a while everything would be bland. Her own place was now spoiled by that word, and one day she told the management to have her room suite redecorated. Between morning and evening its beige walls were painted to a special blue, which Lulu claimed was her best color. Now she lay with her gold head on pale-blue linen, ordering pink roses and red roses from the telephone; the florist at the Yacht Club promised to arrange them himself: She would buy a dress and give it to her maid before she had even worn it, she would complain she had not a thing to wear. Her new convertible she traded in one afternoon for the same model in another color, and yet the exchange cost her close to a thousand dollars. When I reminded her that she had to drive the new car slowly until it accumulated the early mileage, she hired a chauffeur to trundle it through the desert and spare her the bother. Her first phone bill from the Yacht Club was five hundred dollars.

Yet when it came to making money she was also a talent. While I knew her, negotiations were on for a three-picture contract. She would phone her lawyers, they would call her agent, the agent would speak to her lawyers, they would call her agent, the agent would speak to Teppis, Teppis would speak to her. She asked an outrageous price and received more than three-quarters of it. "I can't stand my father," she explained to me, "but he's a gambler at business. He's wonderful that way." It developed that when she was thirteen and going to a school for professional children in the capital, Magnum Pictures had wanted to sign her to a seven-year contract. "I'd be making a stinking seven hundred and fifty a week now like all those poor exploited schnooks, but Father wouldn't let me. 'Free-lance,' he said, he talks that way, 'this country was built on free-lancing.' He's just a chiropodist with holdings in real estate, but he knew what to do for me." Her toes nibbled and twisted at the telephone cord. "I've noticed that about men. There's a kind of man who never can make money for himself. Only for others. That's my father."

Of her father and mother, Lulu's opinion changed by the clock. One time it would be her father who was marvelous. "What a bitch my mother is. She just squeezed all the manhood out of him. Poor Daddy." Her mother had ruined her life, Lulu explained. "I never wanted to be an actress. She made me one. It's her ambition. She's just an . . . octopus." Several phone calls later, Lulu would be chatting with her mother. "Yes, I think it gives me hives," she would say of some food, "glycerine, will that do, Mommie? . . . He's what? . . . He's acting up again. . . . Well, you tell him to leave you alone. I wouldn't put up with it if I were you. I would have divorced him long ago. I certainly would.

"I don't know what I'd do without her," Lulu would say on hanging up the phone, "men are terrible," and she would have nothing to do with me for the next half hour.

It took me longer than it need have taken to realize that the heart of her pleasure was to display herself. She abhorred concealing an impulse. If Lulu felt like burping, she would burp; if it came to her mind that she

Teppis, Teppis would speak to her. She asked a big price
and got more than three-quarters of it. "I can't stand my
father," she explained to me, "but he's a gambler at
business. He's wonderful that way." It came out that
when she was thirteen and going to a school for professional children in the capital, Magnum Pictures wanted
to sign her to a seven-year contract. "I'd be making a
stinking seven hundred and fifty a week now like all
those poor exploited schnooks, but Daddy wouldn't let
me. 'Free-lance,' he said, he talks that way, 'this country
was built on free-lance.' He's just a chiropodist with
holdings in real estate, but he knew what to do for me."
Her toes nibbled at the telephone cord. "I've noticed
that about men. There's a kind of man who never can
make money for himself. Only for others. That's my father."

Of her father and mother, Lulu's opinion changed by
the clock. One round it would be her father who was
marvelous. "What a bitch my mother is. She just
squeezed all the manhood out of him. Poor Daddy." Her
mother had ruined her life, Lulu explained. "I never
wanted to be an actress. She made me one. It's her ambition. She's just an . . . octopus." Several phone calls later,
Lulu would be chatting with her mother. "Yes, I think it
gives me hives," she would say of some food, "glycerine,
will that do, Mommie? . . . He's what? . . . He's acting up
again. . . . Well, you tell him to leave you alone. I
wouldn't put up with it if I were you. I would have
divorced him long ago. I certainly would. . . .

"I don't know what I'd do without her," Lulu would
say on hanging up the phone, "men are terrible," and
she would have nothing to do with me for the next half
hour.

It took me longer than it need have taken to realize
that the heart of her pleasure was to show herself. She
hated holding something in. If Lulu felt like burping, she
would burp; if it came up that she wanted to put cold
cream on her face, she would do it while entertaining

wished to put cold cream on her face, she would do it while entertaining half a dozen people. So it went with her acting. She could say without embarrassment to the most casual acquaintance that she wished to be the greatest actress in the world. Once, talking to a stage director, she was close to tears because the studio never gave her a part in a serious picture. "They ruin me," she complained. "People don't want glamour, they want acting. I'd take the smallest role if it was something I could get my teeth into." Still, she quarreled for three days running, and how many hours of telephone calls I could not guess, because Munshin who was producing her next picture would not enlarge her part. Publicity, she announced, was idiotic, but with her instinct for what was pleasing to an adolescent, she did more than co-operate with photographers. The best ideas always came from Lulu. One occasion when she was photographed sipping a soda she shaped the second straw into a heart, and the picture as it was printed in many hundreds of newspapers showed Lulu peeping through the heart, at once coy, chaste, hoydenish and lovable. On those few times I would be allowed to sleep the night with her, I might awaken to see Lulu writing an idea for publicity in the notebook she kept by her bed table, and I had a picture of her marriage to Eitel, each of them with his own notebook and own bed table. With pleasure, she would expound to me the subtleties of being well photographed. I learned that the core of her dislike for Teddy Pope was that each of them was photographed best from the left side of the face, and when they played a scene together Teddy was as determined as Lulu not to expose his bad side to the camera. "I hate to play with queers," she complained. "Teddy pulled seniority and they gave him his way. I thought I had mumps when I saw myself. Boy, I threw a scene." Lulu acted it out for me. "You've ruined me, Mr. Teppis," she shrieked to my private ear. "There's no chivalry left."

In bed, in those interludes she permitted me at her

half a dozen people. So it went with her acting. She could say to a stranger that she was going to be the greatest actress in the world. Once, talking to a stage director, she was close to tears because the studio never gave her a part in a serious picture. "They ruin me," she complained. "People don't want glamour, they want acting. I'd take the smallest role if it was something I could get my teeth into." Still, she quarreled for three days running, and how many hours on the telephone I could never guess, because Munshin who was producing her next picture would not enlarge her part. Publicity, she announced, was idiotic, but with her instinct for what was good to an adolescent, she did better than co-operate with photographers. The best ideas always came from Lulu. One sortie when she was photographed sipping a soda she shaped the second straw into a heart, and the picture as it was printed in the newspapers showed Lulu peeping through the heart, coy and cool. On the few times I would be allowed to spend the night with her, I would wake up to see Lulu writing an idea for publicity in the notebook she kept on her bed table, and I had a picture of her marriage to Eitel, each of them with his own notebook and own bed table. With pleasure, she would expound the subtleties of being well photographed. I learned that the core of her dislike for Teddy Pope was that each of them photographed best from the left side of the face, and when they played a scene together Teddy was as quick as Lulu not to expose his bad side to the camera. "I hate to play with queers," she complained. "They're too smart. I thought I had mumps when I saw myself. Boy, I threw a scene." Lulu acted it for my private ear. "You've ruined me, Mr. Teppis," she shrieked. "There's no chivalry left."

For odd hours, during those interludes she called at her caprice, things had come around a bit. To my idea of an interlude which must have left her exhausted, she coached me by degrees to something different. Which was all right with me. Lulu's taste was for games, and if

caprice, matters had altered considerably. To my idea of sport which must have left her exhausted, she directed me by degrees to something quite different. Lulu's taste was for games, and if she lay beneath me like a captive, pallid before the fury she aroused, her spirits improved with a play. In my innocence, there seemed a fabulous lewdness to her imagination, and I thought I had managed at a coup to reach the heart of sexual delights. I was convinced no two people ever had shared such excesses, nor even conceived of them. We were extraordinary lovers I felt in my pride; I had pity for those hordes who could know none of this. Yet, like the Oriental monarch who feels a subtle malaise on seeing the beggars of his kingdom, I was at a pitch of greediness to prove everyone else a beggar. For that, Lulu was the sweetest of mistresses. She would never allow comparisons. This was completely the best. I was superb. She was superb. We were beyond all. Unlike Eitel who now could not bear a word of Elena's former lovers, I was more than charitable to all of Lulu's. Why should I not be? She had sworn they were poor sticks to her Sugar. I was even so charitable that I argued in Eitel's defense. She had marked him impossible as a lover, and in a breach of friendship my heart had quickened with spite. I overcame that quickly enough, I wished to set Eitel at the place nearest my feet, vizier to the potentate, and it charmed me that in my first big affair I should be so proficient.

We played our games. I was the iceman and she was the housewife; she was the movie star and I was the bellhop; she the queen, I the slave; or in reverse of those situations she adored so well, Lulu mimed the prostitute to my client. We even met in equality. The game she cherished was to play the bobby-soxer who petted with a date in the living room and was finally seduced, always for the first time naturally enough. She was never so happy as when we acted at theater and fornicated on clouds of myth. I was exactly young enough to wish noth-

NORMAN MAILER

she lay like a cinder under the speed of my sprints, her spirits improved with a play. I was sure no two people ever had done such things nor even thought of them. We were great lovers I felt in my pride; I had pity for the hordes who could know none of this. Yes, Lulu was sweet. She would never allow comparison. This was the best. I was superb. She was superb. We were beyond all. Unlike Eitel who now could not bear to hear a word of Elena's old lovers, I was charitable to all of Lulu's. Why should I not be? She had sworn they were poor sticks to her Sugar. I was even so charitable that I argued in Eitel's defense. Lulu had marked him low as a lover, and in a twist of friendship my heart beat with spite. I stopped that quickly enough, I had an occasional idea by now of when Lulu was lying, and I wanted to set Eitel at my feet, second to the champion. It pleased me in my big affair that I had such a feel for the ring.

We played our games. I was the photographer and she was the model; she was the movie star and I was the bellhop; she did the queen, I the slave. We even met even to even. The game she loved was to play the bobby-soxer who sat with a date in the living room and was finally convinced, always for the first time naturally enough. She was never so happy as when we acted at theater and did the mime on clouds of myth. I was just young enough to want nothing but to be alone with her. It was not even possible to be tired. Each time she gave the signal, and I could never know, not five minutes in advance, when it would happen, my appetite was sharp, dressed by the sting of what I suffered in public.

To eat a meal with her in a restaurant became the new torture. It didn't matter with what friends she found herself nor with what enemies, her attention would go, her eye would flee. It always seemed to her as if the conversation at another table was more interesting than what she heard at her own. She had the worry that she was missing a word of gossip, a tip, a role in a picture, a

ing else ever than to be alone with her. It was not even possible to be sated. Each time she gave herself, and I could never know, not five minutes in advance, when it would happen, my appetite was sharp, dressed by the animus of what I had suffered in public.

To eat a meal with her in a restaurant became a torture. It never mattered with what friends she found herself nor with what strangers, her attention would flee, her eye would wander with impatience. It always seemed to her as if the conversation at another table was more interesting and more provocative than what she heard at her own. She suffered the intolerable anxiety that she was missing a word of gossip, a tip, a role in a picture, a financial transaction, a . . . it did not matter; something was happening somewhere else, something of importance, something she could not afford to miss. Therefore, eating with her was like sleeping with her; if one was interrupted by the telephone, the other was broken by her need to visit from table to table, sometimes dragging me, sometimes parking me, until I often wondered what mathematical possibility there was for Lulu to eat a meal in sequence since she was always having a bit of soup here and a piece of pastry there, joining myself and her friends for breast of squab, and departing to greet new arrivals whose crabmeat cocktail she nibbled. There was no end, no beginning, no certainty that one would even see her during a meal. I remember a dinner when we went out with Dorothea O'Faye and Martin Pelley. They had just been married and Lulu treasured them. Dorothea was an old friend, a dear friend, Lulu assured me, and before ten minutes she disappeared. When at last Lulu returned she perched on my lap and said in a whisper the others could hear, "Sugar, I tried, and I couldn't make doo-doo. Isn't that awful? What should I eat?"

Five minutes later she insisted upon picking up the check.

PUTNAM EDITION (Pages 134-139) continued

financial transaction, a . . . it did not matter; something was happening somewhere else, something of importance, something she could not afford to miss. Therefore, eating with her was like sleeping with her; if one was cut by the telephone, the other was rubbed by her itch to visit from table to table, sometimes dragging me, sometimes parking me, until I had to wonder what mathematical possibility there was for Lulu to eat a meal in sequence since she was always having a bit of soup here and a piece of pastry there, joining me for breast of squab, and taking off to greet new arrivals whose crabmeat cocktail she nibbled on. There was no end, no beginning, no surety that one would even see her during a meal. I remember a dinner when we went out with Dorothea O'Faye and Martin Pelley. They had just been married and Lulu treasured them. Dorothea was an old friend, a dear friend, Lulu promised me, and before ten minutes she was gone. When Lulu finally came back, she perched on my lap and said in a whisper the others could hear, "Sugar, I tried, and I couldn't make doo-doo. Isn't that awful? What should I eat?"

Five minutes later she outmaneuvered Pelley to pick up the check.

Tentatively, she reached out a hand to caress his hair, and at that moment Herman Teppis opened his legs and let Bobby slip to the floor. At the expression of surprise on her face, he began to laugh. "Just like this, sweetie," he said, and down he looked at that frightened female mouth, facsimile of all those smiling lips he had seen so ready to be nourished at the fount of power and with a shudder he started to talk. "That's a good girlie, that's a good girlie, that's a good girlie," he said in a mild lost little voice, "you're just an angel darling, and I like you, and you understand, you're my darling darling, oh that's the ticket," said Teppis.

1952–4

PUTNAM EDITION (Page 284)

Tentatively, she reached out a hand to finger his hair, and at that moment Herman Teppis opened his legs and let Bobby fall to the floor. At the expression of surprise on her face, he began to laugh. "Don't you worry, sweetie," he said, and down he looked at that frightened female mouth, facsimile of all those smiling lips he had seen so ready to serve at the thumb of power, and with a cough, he started to talk. "That's a good girlie, that's a good girlie, that's a good girlie," he said in a mild little voice, "you're an angel darling, and I like you, you're my darling darling, oh that's the ticket," said Teppis.

1955